The Best American Short Plays

2005–2006

The Best American Short Plays

2005–2006

edited with an introduction by
Barbara Parisi

APPLAUSE THEATRE & CINEMA BOOKS
An Imprint of Hal Leonard Corporation
New York

The Best American Short Plays 2005–2006
Edited with an introduction by Barbara Parisi

Published in 2008 by Applause Theatre & Cinema Books
An Imprint of Hal Leonard Corporation
7777 West Bluemound Road
Milwaukee, WI 53213

Trade Book Division Editorial Offices
19 West 21st Street, New York, NY 10010

Printed in the United States of America
Book composition by UB Communications

ISBN 978-1-55783-713-4 [cloth]
ISBN 978-1-55783-714-1 [paper]
ISSN 0067-6284

www.applausepub.com

To William and Gloria Parisi,
Rochelle Martinsen,
and my husband—
Michael Ronald Pasternack

contents

introduction
by Barbara Parisi

While compiling my second edition of Best American Short Plays, I have
had the opportunity to read many new one-act plays, taking me through a
fascinating selection process. One-act plays—why write them? Who writes
them and who produces them? On August 8, 1920, Brander Matthews
wrote an article in the *New York Times* Sunday edition's book review section,
"Why the One-Act Play Grows in Popularity; The One-Act Play." Today,
in many theatre venues, one-act plays are being produced in festivals and as
evenings of theme-related one-acts.

Contemporary playwright Sam Shepard is quoted in an Internet article
written by Richard Toscan, entitled "One-Act Tips—The Playwriting Sem-
inars—2007," as saying:

> I wrote all the time. Everywhere. When I wasn't writing, I was thinking
> about it or continuing to "write" in my head. . . . I wasn't very good com-
> pany. At that time, a major critic commented that I wrote "disposable
> plays," and in some sense he was probably right. But nothing mattered to
> me then except to get the stuff down on paper. . . . There was never a
> sense . . . of evolving a style or moving on to a bigger, longer, "more
> important" form. Each play had a distinct life of its own and seemed
> totally self-contained within its one-act structure.

Toscan's article goes on to say that there wasn't a strong interest
among regional theatres for one-acts. Even one-acts connected by themes

creating a full evening of theatre hardly make it into a rep theatre's season. Contemporary playwright David Ives is considered the exception in this genre.

The one-act play—how do you start to write one? Do playwrights think about the theme before they write? This seems to be a debatable question. In Richard Toscan's article "Themes and the Meanings of Plays—2007," contemporary playwright Beth Henley said: "I don't believe in a message. I think it would be disastrous if you could say what the message of *Hamlet* was. Even with a minor play, everyone is going to come away with something different depending on if they've just left their lovers or if they've just had a child or if they've just been fired." So, do you need a theme or not?

What is a theme? Theme is the meaning created when we consider all aspects of the play. It is the human experience that the author wishes to express. The theme expresses the author's opinion, which raises major questions about human nature. The theme lets authors share their perceptions about life as they experience it. The theme should be felt by an audience. Playwrights think about characterization, subtext, plot, events, setting, motivation, style, tone, point of view, irony, imagery, and values. To create a theme you need to see the meaning of the relationship of all of these areas.

During my selection process, I focused an author's thematic point of view. One-act plays do not have a break in the action and reveal their themes through the challenge of character development, plot, and resolution of the conflict. They must develop engaging, believable characters. A meaningful theme is revealed by solid action.

One-act plays were making a successful entrance on the theatrical scene in the 1920s. In the book *Contemporary One-Act Plays* by B. Roland Lewis, written in 1922, he states, in the chapter entitled "Dramatic Analysis and Construction of the One-Act Play":

> The one-act play, like the short story, is a work of literary art, and must be approached as such. Just like a painting or a poem . . . the one-set play aims at making a singleness of effect upon the reader or observer. One does not

judge . . . any work of art, by the appearance of any isolated part of it, but by the sum-total effect of the whole. . . . In approaching a one-act play . . . the very first consideration should be to determine what the purpose and intent of the play is—to determine its theme. This demands that the play be read through complete at one sitting and that no . . . conclusions be drawn. Once the play is read, it is well to subject the play to certain leading questions. What has the author intended that his reader . . . shall understand, think, or feel? What is the play about? What is its object and purpose? With what fundamental element in human nature does it have to do: Love? Patriotism? Fear? Egotism and self-centeredness? Sacrifice? Faithfulness? Or what? A word of warning should be given. The student should not get the idea that by theme is meant the moral of the play. A good play may be thoroughly moral without its descending to commonplace moralizing. Good plays concern themselves with the presentation of the fundamentals of life rather than a creed of morals, theories, and propagandas. Art concerns itself with larger things than didactic and argumentative moralizing.

The art of teaching playwriting suggests that playwrights should be clear in their mind what their theme is. Not all theatre academic artists agree on this concept even though the heart of dramatic writing is conflict reflecting the theme. Characters want something and there is usually something standing in their way of getting what they need. The writer should know what the conflict is and how the theme is felt throughout the one-act play. It's interesting that many famous, and infamous, playwrights will tell you they don't think about theme when they write, but theatre critics and reviewers describe and analyze plays in terms of theme, plot, and characterization.

In analyzing the complex and diverse plays that are part of this edition, many themes that reflect the current social and personal issues of our society are prevalent. With the current political state of the United States, many of the plays in this anthology reflect the pressing concerns of Americans. I would like to leave you with a final thought from Richard Toscan's article quoting David Ives, the most successful playwright of related one-act plays: "With my plays, when the lights go down, at least the audience isn't thinking, Oh God, two more hours of this." In writing this introduction, I asked the playwrights to express their themes, plots, and inspirations for writing their one-act plays.

David Ives

In *The Other Woman*, David Ives poses a peculiar question—Can you cheat on your wife with your wife? On May 29, 2006, in a theatre review entitled "Marathon 2006: That Was No Wraith, That Was My Wife," critic Charles Isherwood stated:

> Like the short story, the brief one-act play can be tricky to master. Mr. Ives is one of the few contemporary playwrights to specialize in the form. . . . From him we expect a brainy, possibly zany comic jape, not this shiver-inducing erotic pas de deux. . . . *The Other Woman* generates both edge-of-your-seat suspense and a measure of compassionate wonder about the mysterious frailty of the mind, and of the married state. . . . It's a sensitive, sorrow-tinged parable about the secrets and lies that can create dangerous fissures in a seemingly firm relationship.

David Ives says: "*The Other Woman*'s plot reveals a man visited in the night by his sleepwalking wife. He has a love affair with her, unbeknownst to her rational, waking self. I have no idea what the theme is, even having written the thing. I never think about the theme of anything I'm writing. Now that I think about it, is there really a theme? Or is it just a good story? The inspiration came from the rather spooky experience of once seeing a look on a woman's face that so transformed the woman that I didn't recognize her."

Quiara Alegría Hudes

A critical review, dated April 2007, published in *The Scene*—"*Elliot* examines three generations of soldiers" by Pamela Fernandez—stated:

> Three wars, three generations of Puerto Ricans and the fight for one country that is not theirs: the United States. *Elliot, a Soldier's Fugue* and its up-and-coming Hispanic playwright Quiara Alegría Hudes give a voice to the loyal soldiers who cannot elect the president nor have voice in the congress but

still join the US Army Forces with patriotism.... Moving and touching on many levels, Elliot grabs the audience, takes them close to tears and then offers some comic relief, because that is the only thing left when nightmares rob ones sleep at night.

From the *New York Times* review of *Elliot, a Soldier's Fugue*, by Phoebe Hoban, February 7, 2006, this play is described as a

rare and rewarding thing: a theatre work that succeeds on every level, while creating something new.... *Elliot* ... is composed like a fugue, with several strands of narrative playing in point and counterpoint around a single theme: a soldier's personal experience of war.... As the play unfolds, the individual and overlapping voices weave a vivid web of images.... Without ever invoking current politics, *Elliot, a Soldier's Fugue* manages to be a deeply poetic, touching and often funny indictment of the war in Iraq.

On February 7, 2006, critic Victor Gluck of *Backstage* said: "This new play approximates verbally the musical composition in which one or more themes are developed by different voices "contrapuntally." Mark Blankenship from *Variety* (February 5, 2006) said: "A play which models its plot on the musical structure in which different voices sing similar themes." Kate Taylor of the *New York Sun*, in a review entitled "Everything Old Is New Again" (October 6, 2006), said that Ms. Hudes said she was inspired to write the play because "her cousin fought in Iraq. He was injured and went to recuperate in California, where Ms. Hudes visited him. He had always been the clown of the family, with a big smile, she said. While he hadn't lost his sense of humor, she had a sense that he had changed, and that his personality would never be the same as it was before." *Elliot*'s success is clearly demonstrated by the number of productions and performances it has given in its early life.

Jules Tasca

The theme and inspiration of *The Rapture of Mammon* is based on the story of Anna Nicole Smith, who in her twenties married a ninety-year-old man and told the world that she did it for love. This prompted the writing of *The Rapture of Mammon*.

The plot finds Uncle Henry Walmont, up in his eighties, as a lustful old man who is worth more millions than anyone can count. His nephew, Clarence, and Clarence's wife, Cielia, cannot wait for Uncle Henry to die, so they hatch a plot to kill Uncle Henry. Their plan is to hire the most desirable, yet not too bright, young woman they can find to become Uncle Henry's housekeeper. Then, they presume, he will attempt to make love to her, thus killing himself. They find a housekeeper, Cindy Anne Dibbs, voluptuous enough and, they think, dense enough to take the job as companion/housekeeper to rich Uncle Henry. However, the rich old guy does not expire. Instead the relationship with Cindy Anne revitalizes him.

The major idea that I strived for in *The Rapture of Mammon* was that human beings have always been driven completely by avarice. It is a vice that, unlike some others, completely severs man from his humanity. Because of this, it is comic in its tragic consequences. The vice probably has roots in evolutionary struggle, where the animal would, for reasons of survival, put a premium on personal acquisition. Hence in yesteryear we had Enron, and today we have mortgage company fraud. Sadly, avaricious man will never stop, even if we laugh heartily at his foibles. Cindy Anne Dibbs selling her body and Clarence and Cielia selling their souls are simply stand-ins for us all, and I had great fun in poking fun at us.

Pamela Sneed

Kong developed after seeing the recent remake of the film *King Kong* by Peter Jackson in 2005. I was appalled at such racist images still being perpetuated, but at the same time there were parts of the film I liked. *Kong* is both satire and protest, and explores the complexities of activism in 2006.

Kong is a political tapestry that weaves together current events and trends in cinema, and retells the important history of black lesbian and gays in New York City in the early 1990s, who formed a literary movement akin to the Harlem Renaissance. *Kong* addresses cinema and the racial images pervasive in new and remade films like *King Kong*, *Hustle and Flow*, and *Freedomland*. I also tackle the current political landscape of war in Iraq, the crisis in New Orleans, the lack of American health care, and finally the need for new kinds of activism.

Carol K. Mack

For those of us in New York City on September 11, 2001, everything changed. For the month that followed, the city was silent. There were no car horns, no loud cell phone monologues, no arrogant behavior: instead each person walked slowly with profound awareness of each stranger/neighbor we passed, of our beautiful "mongrel" city and each of its diverse inhabitants. The music of its many languages. Our very way of being was threatened. We hugged strangers, wept openly, appreciated our way of life, and took nothing for granted-as we might lose all of it, and yes, we idealized what our country could be, what we thought we stood for, and we recognized all that we had failed to do. We stood at a crossroads. While we were preoccupied, a bill called "Uniting and Strengthening America by Providing Appropriate Tools Required to Intercept and Obstruct Terrorism Act of 2001" was passed. The bill is better known as the U.S.A. Patriot Act. That crossroad might have been in any other administration a wake-up call to our global connections, responsibility, failures, and the work ahead on the hard road to peace. Instead we were led through fear onto a path that has led us to brutal behavior, secrecy, lies, and as far from genuine patriotism (which is love of our country, its constitution, civil rights, and potential) to a new place that is as close to fascism as this country has ever come. Who are we? Who has led us here? Can we turn back, change paths, redefine our goals, work with our neighbors to realize our vision of what the best of America represents? Can we ever become that America?

Michael Roderick

The plot of *Props* begins after a brutal breakup that forces a properties artist to dive desperately into his work. His friends begin to worry as he becomes more and more obsessed with his newest project: a woman. When the prop he's working on comes to life, he is forced to make some painful decisions about love and relationships before everything starts burning up around him.

Inspiration for *Props:* I wrote this play after a very difficult breakup. I was listening to an R.E.M. song and was fascinated by the idea of referring to someone as a prop. I decided to thematically explore this idea.

Jeni Mahoney

I have to admit, as a playwright I find it difficult to talk about my work in terms of theme. It is not something that I consider as I work on a play. That being said, I hope *Come Rain or Come Shine* offers a reflection on the "American family" in the aftermath of the 2004 elections. Perhaps something closer to "theme" can be found in the "what inspired me" section.

The plot finds a mom who doesn't know why it's taken Luke so long to break the news. She's liberal after all. But she's thrilled that after years away Luke is finally coming home to tell her he's gay. He's even bringing his new boyfriend, Chris! Chris is his boyfriend . . . right?

I think I was inspired by my own struggle to come to terms with my "American family" after the re-election of George W. Bush in 2004. Of course, this play is more about that moment of realization—the kick in the gut that many Democrats felt that day—than it is about the struggle that followed. I have to say that I'm not really proud of Mom's response to her son—it's quite sad actually. But the depth and power of her disappointment, and her inability to accept her son, surprises her so sharply that she is overwhelmed.

Dano Madden

The theme of *Beautiful American Soldier* reveals two sisters, unexpectedly lost along a quiet roadside in war-torn Iraq, who find an unexpected friend in a man peddling junk. Together, their shattered hearts must find a way to deal with the consequences of war.

The plot begins with Lamiya and her older sister, Ula, who are lost along a quiet roadside on the way home to their sister's wedding. Lamiya desperately tries to convince her sister to get moving so they can make it to the wedding on time, but Ula seems to have given up. Lamiya tells Ula about her secret love for an American soldier in order to get a rise out of her, but Ula will not move or speak. Lamiya is at her wits end with her sister when a young man, Bahlool, shows up. He is peddling junk that he has salvaged from bomb sites across Iraq. Lamiya asks Bahlool to help her and Ula find the wedding. The exchange: if Bahlool successfully locates the site of the festivities, he can attend the reception and eat plentifully. Bahlool agrees, but even as he tries to figure out the proper direction to travel, Lamiya begins to get distracted by thoughts of the American soldier she loves. She wants to practice her dancing. Frustrated and hungry, Bahlool gives up on the two women and begins to leave. In this moment, Ula finally speaks. She reveals what is really going on: they are already at the site of the wedding, which was bombed by American war planes three days ago, killing everyone. It becomes clear that Lamiya is existing in a deep state of shock and Ula cannot move her. Bahlool decides to leave in an attempt to get help for the two women. Lamiya and Ula are left alone, much as they were in the beginning, underneath a tree as the sun sets.

For a long time, I wanted to write a play about the war in Iraq, but I didn't know how. All of the news I took in about what was happening filled me with anger, disbelief, frustration, and sadness. Inspired, but still having no idea how to transform all that I was feeling into a play, the idea came to me. One day, swamped with several other projects, I realized what I wanted the play to be about. I wanted to write a simple story about the one element of the war in Iraq that, in my mind, is grossly overlooked: the Iraqi civilians. In Iraq, and all over the world, I believe that people pretty much want the same thing: a long life filled with love and happiness. This is not a new revelation by any means. But the more I hear Americans saying "God bless America," the more I wonder if we've forgotten the rest of the people on this planet. In Iraq, there are people pretty much like us with families and dreams and a simple desire to live happy lives. In Iraq, there is someone almost exactly like you and someone like me. Except they are living through horrific circumstances that none of us can imagine. I think it is my job as a playwright to try to imagine. *Beautiful American Soldier* contains elements that are based on actual events. Mostly, though, it is me trying to imagine what the people in Iraq are going through.

James Armstrong

The plot of *The Mysteries of the Castle of the Monk of Falconara* begins on All Hallows' Eve 1793, as three strangers come to the Castle of Falconara in response to a mysterious letter. They are Ann Radcliffe, Horace Walpole, and Matthew G. Lewis, three of the great Gothic novelists of the late eighteenth century. As their host has warned them, each has a dark secret capable of destroying everything. Their secrets, however, are not what they think, and the three writers end up battling the personal nightmares that haunt their fiction.

What inspired me: I've been a fan of Gothic literature ever since reading Horace Walpole's *The Castle of Otranto*, a brilliant little book that managed to launch a whole movement in literature, ultimately giving rise to horror, mystery, fantasy, basically all of what we now consider "genre" fiction. I began wondering what might have inspired authors such as Walpole, Radcliffe, and Lewis to create such imaginative worlds, so in the spirit of their novels, I wrote this play as a wild fantasy of my own.

Cary Pepper

Two things inspired me to write *Small Things*. The first was door-to-door proselytizers, who would interrupt my day to confidently proclaim that their belief system was The Answer, inherently invalidating mine. And apparently having no awareness that that's what they were doing. The second was meeting a young man who became the basis for the character Drew.

The plot of *Small Things* begins with Hoyt, who has lost everything. With no job, no money, and no hope that things are going to get better, he's given up and is sitting alone in his apartment cleaning a revolver. He's going to kill himself. But the bell rings, And there stands Drew, who's going door-to-door proselytizing for the Assembly of Hubristic Evangelicals. "If you'll give me just a few minutes, I'll tell you how you can experience the one true God."

Hoyt steps aside and invites Drew in, which amazes Drew. No one's ever let him in before. As the two of them talk, they both find themselves deeply challenged, though in vastly different ways. They are each, in their own fashion, in crisis. And thematically finding each other, at this particular point in their lives, will prove pivotal for both of them.

Adam Kraar

Love on the B-Line is a romantic serio-comedy about a young man, Robbie, who wants to take his passionate relationship with a young woman, Marie, to the next level. That "next level" isn't sex—which is already part of their relationship—but rather for Marie to spend the whole night with Robbie. The play, originally written for the H.B. Playwrights' Foundation's "Subway Plays," grew out of many late nights waiting for trains in Brooklyn. A deserted subway platform in the wee hours of the morning can feel like the end of the world, where yearning and hidden things threaten to drive one mad. In the play, Robbie and Marie confront the darkness and reach a deeper understanding of each other.

Joan Lipkin

The inspiration for *Crab Cakes* began with the economy tanking. I wondered about the psychic fallout for upper-level management having to fire people. Those who are assigned the odious task of passing out the pink slips are rarely the CEOs, but they are generally not middle management, either. How might someone feel about laying off people who are an essential part of the team? What effect does implementing decisions that are not of their making have on their sense of themselves? On their intimate relationships? Or on their libido? How might it feel to struggle with the subsequent ambivalence and guilt? With whom might one share their feelings? When and where?

As with many tragic circumstances, I turned to comedy and, more specifically, the capacity of the human psyche to adapt. In the plot, our protagonist, Franklin, feels so bad about his role in firing people that he wants to be punished. His choice of punishment? A little bondage, with his wife using her shoe, as long as she doesn't break the skin (or her heel). As with all things relational, Franklin's work circumstances affect his wife. This deceptively light comedy asks what happens when the needs of one half of a long-term partnership shift? Can the other understand? Can they adapt? And are there any mutual advantages to this adaptation and change?

The play is simultaneously about the challenges of the economy, the capacity for change, and is ultimately a love story with rousing good roles for two middle-age actors. It is a story for our times.

Cara Restaino

The plot of *It's a . . . Baby!* finds Cara telling the story of her sister's miraculous and surprise delivery of a baby no one excepted, not even her sister.

With a theme of happy accidents, the playwright was inspired by the true and ridiculous events leading up to and surrounding the birth of her niece, Angelina. Literally a little angel, Angelina was born into this world just twenty minutes after her less-than-prepared mother found out that she was even pregnant.

Julia Jarcho

The Highwayman was inspired by Alfred Noyes's romantic ballad "The Highwayman." I first heard about the poem from my grandmother, who'd won a prize for reciting it when she was a child. In the original poem, Bess is the beloved of the Highwayman, a notorious bandit. When a jealous admirer of Bess informs the authorities of this relationship, soldiers come to the inn and tie Bess up, waiting for the Highwayman in ambush. So that she won't move, they fasten a rifle to her heart. When she hears her love approaching, Bess realizes the only way to save him is to set off the gun herself so he'll know something is up and ride away to safety. She does so, killing herself.

In my play, Bess is a character in her own dream. The "story" of the poem becomes a fantasy she uses to navigate the suffering of her everyday life. In this fantasy, she's able to imagine a life made almost entirely of waiting, a passivity so intense it becomes active on its own terms, an entirely romantic self-erasure. I wanted to explore the ways in which a certain traditional image of feminine virtue resonates and collides with contemporary desires— sometimes painfully, sometimes beautifully.

Murray Schisgal

It is my belief that all those who pretend to the title of artist are deformed. The plot of *The Hunchback of Central Park* reveals a deformed, name-recognizable playwright, for the first time in his career, tormented by an interminable spell of writer's block. He is interviewed at length by a spectral entertainment journalist in his Central Park West apartment.

My inspiration for the play came when I received a phone call from a journalist working for a national magazine. He asked for a phone interview, wanting to write a column on what I was into since I hadn't had anything produced in New York City over the past half-dozen or so years. I agreed to the interview and we spoke at the prearranged time. After a number of general questions, he asked me how it felt to be a senior citizen. When I expressed my surprise, he said: "Well, the fact is, I'm writing a column about aging and I thought you might have something of interest to say about it. I mumbled a number of fatuous observations before hanging up. At once I had to acknowledge that I had acted like a wimp, a putz. I regretted not hanging up on him as soon as he told me the true reason for his call. My regret simmered into self-anger, my self-anger morphed into *The Hunchback of Central Park*.

I have carried within me since childhood the shadow of Quasimodo. I saw *The Hunchback of Notre Dame* when it was first released in 1939. I was mesmerized by Charles Laughton's performance. I shared with Mr. Laughton's Quasimodo certain, definitive characteristics. I was, inescapably, the outsider. I was locked for the length of my days in the dungeons of my imagination. I was, if not grossly unattractive, painfully aware of my slouching ordinariness. I pined for attention. I longed for bells to ring, for songs to sing, for dances to dance, all, for the love of an Esmeralda.

The Best American Short Plays

2005–2006

The Other Woman

David Ives

David Ives

David Ives was born in Chicago and educated at Northwestern University and the Yale School of Drama, where he received an MFA in playwriting. His first play in New York was *Canvas* at the Circle Repertory Company in 1972. *Saint Freud* was then produced by Circle Rep in 1975.

The critics noticed him in the late 1980s for a series of original one-act comedies that began to appear every season at the Manhattan Punch Line's one-act play festivals. Those plays, along with others written later, created full evenings of theatre—the series *All in the Timing, Mere Mortals,* and *Lives of the Saints.* His best-known one-act comedies are *Sure Thing; Words, Words, Words; Variations on the Death of Trotsky; Philip Glass Buys a Loaf of Bread;* and *The Universal Language.* In the early 1990s, he started working in music theatre with the libretto for an opera based on Frances Hodgson Burnett's *The Secret Garden,* which premiered in Philadelphia in 1991 at the Pennsylvania Opera Theatre. In the mid-1990s, after having been a contributor to *Spy* magazine, he wrote occasional humor pieces for the *New York Times Magazine* and the *New Yorker.*

Ives's most popular series of plays is *All in the Timing,* which originated as an evening of one-act comedies that premiered at Primary Stages in 1993, moved to the larger John Houseman Theatre, and ran for two years, giving 606 performances. This series won him the Outer Critics Circle John Gassner Award for Playwriting. In the 1995–1996 season, this production was the most-performed play in the country after Shakespeare productions.

His short plays are collected in two anthologies, *All in the Timing* (Vintage) and *Time Flies* (Grove). His full-length works for theatre are available in *Polish Joke and Other Plays* (Grove). He is also the author of a young adult novel, *Monsieur Eek* (HarperCollins), the almost-true story of how a chimpanzee got mistaken for a Frenchman.

David Ives is an artistic associate at Encores! at City Center, New York, where to date he has adapted fifteen of their shows. He is a regular adapter in New York's celebrated Encores! series of classic American musicals in concert, working on two or three a year for over a dozen years. His adaptation of *Wonderful Town* moved to Broadway at the Martin Beck Theatre in 2003, directed by Kathleen Marshall. In the late 1990s, he adapted David Copperfield's magic show *Dreams and Nightmares* for Broadway, which also played at the Beck. He also adapted Cole Porter's *Jubilee* and Rodgers and Hammerstein's *South Pacific*, starring Reba McEntire, for concert performances at Carnegie Hall. In 2002, he worked on the German transfer *Dance of the Vampires*. He co-wrote the book for *Irving Berlin's White Christmas*, which premiered in San Francisco in 2004 to great acclaim, and this musical has toured across the country. Mr. Ives did a new translation of Georges Feydeau's classic farce *A Flea in Her Ear*, which premiered in Chicago in 2006. Mr. Ives lives in New York City with his wife, Martha.

···production note···

The Other Woman premiered at Ensemble Studio Theatre, New York (Curt Dempster, artistic director). It was directed by Walter Bobbie, and the cast was Ruthie Henshall as Emma and Scott Cohen as Thomas.

···

[*In the dark: a clock chimes three times.*]

[*Lights fade up on* THOMAS'*s study. Middle of the night. A desk with books, papers, a small lamp. A chair in front of the desk. Books.*]

[THOMAS *sits in the glow of the desk lamp, writing at a laptop. Darkness around* THOMAS.]

[EMMA *enters out of the dark from right, barefoot, in a nightgown.* THOMAS *doesn't notice and keeps working a moment.*]

EMMA   It's too dark.

THOMAS   Jesus, you spooked me. What are you doing up? Time is it . . . ? Three . . . ? I was just going to wrap up and come to bed. Three hours, three paragraphs. I shouldn't have drunk so much at that party . . .

[EMMA *says nothing, looking at him steadily.*]

What's the matter? Emma?

[*No response.*]

Emma . . . ?

EMMA   I'm so afraid.

[*She sits on the edge of the chair.*]

I'm so afraid.

THOMAS   Emma . . . You're sleeping, honey. You're asleep. Don't you want to go back to bed? Come back to bed, honey. Come on.

EMMA   [*Who seems to us in no way somnambulistic.*]

I'm so afraid.

THOMAS   What are you afraid of? What is it? Emma, what's the matter?

EMMA   Not here.

THOMAS What?

EMMA Not here.

THOMAS What's not here?

EMMA Is it still night?

THOMAS Yes.

EMMA How night?

THOMAS Very night. It's late. Come on.

EMMA *Don't you patronize me. I'm afraid.*
[*That stops him.*]
I'm so afraid.

THOMAS Okay. Okay...

EMMA Where are you going?

THOMAS [*Who has not moved.*]
Nowhere. I'm right here.

EMMA Will it be morning soon?

THOMAS Come back to bed. Everything's going to be all right.

EMMA Nothing bad can happen in the daylight.

THOMAS What...?

EMMA Nothing bad can happen in the daylight.

THOMAS I know.

EMMA Will you tell her that?

THOMAS Tell who?

EMMA Tell her that.

THOMAS I will. I'll tell her tomorrow. Now everything is fine. Go back to bed.

EMMA [*Sighs heavily; reluctant, resigned.*]
All right. All right...

THOMAS Everything is fine. Everything is good.

EMMA   Not you. Not you.

[*EMMA exits.*]

THOMAS   It's so unreal, it's so wild, for a second I can hardly believe it happened. Everything's the way it was before. I'm alone. The room is empty. The laptop is on the desk. I write it all down, of course—as much as I can remember—just so I won't forget it. This visitation. And when I go upstairs a while later, Emma is in bed, fast asleep. Peaceably asleep. The way she always sleeps. The way she lives. With a kind of preternatural calm, a serenity that I admire but never seem able to attain myself. Unruffled, and unrufflable. That's Emma. And afraid—? Never. Not Emma.

[*Lights change to morning. EMMA enters in a robe.*]

EMMA   Good morning.

THOMAS   Good morning.

[*Kiss.*]

EMMA   You're up early.

THOMAS   Yeah. Sort of a restless night.

EMMA   Too excited. The new book.

THOMAS   Must be. How did *you* sleep?

EMMA   Wonderfully. Gone with the light.
    [*Sits in the chair.*]
    What a fun party.

THOMAS   Yeah. Very fun.

EMMA   A lot of people I didn't know. Interesting people. The Nielsens always have such good parties. You know Terry's going around the world in June. I should call her. So you did good work?

THOMAS   Yeah. I think I might've cracked it.

EMMA   Good.
    [*Off his look.*]
    What's the matter?

THOMAS Nothing. Nothing.

EMMA Full day today. Meeting about the power plant.

THOMAS The power plant. . . .

[*A small pause.*]

EMMA The leakage. The river, the chemicals? You remember?

THOMAS Yes, I remember.

EMMA The way you were looking at me . . .

THOMAS Darling, I hear every word you say.

EMMA . . . like I was crazy. How about you? What's on the docket?

THOMAS Emma, you don't have something on your mind, do you?

EMMA Something on my mind . . . ?

THOMAS I mean, you're not worried about anything. Anxious, or afraid . . . ?

EMMA No, why? "Afraid"? That's a strong word. Why do you ask?

THOMAS I don't know, you just seem . . . anxious, lately. A bit on edge.

EMMA I'm sorry. When?

THOMAS No particular time. Just . . .

EMMA No. I feel good. I feel *very* good. That power plant certainly troubles me.

THOMAS Maybe something about me?

EMMA What is all this? Did I miss a chapter?

THOMAS No, I'm just . . . You were talking in your sleep last night.

EMMA I was? God, did I say anything embarrassing?

THOMAS No. Well, I didn't know you were sleeping with that car mechanic.

EMMA No, come on. What did I say?

THOMAS I don't know. I couldn't quite make it out. You seemed pretty worked up, pretty tense about something. Afraid.

EMMA I didn't know I talk in my sleep.

THOMAS You never have. I mean, not to my knowledge.

EMMA Huh. Funny. So she's going mad at last, huh. Just tell them the chemicals from the power plant did it. Then sue those bastards for everything they've got.

THOMAS Well, it's daylight now. Nothing bad can happen in the daylight.

[*Pause.*]

EMMA What?

THOMAS I just mean—I wouldn't worry about it.

EMMA I'm not worried. Talking in my sleep. How *odd*. I'm not talking in my sleep right now, am I? I mean, how would I know?

THOMAS But you would tell me if there was something. I mean something more personal than the power plant—?

EMMA Darling, I tell you everything. And you hear every word I say.

THOMAS Right.

EMMA It's a nice arrangement.
    [*Kisses him.*]
    Dinner out tonight? What do you say?

THOMAS Sure.

EMMA Anton's? For the amazing appetizers?

THOMAS Sounds good to me.

EMMA [*Stretches; sighs happily.*]
    All right. All right. I'm going to clean up.
    [*He's still staring at her. She snaps her fingers in front of his face.*]
    Wake up!

[EMMA *exits.* THOMAS *watches her go.*]

THOMAS The day is uneventful, the amazing appetizers are eaten, night falls, and Emma slips peaceably off to bed.

[*Lights change back to night. Music comes back up.*]

Needless to say, I get no work done. No real work. Because after Emma goes to bed I spend the night waiting, listening for something. A sound. A footstep in the hall. A strange woman wandering the house.

[*Clock strikes three, offstage.*]

Three o'clock chimes.

[EMMA *enters, barefoot, in her nightgown.*]

EMMA Don't let me be in there.

THOMAS Be where?

EMMA It's too dark.

[THOMAS *turns off the music.*]

So will I be hanging off the ceiling upside-down? Otherwise?

[*She waits urgently for an answer.*]

So? *Otherwise?*

THOMAS Otherwise . . . I think you're fine.

EMMA If brain matter was equal to landscape, Portugal would extend from the cerebral cortex all the way to mistake.

THOMAS I never thought of it that way.

EMMA What are you going to do about it?

THOMAS What do you want me to do?

EMMA Will you help? Or is the gray jacket?

THOMAS I'll help you. I just need to know how.

EMMA Useless. Pathetic. Men men men.

[*Deep sigh.*]

Is it still night?

THOMAS Honey . . .

EMMA Fake. Fraud.

THOMAS Honey, wake up.

EMMA The orange isn't *on* the orange, the orange *is* the orange. In the basket on the cat. If I could only...

THOMAS What? What do you want? What are you afraid of?

EMMA If I could only.

THOMAS Only what.

EMMA I forgot to take my perfume.

THOMAS What perfume?

EMMA My *perfume*. My necessary *perfume*. By prescription.

THOMAS Nothing bad can happen in the daylight.

[That catches her attention.]

EMMA Nothing bad...

THOMAS ... can happen in the daylight. Do you know who I am? What's my name?

EMMA Book.

THOMAS Who are you? What's your name?

EMMA You know my name.

THOMAS What name?

EMMA Secret prescription.

THOMAS Where do you come from?

EMMA From sleep.

THOMAS Do you know where you are? Do you recognize this place?

EMMA No...

THOMAS Do you know Thomas and Emma? Emma and Thomas?

EMMA That would be fine. Amazing appetizers if all the world was a restaurant.

THOMAS So you remember the appetizers at Anton's—

EMMA *No. Help. At. All.*

THOMAS I'll help you. What can I do? What do you want? Tell me.

EMMA [*Runs a hand along his cheek.*]
>   So sweet.
>   [*Kisses him.*]
>   Love me.

THOMAS I do.

EMMA Love me.
>   [*Throws her arms around his neck and kisses him again.*]
>   Love me.

THOMAS It's like kissing another woman who also happens to be my wife.

EMMA Love me.

[*She exits.*]

THOMAS We make love right there on the floor, and she's warm and deep and delicious. It's like I'm in the back room at some crazy drunken party—out of my mind and making love to a total stranger who wraps herself around me like a vine. Our first time but not our first time. Emma but not Emma. Emma but anonymous. It's not even Emma's body—not quite. The same body, but with different eyes looking at me. Familiar but unknown. All the while we're making love I'm terrified that she'll wake up. Yet somehow the danger of it all excites me. Nothing in my life tells me I could ever do such a thing, or that it would excite me. But I can and I do and it does, and the woman in my arms is amazing. When she leaves the room, trailing her nightgown behind her, I feel bereft. Bereft the way you feel when you've said good-bye to a lover. Ashamed the way you feel when you've betrayed her. Which I have done. I lie awake until dawn in a universe that feels light-years wider, and infinitely more fragile.

[*Morning. EMMA enters, dressed for the day.*]

EMMA I missed you.

THOMAS I'm sorry?

EMMA You didn't come to bed last night.

THOMAS No, I fell asleep on the couch.

EMMA Working till dawn now, huh.

THOMAS Yeah. Type type type. That couch isn't meant for sleeping, I'll tell you that. I'm sort of out of it. How are you? Besides smart and strong and incredibly alluring.

EMMA Do you know I woke up naked this morning?

THOMAS Naked. Really.

EMMA Naked in bed, with my nightgown at the bottom of the stairs.

THOMAS Huh. You don't remember taking it off?

EMMA Just sort of dropped there. I don't even remember *being* on the staircase.

THOMAS Funny.

EMMA Which means I would have had to be downstairs sometime during the night. But I don't remember that either.

THOMAS Huh.

EMMA You don't remember hearing me or anything? Moving around the house?

THOMAS No.

EMMA I don't walk in my sleep, do I? You said I was talking in my sleep the other night.

THOMAS Maybe you're trying to tell yourself to sleep in the nude.

EMMA It's just so creepy. To have done something and be totally unaware of it. To be somewhere, or have been somewhere, walking around—and have no memory of it all.

THOMAS You slept all right otherwise? Apart from waking up naked?

EMMA It's like I just got home from Saks and found I'd dropped a perfume bottle in my purse. A secret klepto.

THOMAS Who knows what we do that we're not aware of. We could have whole other lives. We've done plenty of things in the past that we don't remember. It's like a whole life that we've lived and what percentage of it do we remember? A billionth of one percent? It's like we've never lived it at all. Or only the few nanoseconds left scattered in our memory.

EMMA Tom, you're not hiding something from me?

THOMAS No.

EMMA *Do* I walk in my sleep?

THOMAS No. I mean . . .

EMMA Not to your knowledge. I guess I could've been walking around at three a.m. for years.

THOMAS Three a.m.?

EMMA What?

THOMAS Nothing. Three a.m. That's very specific.

EMMA Wait a minute. Wait a minute . . .

[*She looks around the room.*]

THOMAS What . . .

EMMA Nothing. Part of a dream, I guess. A flash on something. Gone . . . Maybe I am going off my rocker.

THOMAS Great material if you do.

EMMA Don't you dare. Pinned and wriggling to the page of a book?

THOMAS Could be a big bestseller.

EMMA No thank you.

THOMAS I'll cut you in for twenty percent. And buy you a new rocker. A house in Aruba.

EMMA [*Reading from the papers on the desk.*]
". . . we make love right there on the floor, and she's warm and deep and delicious . . . "

THOMAS [*Trying to move her away from the papers.*]
No peeking.

EMMA "I'm in the back room at some crazy drunken party—out of my mind and making love to a total stranger who wraps herself around me like a vine . . . "

THOMAS No peeking.

EMMA Looks like the book's taken a turn to the sexy.

THOMAS Yeah.

EMMA So. An erotic novel.

THOMAS No. I don't know.

EMMA That's a change.

THOMAS Erotic elements. I'm still sort of fumbling around.

EMMA Does it turn you on?

THOMAS What.

EMMA Writing sexy scenes, late at night.

THOMAS Well—sure.

EMMA So wake me up sometime and do something about it.

THOMAS All right. It's a deal. Sleeping Beauty.

[*He kisses her.*]

EMMA What was that?

THOMAS What . . .

EMMA What was that all about?

THOMAS [*Moving back in.*]
   You just said . . .

[*She pushes him away and looks at him a moment.*]

EMMA I don't get it.

THOMAS Get it? Get what?

EMMA That kiss was so funny.

THOMAS Just a kiss.

EMMA   It didn't even feel like you. It didn't feel like you at all.

THOMAS   How'd you like it?

EMMA   I didn't, really. I don't want a stranger on a floor in a back room. I want you.

THOMAS   You've got me already.

EMMA   You're supposed to say you don't want a stranger either.

THOMAS   I don't want a stranger either. I want you.

EMMA   Thank you.

THOMAS   [*Unbuttoning her blouse.*]
So are we saving the spotted owl today?

EMMA   We're supposed to be.

THOMAS   Maybe we could save the spotted owl for another time and save ourselves instead.

EMMA   Save ourselves?

THOMAS   From the ravages of unrequited desire. Nice bra.

EMMA   Tom, do you hate my name?

THOMAS   *What?* Do I *what?*

EMMA   I'm just asking. Do you hate my name?

THOMAS   What put that into your head?

EMMA   I don't know. *Do* you?

THOMAS   No. Am I supposed to?

EMMA   I was just wondering if you did.

THOMAS   You just happened to be wondering?

EMMA   Say my name.

THOMAS   [*Says nothing.*]

EMMA   Go on. Say my name.

THOMAS   Emma.

EMMA   Say it again.

THOMAS   Emma. Emma. Emma.

EMMA   I feel like crying today. I feel like weeping and I don't know why.
I felt like it when I woke up. A feeling of loss. Absence. I don't
know . . .
[*Pause.*]
I'm sorry.

THOMAS   No. Don't be.

EMMA   [*Rebuttoning.*]
Maybe later?

THOMAS   Absolutely. Say hello to the spotted owl for me.

EMMA   Actually it's a kind of dove.

THOMAS   Dove.

EMMA   [*Putting a hand to his cheek.*]
So sweet. Later?

THOMAS   Yes.

EMMA   Bye.

THOMAS   Bye.

[*Kiss.* EMMA *exits. Lights change to night.*]

THOMAS   We do make love later that evening. Not very happily. In the
midst of it, Emma begins to cry. To weep, I should say. Great
horrible sobs that shake her. And me. All her unruffledness, all
that serenity is gone, and nothing I say can calm her. She says
over and over again that it's her, but she doesn't know why it's her.
She keeps apologizing for weeping. After midnight sometime she
drifts off to sleep and I slip downstairs to wait . . . Shuffle some
sentences around. Stare at the screen.
[*Clock chimes three.*]
Three o'clock. Nobody. I still wait. At four-thirty I turn out all
the lights and find my way through the house and up the stairs

with my arms out in the dark in front of me—like a child
imitating a ghost. I wait the next night, and the next night.
Writing almost nothing. The next night. A month passes. The
clock chimes. I wait.

[*Clock chimes three.* EMMA *enters, barefoot, in her nightgown.*]

EMMA   It's too dark up there. I'm so afraid.

[*Sits on the edge of the chair.*]

I'm so afraid . . .

THOMAS   I've missed you.

EMMA   I couldn't be up there anymore. Hanging off the ceiling in the
dark . . .

[THOMAS *says nothing.*]

Well? Mr. Book?

[*He goes to her and tries to embrace her. She pulls away.*]

What are you doing?

[*He tries again and she pulls away.*]

Thomas. What are you doing?

THOMAS   Sorry . . .

EMMA   So who is she?

THOMAS   Who is who?

EMMA   Who is she? Isn't there somebody? The woman in your book.

THOMAS   Emma—that was . . . There is nobody.

EMMA   The Nielsens' party?

THOMAS   What?

EMMA   The warm and deep and delicious stranger in the back room at a
party?

THOMAS   Emma, it's *fiction.*

EMMA   I was looking for you at one point during that party and I
couldn't find you.

THOMAS   The Nielsens' party doesn't have anything to do with anything.

EMMA   So which party?

THOMAS   *No* party. *No* woman. *Nowhere.* There's nobody but you.

EMMA   And I stupidly thought it could never happen to us. Not here. Not in this house. Not you.

THOMAS   I kissed *you* in the bedroom at the Nielsens' party, just before we left. Do you remember? The mix-up with the coats?

EMMA   Do you love her, or is it just fucking?

THOMAS   There is nobody but you.

EMMA   Can I read this book?

THOMAS   I destroyed it. What there was of it.

EMMA   The whole book?

THOMAS   The whole book.

EMMA   Why?

THOMAS   I don't know. The direction it was taking. Honey, if I've hurt you or confused you or made you worry—I'm sorry. But look, everything's going to be all right. Everything's fine.

EMMA   Don't you patronize me. *I'm afraid.*

THOMAS   I'm sorry.

EMMA   Is it still night?

THOMAS   What...?

EMMA   Is it still night?

THOMAS   Yeah...

EMMA   How night?

THOMAS   Very night. It's three o'clock in the morning...

EMMA   Will you tell her that?

THOMAS   Sure, I'll tell her in the morning.

EMMA Something tells the bell tower to scream at England every hour. Depending on circumstances.

THOMAS Emma...

EMMA And what about the circumference of all that noise? Where does that go?

THOMAS Emma, it's time to go to bed. Come on, honey.

EMMA I told you, I'm afraid. I'm afraid. I'm so afraid.

THOMAS Emma...

EMMA Love me.

EMMA Love me. Love me.   **THOMAS** Emma. Emma. *Emma.*
Love me. Please love me.   Wake up! Wake up, Emma!
Please. Please. Love me.   Wake up! Wake up!
Love me. Love me.

THOMAS *Emma—WAKE UP!*

EMMA [*Running a hand along his cheek.*]
So sweet...

[*Blackout.*]

• • •

Elliot,
a Soldier's
Fugue

Quiara Alegría Hudes

Quiara Alegría Hudes

Quiara Alegría Hudes wrote the book for the musical *In the Heights*, presented on Broadway at the Richard Rodgers Theatre. In its original Off-Broadway incarnation, *In the Heights* received the Lucille Lortel Award and Outer Critics Circle Award for Best Musical, was named Best Musical of 2007 by *New York Magazine* and Best of 2007 by the *New York Times*, and garnered Quiara an HOLA Award for Outstanding Achievement in Playwriting. Her play *Elliot, a Soldier's Fugue* was a Pulitzer Prize finalist in 2007 and has been performed around the country and in Romania and Brazil. Her newest play, *26 MILES*, received its world premiere at the Alliance Theatre in Atlanta during the 2008–2009 season. She is currently writing a musical called *The Adventures of Barrio Grrrl!* for the Kennedy Center. Her first play, *Yemaya's Belly*, received the Clauder Prize, the Paula Vogel Award in Playwriting, and the Kennedy Center/ACTF Latina Playwriting Award and had numerous productions around the country. As an author, Hudes' first children's book will soon be published by Arthur Levine Books, an imprint of Scholastic Inc. Hudes has studied music composition (BA, Yale University) and playwriting (MFA, Brown University), is a resident writer at New Dramatists, and a previous Page 73 playwriting fellow. She was born and raised in West Philadelphia, where she began composing music and writing; she now maintains residencies in New York and Philadelphia with her husband and daughter.

··· production note ···

Elliot, a Soldier's Fugue was first produced by Page 73 Productions in New York on January 4, 2006, directed by Davis McCallum.

characters

> **ELLIOT**, serving in Iraq, 1st Marine Division, 19
> **POP**, Elliot's father, served in Vietnam, 3rd Cavalry Division, various ages
> **GRANDPOP**, Elliot's grandfather, served in Korea, 65th Infantry Regiment of Puerto Rico, various ages
> **GINNY**, Elliot's mother, served in Vietnam, Army Nurse Corps, various ages

set

The set has two playing areas. The "empty space" is minimal, it transforms into many locations. It is stark, sad. When light enters, it is like light through a jailhouse window or through the dusty stained glass of a decrepit chapel. The "garden space," by contrast, is teeming with life. It is a verdant sanctuary, green speckled with magenta and gold. Both spaces are holy in their own way.

note to actors

Fugues

In the "fugue" scenes, people narrate each other's actions and sometimes narrate their own. For instance:

•••

ELLIOT   A boy enters.

[ELLIOT *enters.*]

GRANDPOP   Clean, deodorized.
>   Some drops of water plummet from his nose and lips.
>   The shower was ice cold.

[ELLIOT *shivers.*]

Elliot's action should mirror what the narrator, Grandpop, says. The narrator steps in and out of the scene as necessary.

Pop's letters

Pop's letters are active and alive. They are not reflective, past-tense documents. They are immediate communication. Sometimes the letters are shared dialogue between Pop and Grandpop, but it should always be clear that it is Pop's story being spoken.

Music

Flute. Bach, danzónes, jazz, etudes, scales, hip-hop beats. Overlapping lines.

Other

Please do not use actual barbed wire or vines in the wrapping scenes. The stage directions in these moments are an important part of the soul of the piece, but should not be staged literally.

··· 1/fugue ···

[*The empty space, very empty. A pair of white underwear is on the ground. That's all we see.*]

GINNY A room made of cinderblock.
  A mattress lies on a cot containing thirty-six springs.
  If you lie on the mattress, you can feel each of the thirty-six springs.
  One at a time.
  As you close your eyes.
  And try to sleep the full four hours.

POP A white sheet is on the mattress.
  The corners are folded and tucked under.
  Tight, like an envelope.

GRANDPOP Military code.
  The corner of the sheet is checked at 0600 hours, daily.
  No wrinkles or bumps allowed.

ELLIOT   A man enters.

[ELLIOT *enters in a towel. It's 2003. He's 18.*]

GRANDPOP   Clean, deodorized.

Some drops of water plummet from his nose and lips.

The shower was ice cold.

[ELLIOT *shivers. He picks up the underwear.*]

GINNY   He performs his own military-style inspection.

[ELLIOT *looks at the front and back of the underwear. No apparent stains. He sniffs them. They're clean.*]

ELLIOT   Nice.

[ELLIOT *puts them on under the towel, removes the towel.*]

POP   There's little bumps of skin on his arm.

His pores tighten.

His leg hair stands on end.

Cold shower spray.

[ELLIOT *drops to the ground and does ten push-ups. He springs to his feet and seems invigorated.*]

ELLIOT   One two three four five six seven eight nine ten. Rah!

POP   The mirror in the room reflects a slight distortion.

[ELLIOT *peers into the mirror-the audience.*]

GINNY   The chin.

The teeth.

Uppers and lowers.

The molars.

The one, lone filling.

[*He clenches his jaw, furrows his eyebrows. Holding the face, he curls a bicep, showing off a round muscle.*]

ELLIOT   [*To the mirror adversary.*]

What? You want to step? You're making Subway hoagies. I'm a marine. Who are you?

[*He shakes out that pose. Now, he smiles like a little angel into the mirror.*]

[*To the mirror mommy.*]

Mami, quiero chuletas. Pasteles. Morsilla. Barbecue ribs. Sorullito. Macaroni salad. Sopa de fideo. When I make it back home, you gonna make me a plate, right? A montón of ribs. But no pigs feet. Ain't no other Puerto Rican on this earth be cookin' no pigs feet.

[ELLIOT *shakes out that pose. He leans in, an inch away from the mirror. He pops a pimple. He wipes it on his underwear. He scrutinizes his face for more pimples. There are none. He fixes his nearly-shaved hair. He stands in a suave posture, leaning sexy. He blows a subtle kiss to the mirror.*]

You know you like it. Navy nursee want mi culito?

[*He turns around, looks at his butt in the mirror. He clenches his butt muscles and releases. Then he does this about ten times in a quick succession, watching the mirror the whole time. He stops.*]

POP   Blank.

He's nervous about something.

GRANDPOP   He will board the ship to Iraq at 0700 hours.

[ELLIOT *starts to put on his uniform under. . .*

The room is empty. A towel is on the floor.]

GINNY   A room with steel doors.

Steel walls, steel windows.

The room sways up and down.

Hammocks on top of hammocks swing back and forth.

GRANDPOP   The room is inside a boat.

That's on the ocean to Vietnam.

GINNY   The floors of the USS *Eltinge* are inspected at 0530 daily.

POP and **GRANDPOP**   Military code.

No dirt allowed.

GINNY   But the floor is wet.

It's the Pacific Ocean, seeping inside.

POP   A young man enters.

[POP *enters. It's 1966. He wears a uniform and catches his breath.*]

GINNY   The 0400 deck run was hot.

The shower will be warm.

640 muscles will relax.

GRANDPOP   Military code.

No bare chests.

[POP *untucks his shirt, unbuttons it, throws it to the floor.*]

POP   [*Imitating a drill sergeant under his breath. Faux Southern accent.*]

Keep up the pace, Ortiz. You can't hear me, Ortiz? Are you deaf, Ortiz? Corporal Feifer, is Corporal Ortiz deaf?

GRANDPOP   Military code.

No bare feet.

[*He takes off his boots, peels off his socks.*]

POP   You're the best damn shot in the marines, Ortiz. You could kill a fly. Does your momma know what a great shot you are?

GINNY   Reflect honor upon yourself and your home country.

[*He peels off his undershirt.*]

POP   Where are you from, Ortiz? What's your momma's name? Eh? Is she fat like you? Your momma got a fat ass, Ortiz?

[ELLIOT *is fully dressed. He salutes the mirror.*]

ELLIOT   Lance Corporal Elliot Ortiz Third Light Armored Recon Battalion First Marine Division. Mutha fucka.

[POP *finds a paper and pencil. He taps the pencil, thinking of what to write.* ELLIOT *checks inside his duffel bag.*]

GINNY   The duffel is heavy, full of boots and pants.

A map of Iraq.

A Bible with four small photographs.

GRANDPOP   Military code.

No electronic devices.

ELLIOT   Got my Walkman.

GRANDPOP   Military code.
　　　No valuables.

ELLIOT   My Nas CD. Jay Z. Slow Jams. Reggaetón 2002.

POP   April 12, 1966 . . .

[ELLIOT *opens a little green Bible, looks at photos.*]

ELLIOT   My photos. Mom. In your garden.
　　　[*He kisses the photo. Finds a new one.*]
　　　Grandpop. Senile old head.
　　　[*Taps the photo. Finds a new one.*]
　　　Pops. With your beer-ass belly.

POP   [*Writing.*] Dear pop . . .

ELLIOT   [*Still to the photo.*] When I get home, we gonna have a father and
　　　son. Chill in mom's garden. Drink some Bud Light out them mini
　　　cans. I don't want to hear about no "leave the past in the past."
　　　You gonna tell me your stories.

[ELLIOT *puts on headphones and starts bobbing his head to the hip-hop beat.*
POP *continues to write under . . .*
The room is empty. A towel is on the floor.]

GINNY   A tent.
　　　No windows, no door.
　　　Walls made of canvas.
　　　A floor made of dirt.
　　　The soil of Inchon, Korea, is frozen.

GRANDPOP   Sixteen cots they built by hand.
　　　Underwear, towels, unmade beds.
　　　Dirty photos.

GINNY   That is, snapshots of moms and daughters and wives
　　　That have dirt on them.

GRANDPOP   A boy enters.

[GRANDPOP *enters. It's 1950. He's wearing heavy soldier clothes. He rubs his arms for warmth. He puts on additional clothing layers.*]

GINNY   His breath crystallizes.

His boots are full of icy sweat.

The 0500 swamp run was subzero.

[GRANDPOP *blows into his hands for warmth. He bends his fingers.*]

GRANDPOP   One two three four . . . five. My thumb is as purple as a flower.

[*He pulls a black leather case from his cot. He opens it, revealing a flute. He pulls out pieces of the flute, begins to assemble them, cleaning dirt from the joints.*]

Ah, this Korean dirt is too damn dirty. We lost another man to frostbite this week. These guys deserve some Bach. Light as a feather,

POP   [*Finishing the letter.*] Your son,

GRANDPOP   free as a bird.

POP   Little George.

[GRANDPOP *puts the flute to his lips, inhales, begins to play. The melody of a Bach passacaglia.*

POP *folds up the letter, puts it in an envelope. Addresses the envelope.*]

GINNY   Military code.

Make no demands.

Military code.

Treat women with respect.

Military code.

Become friends with fellow soldiers.

No rude behavior.

Pray in silence, please.

[POP *drops the letter, lays down, sings himself to sleep. It overlaps with* GRANDPOP's *flute and* ELLIOT's *head-bobbing.*]

POP   1234

We're gonna jump on the count of four

If I die when I hit the mud
Bury me with a case of bud
A case of bud and a bottle of rum
Drunk as hell in kingdom come
Count off
1234[1]

[ELLIOT *skips forward a few tracks on the Walkman. He finds his jam. Head bobbing, feeling it.*]

ELLIOT   Uh, uh.

And when I see ya I'ma take what I want so	
You tryin to front, hope ya	
Got ur self a gun	
You ain't real, hope ya	
Got ur self a gun	**POP**
Uh, uh, uh, uh.	1234
I got mine I hope ya . . . uh, uh	We're gonna charge on the count of four
You from da hood I hope ya . . .	If my heart begins to bleed
You want beef I hope ya . . .	Bury me with a bag full a' weed
Uh, uh, uh, uh.	A bag full a' weed and a
And when I see you I'ma	Bottle of rum
Take what I want so	Laugh at the devil in kingdom come
You tryin to front, hope ya . . .	Count off
You ain't real, hope ya . . .	Bud bud bud bud
Uh, uh, uh, uh.[2]	Bud bud bud bud

[*It is three-part counterpoint between the men. Lights fade, counterpoint lingers.*]

---

[1] Based on traditional military cadences.
[2] From Nas, "Got Yourself a Gun."

··· 2/prelude ···

[*The empty space. A flashbulb goes off.*]

SPORTSCASTER VOICE   Thanks, Harry. I'm standing outside the Phillies locker room with hometown hero Lance Corporal Elliot Ortiz. He'll be throwing out tonight's opening pitch.

ELLIOT   Call me Big El.

SPORTSCASTER VOICE   You were one of the first marines to cross into Iraq.

ELLIOT   Two days after my eighteenth birthday.

SPORTSCASTER VOICE   And you received a Purple Heart at 19. Big El, welcome home.

ELLIOT   *Philly!*

SPORTSCASTER VOICE   You're in Philadelphia for a week and then it's back to Iraq for your second tour of duty?

ELLIOT   We'll see. I got until Friday to make up my mind.

SPORTSCASTER VOICE   Did you miss the City of Brotherly Love?

ELLIOT   Mom's food. My girl, Stephanie. My little baby cousin. Cheese steaks.

SPORTSCASTER VOICE   Any big plans while you're home?

ELLIOT   Basically eat. Do some interviews. My mom's gonna fix up my leg. I'm a take my pop out for a drink, be like, alright, old head. Time to trade some war stories.

SPORTSCASTER VOICE   I hope you order a Shirley Temple. Aren't you 19?

ELLIOT   I'll order a Shirley Temple.

SPORTSCASTER VOICE   Big Phillies fan?

ELLIOT   Three years in a row I was Lenny Dykstra for Halloween.

SPORTSCASTER VOICE   A few more seconds to pitch time.

ELLIOT   Hold up. Quick shout out to North Philly. 2nd and Berks, share the love! To my moms. My pops. I'm doing it for you.

Grandpops—videotape this so you don't forget! Stephanie. All my friends still out there in Iraq. Waikiki, one of these days I'm going to get on a plane to Hawaii and your mom better cook me some Kahlua pig.

SPORTSCASTER VOICE   Curve ball, fast ball?

ELLIOT   Wait and see. I gotta keep you on your toes. I'm gonna stand on that mound and show ya'll I got an arm better than Schilling! Record lightning speed!

···3/prelude···

[*The garden.* GRANDPOP *opens a letter and reads.* POP *appears separately.*]

GRANDPOP and **POP**   May 24, 1966

POP   Dear pop,
　　　It's hot wet

GRANDPOP   cold muddy

POP   miserable. Operation Prairie has us in the jungle, and it's a sauna.

GRANDPOP   One hundred twenty degrees by 1100 hours,

POP   you think you're gonna cook by 1300. Then yesterday it starts to rain.

GRANDPOP   Drops the size of marbles—

POP   my first real shower in weeks. Monsoon. They said,

GRANDPOP   "Get used to it." Corporal shoved a machete in my hand and told me to lead.

POP   He's the leader, but I get to go first!

GRANDPOP   I cut through the vines, clear the way. We get lesions,

POP   ticks,

GRANDPOP   leeches.

POP   At night we strip down, everybody pulls the things off each other. We see a lot of rock ape.

GRANDPOP   They're bigger than chimps and they throw rocks at us.

POP   They've got great aim! You just shoot up in the air, they run away.

GRANDPOP   At night you can't see your own hand in front of your face.

POP   I imagine you and Mom on the back stoop, having a beer. Uncle Tony playing his guitar. My buddy Joe Bobb,

GRANDPOP   from Kentucky.

POP   He carries all his equipment on his back, plus a guitar, and he starts playing these hillbilly songs.

GRANDPOP   They're pretty good.

POP   I think Uncle Tony would like them. I pulled out your flute and we jammed a little. C-rations, gotta split,

POP and **GRANDPOP**   Little George.

···4/prelude···

[GINNY *in the garden.*]

GINNY   The garden is twenty-five years old. It used to be abandoned. There was glass everywhere. Right here, it was a stripped-down school bus. Here, a big big pile of old tires. I bought it for one dollar. A pretty good deal. Only a few months after I came back from Vietnam. I told myself, you've got to *do* something. So I bought it. I went and got a ton of dirt from Sears. Dirt is expensive! I said, when I'm done with this, it's going to be a spitting image of Puerto Rico. Of Arecibo. It's pretty close. You can see electric wires dangling like right there and there. But I call that "native Philadelphia vines." If you look real close, through the heliconia you see anti-theft bars on my window.

Green things, you let them grow wild. Don't try to control them. Like people, listen to them, let them do their own thing. You give them a little guidance on the way. My father was a mean bastard. The first time I remember him touching me, it was to whack me with a shoe. He used to whack my head with a wooden spoon

every time I cursed. I still have a bump on my head from that.
Ooh, I hated him. But I was mesmerized to see him with his
plants. He became a saint if you put a flower in his hand. Secrets,
when things grow at night. Phases of the moon. He didn't need a
computer, he had it all in his brain. "I got no use for that." That
was his thing. "I got no use for church." "I got no use for a
phone." "I got no use for children." He had use for a flower.

There are certain plants you only plant at night. Orchids. Plants
with provocative shapes. Plants you want to touch. Sexy plants.
My garden is so sexy. If I was young, I'd bring all the guys here.
The weirdest things get my juices going. I sit out here at night,
imagine romances in the spaces between banana leaves. See
myself as a teenager, in Puerto Rico, a whole different body on
these bones. I'm with a boyfriend, covered in dirt.

When I was a nurse in the Army Nurse Corps, they brought men
in by the loads. The evacuation hospital. The things you see.
Scratched corneas all the way to . . . a guy with the back of his
body torn off. You get the man on the cot, he's screaming. There's
men screaming all around. Always the same thing, calling out for
his mother, his wife, girlfriend. First thing, before anything else, I
would make eye contact. I always looked them in the eye, like to
say, hey, it's just you and me. Touch his face like I was his wife.
Don't look at his wound, look at him like he's the man of my
dreams. Just for one tiny second. Then, it's down to business. Try
to keep that heart going, that breath pumping in and out, keep
that blood inside the tissue. Sometimes I was very attracted to the
men I worked on. A tenderness would sweep through me. Right
before dying, your body goes into shock. Pretty much a serious
case of the shakes. If I saw a man like that, I thought, would he
like one last kiss? One last hand on his ass? Give him a good
going away party.

Just things in my mind. Not things you act on.

With George, though. We had a great time when he was in the
evacuation hospital. I stitched his leg up like a quilt and we stayed
up all night smoking joints. Everyone in the hospital was passed

out asleep. The first time George got up and walked to me, I took his head in my right hand and I kissed him so hard. That kiss was the best feeling in my body. Ooh. You see so much death, then someone's lips touches yours and you go on vacation for one small second.

Gardening is like boxing. It's like those days in Vietnam. The wins versus the losses. Ninety percent of it is failures but the triumphs? When Elliot left for Iraq, I went crazy with the planting. Begonias, ferns, trees. A seed is a contract with the future. It's saying, I know something better will happen tomorrow. I planted bearded irises next to palms. I planted tulips with a border of cacti. All the things the book tells you, "Don't ever plant these together." "Guide to Proper Gardening." Well, I got on my knees and planted them side by side. I'm like, you have to throw all preconceived notions out the window. You have to plant wild. When your son goes to war, you plant every goddamn seed you can find. It doesn't matter what the seed is. So long as it grows. I plant like I want and to hell with the consequences. I planted a hundred clematis vines by the kitchen window, and next thing I know sage is growing there. The tomato vines gave me beautiful tomatoes. The bamboo shot out from the ground. And the heliconia!

[She retrieves a heliconia leaf.]

Each leaf is actually a cup. It collects the rainwater. So any weary traveler can stop and take a drink.

··· 5/prelude ···

[The garden. GRANDPOP *opens a letter and reads.* POP *appears separately.]*

POP   October 7, 1966

GRANDPOP   Dear dad and all the rest of you lucky people,

POP   Got my next assignment. All those weeks of waiting and boredom? Those are the good old days! They marched us to Dong Ha for Operation Prairie 2. I'm infantry. Some guys drive, go by tank. Infantry walks. We walk by the side of the tank. Two days straight, we've been scouting for body parts. You collect what you find, throw it in the tank, they label it and take it away. Where they take it? You got me. What they write on the label? It's like bird watching. You develop your eye.

GRANDPOP   Don't show this letter to mom, please. And don't ask me about it when I get home. If I feel like talking about it I will but otherwise don't ask.

POP   Today this one little shrimp kept hanging around, chasing after the tank. Looking at me with these eyes. I gave him my crackers I was saving for dinner. I made funny faces and he called me dinky dow. That's Vietnamese for crazy, I guess. Dinky dow! Dinky dow! He inhaled those crackers, then he smiled and hugged my leg. He was so small he only came up to my knee.

··· 6/fugue ···

[*The empty space. Two wallets are on the ground.*]

GINNY   In my dreams, he said.

Everything is in green.

Green from the night vision goggles.

Green Iraq.

Verdant Fallujah.

Emerald Tikrit.

[ELLIOT *enters. He puts on night vision goggles.*]

ELLIOT   [*To imaginary night patrol partner.*]

Waikiki man, whatchu gonna eat first thing when you get home? I don't know. Probably start me off with some French toast from Denny's. Don't even get me near the cereal aisle. I'll go crazy. I yearn for some cereal. If you had to choose between Cocoa Puffs and Count Chocula, what would you choose? Wheaties or Life? Fruity Pebbles or Crunchberry? You know my mom don't even buy Cap'n Crunch. She buys King Vitaman. Cereal so cheap, it don't even come in a box. It comes in a bag like them cheap Jewish noodles.

GINNY   Nightmares every night, he said.

A dream about the first guy he actually saw that he killed.

A dream that doesn't let you forget a face.

ELLIOT   The ultimate Denny's challenge. Would you go for the Grand Slam or the French Toast Combo? Wait. Or Western eggs with hash browns? Yo, hash browns with ketchup. Condiments. Mustard, tartar sauce. I need me some condiments.

GINNY   Green moon.

Green star.

Green blink of the eye.

Green teeth.

The same thing plays over and over.

[ELLIOT*'s attention is suddenly distracted.*]

ELLIOT   Yo, you see that?

GINNY   The green profile of a machine gun in the distance.

ELLIOT   Waikiki, look straight ahead. Straight, at that busted wall. Shit. You see that guy? What's in his hand? He's got an AK. What do you mean, "I don't know." Do you see him?

[ELLIOT *looks out.*]

We got some hostiles. Permission to shoot.

[*Pause.*]

Permission to open fire.

[*Pause.*]

Is this your first? Shit, this is my first, too. Alright. You ready?

GINNY   In the dream, aiming in.

In the dream, knowing his aim is exact.

In the dream, closing his eyes.

[ELLIOT *closes his eyes.*]

ELLIOT   Bang.

[ELLIOT *opens his eyes.*]

GINNY   Opening his eyes.

　　　　The man is on the ground.

ELLIOT   Hostile down. Uh, target down.

[ELLIOT *gets up, disoriented from adrenaline.*]

GINNY   In the dream, a sudden movement.

ELLIOT   Bang bang. Oh shit. That fucker moved. Did you see that? He moved, right? Mother f—. Target down. Yes, I'm sure. Target down.

GINNY   Nightmares every night, he said.

　　　　A dream about the first guy he actually saw that he killed.

[POP *enters, sits on the ground. He's trying to stay awake. He looks through binoculars.*]

GRANDPOP   In my dreams, he said.

GINNY   Walking toward the guy.

[ELLIOT *walks to the wallet.*]

GRANDPOP   Everything is a whisper.

GINNY   Standing over the guy.

[ELLIOT *looks down at the wallet.*]

GRANDPOP   Breathing is delicate.

GINNY   A green face.

GRANDPOP   Whisper of water in the river.

GINNY   A green forehead.

GRANDPOP   Buzz of mosquito.

GINNY   A green upper lip.

GRANDPOP   Quiet Dong—Ha.

GINNY   A green river of blood.

[ELLIOT *kneels down, reaches to the wallet on the ground before him. It represents the dead man. He puts his hand on the wallet and remains in that position.*]

GRANDPOP   Echo Vietnam.

POP Joe Bobb. Wake up, man. Tell me about your gang from Kentucky. What, back in the Bronx? Yeah, we got ourselves a gang, but not a bad one. We help people on our street. Like some kids flipped over an ice cream stand. It was just a nice old guy, the kids flipped it, knocked the old guy flat. We chased after them. Dragged one. Punched him till he said sorry. We called ourselves the Social Sevens. After the Magnificent Sevens.

GRANDPOP Nightmares every night, he said.

A dream that doesn't let you forget a voice.

The same sounds echoing back and forth.

POP Guns? Naw, we weren't into none of that. We threw a lot of rocks and bottles. And handballs. Bronx Handball Champs, 1964. Doubles and singles. Hm? What's a handball?

GRANDPOP The snap of a branch.

POP Shh.

GRANDPOP Footsteps in the mud.

POP You hear something?

GRANDPOP Three drops of water.

A little splash.

[POP *grabs his binoculars and looks out.*]

POP VC on us. Ten o'clock. Kneeling in front of the river, alone. He's drinking. Fuck, he's thirsty. Joe Bobb, man, this is my first time. Oh shit. Shit. Bang. [*Pause.*] Bang.

GRANDPOP Whisper of two bullets in the air.

Echo of his gun.

A torso falling in the mud.

POP Got him. I got him, Joe Bobb. Man down. VC down.

[POP *rises, looks out.*]

GRANDPOP Hearing everything.

Walking to the guy.

Boots squishing in the mud.

[POP *walks to the second wallet.*]
Standing over the guy.
The guy says the Vietnamese word for "mother."
He has a soft voice.
He swallows air.
A brief convulsion.
Gasp.
Silence.
Water whispers in the river.

POP and **ELLIOT**   Military code.
Remove ID and intel from dead hostiles.

[POP *kneels in front of the wallet. It represents the dead man. He reaches out his hand and touches the wallet.*

ELLIOT *and* POP *are in the same position, each of them touching a wallet. They move in unison.*]

POP   The wallet
The body
The face
The eyes

[ELLIOT *and* POP *open the wallets.*]

ELLIOT   The photo
The pictures
Bullet

[ELLIOT *and* POP *each pull a little photo out of the wallets.*]

POP   Dog tags
The wife

ELLIOT   The children
[*They turn over the photo and look at the back of it.*]
Black ink

POP   A date

POP and **ELLIOT**   Handwriting

> A family portrait

[*They drop the photo. They find a second photo. Lights fade.*]

··· 7/prelude ···

[*The empty space. A flashbulb goes off.* ELLIOT *is in a TV studio. Harsh studio lighting is on him.*]

PRODUCER VOICE   ABC evening local news. And we're rolling to tape in three, two . . .

ELLIOT   [*Tapping a mike on his shirt collar.*]

> Hello? What? Yeah. So where do we start?
>
> [*He presses his fingers against his ear, indicating that a producer or someone is talking to him through an ear monitor.*]
>
> My name? Elliot Ortiz.
>
> [*Listens.*]
>
> Sorry. Lance Corporal Elliot Ortiz, 3rd Light Armored Recon Battalion, 1st Marine Division.
>
> [*Listens.*]
>
> What? How was I injured?

PRODUCER VOICE   [*Impatient.*]

> Someone fix his monitor. Don't worry, Mr., uh, Ortiz. Just tell us the story of your injury, would you?

ELLIOT   Okay. Well. I was on watch outside Tikrit. I don't know. I feel stupid. I already told this story once.

PRODUCER VOICE   You did?

ELLIOT   Just now. In the screen test.

PRODUCER VOICE   Right, right. That was to acclimate you to the camera.

ELLIOT   It loses the impact to repeat it over and over.

PRODUCER VOICE   Was it scary?

ELLIOT People say, oh that must be scary. But when you're there, you're like, oh shit, and you react. When it's happening you're not thinking about it. You're like, damn, this is really happening. That's all you can think. You're in shock basically. It's a mentality. Kill or be killed. You put everything away and your mentality is war. Some people get real gung ho about fighting. I was laid back.

PRODUCER VOICE Yes, Mr., uh Ortiz. This is great. This is exactly it. Let's go back and do you mind repeating a couple sentences, same exact thing, without the expletives?

ELLIOT Say what?

PRODUCER VOICE Same thing. But no *shit* and no *damn*.

ELLIOT I don't remember word for word.

PRODUCER VOICE No problem. Here we go. "But when you're there, you're like, oh shit, and you react."

ELLIOT But when you're there you're like, oh snap, and you react.

PRODUCER VOICE "You're like, damn, this is really happening."

ELLIOT You're like, flip, this is really happening.

PRODUCER VOICE Flip? Do people say "flip" these days?

ELLIOT You're like, FUCK, this is really happening.

PRODUCER VOICE Cut!

ELLIOT It's a marine thing.

···8/prelude···

[GRANDPOP *in the garden.*]

GRANDPOP Of everything Bach wrote, it is the fugues. The fugue is like an argument. It starts in one voice. The voice is the melody, the single solitary melodic line. The statement. Another voice creeps up on the first one. Voice two responds to voice one. They tangle together. They argue, they become messy. They create dissonance. Two, three, four lines clashing. You think, good god, they'll never untie themselves. How did this mess get started in the first place? Major keys, minor keys, all at once on top of each other. [*Leans in.*] It's about untying the knot.

In Korea my platoon fell in love with Bach. All night long, firing eight-inch howitzers into the evergreens. Flute is very soothing after the bombs settle down. They begged me to play. "Hey, Ortiz, pull out that pipe!" I taught them minor key versus major key. Minor key, it's melancholy, it's like the back of the woman you love as she walks away from you. Major key, well that's more simple, like how the sun rises. They understood. If we had a rough battle, if we lost one of our guys, they said, "Eh, Ortiz, I need a minor key." But if they had just got a letter from home, a note from the lady, then they want C major, up-tempo.

"Light as a feather, free as a bird." My teacher always said the same thing. Let your muscles relax. Feel like a balloon is holding up your spine. He was a gringo but he lived with us rural Puerto Ricans. Way in the mountains. He was touring in San Juan with his famous jazz combo, fell in love with a woman, never left. We accepted him as one of our own. He was honorary Boricua. "Light as a feather, free as a bird." I said, you know, if I get any lighter and freer, I'll float to the moon. But that's how you learn. By repeating. Over and over. At Inchon my right hand was purple with frostbite. I developed a technique for left-hand only. In Kunu-Ri? Every night we took our weapons to bed, like a wife. One night I shot myself in the shoulder. So I mastered the left-hand method.

Elliot always wanted to know. "Abuelo, tell me a story." About life in the service, about Puerto Rico. "Abuelo, how old were you when? How old were you when this, when that?" Carajo, I don't remember! All I know is what music I was playing at the time. When I started school, when I was a boy, helping mom in the house, it was etudes and scales. The foundations. The first girl I "danced with," it was danzónes around that time, mambo with a touch of jazz. But in Korea, I played Bach only. Because it is cold music, it is like math. You can approach it like a calculation. An exercise. A routine.

At the airport, I handed the flute to little George. I thought, he
needs a word of advice, but what is there to say? I sent him to
boot camp with a fifty-dollar bill and a flute. That he didn't know
how to play. But without it my fingers grew stiff. I started losing
words. Dates. Names of objects. Family names. Battles I had
fought in. I started repeating words as if I was playing scales.
Practice. Bookmarks to remind myself. "Inchon, Inchon,
Inchon." "Korea, Korea." "Bayamón." "Howitzer."
"Evergreen."

···9/prelude···

[*The garden.* GRANDPOP *opens a letter and reads.* POP *appears separately, in a
good mood.*]

POP   November 30, 1966

Did you ever notice a helmet is an incredibly useful item? I got a
wide range of artistic and practical uses for mine.

GRANDPOP   Today I took a bath, if you want to call it that, out of my
helmet. The newer ones have two parts.

POP   If you take the metal part out, you can cook in it. Tonight we had
two cans of tuna. A hamburgers in gravy. Hess's contribution?

POP and GRANDPOP   Ham with lima beans.

POP   Everyone empties out their cans. Make a little blue campfire with
some minor explosives. Voila,

GRANDPOP   helmet stew.

POP   So that's our Thanksgiving feast. The guys are singing carols.
They're in the spirit!

Jingle bells

Mortar shells

VC in the grass

Take your Merry Christmas

And shove it up your ass

··· 10/fugue ···

[*The empty space. Two cots are there. Elliot lies on the ground.* GRANDPOP, GINNY, *and* POP *wrap* ELLIOT's *legs in barbed wire. They entangle* ELLIOT *in this position, trapping him.* ELLIOT *lies helpless.*]

GINNY   A road outside Tikrit.

A mile short of Saddam's hometown.

GRANDPOP   Cars are allowed out, but not back in.

POP   The boy was standing guard.

GRANDPOP   He saw an incoming car.

GINNY   The headlights approached.

POP   He fired into the car.

GRANDPOP   The horn sounded.

POP   The car collided into the barricade.

GINNY   The concertina wire slinkied onto his legs.

GRANDPOP   Two seconds ago.

ELLIOT   Sarge! Sarge! Waikiki!

GINNY   Seventy-four thorns dig deep into his skin.

POP   Seventy-four barbs chew into his bone.

GRANDPOP   It is not a sensation of rawness.

GINNY   It is not excruciating pain.

POP   It is a penetrating weakness.

GRANDPOP   Energy pours out of his leg.

GINNY   Like water from a garden hose.

ELLIOT   Sarge!

POP   The boy knows he is trapped.

GRANDPOP   He doesn't know he is injured.

GINNY   He does a military-style inspection.

[ELLIOT *reaches up his pants leg.*]

GRANDPOP   His hand enters the warm meat of his calf.

ELLIOT   Oh shit. Stay calm. Put the tourniquet on. Lay back. Drink a cup of water.

[ELLIOT *pulls a strip of cloth from his pocket. He wraps it like a tourniquet around his thigh. Tight.*]

GINNY   Forty-one percent of all injuries are leg wounds.

POP   Military code.

GRANDPOP   Carry a tourniquet at all times.

GINNY   Instructions in the event of rapid blood loss.

GRANDPOP   One.

ELLIOT   Stay calm.

POP   Two.

ELLIOT   Put the tourniquet on.

GRANDPOP   Three.

ELLIOT   Lay back.
　　　Four...Four?

GINNY   Drink a cup of water.

ELLIOT   Someone get me a cup of water.

POP   Stay

GRANDPOP   Calm
　　　Put

POP   Tourniquet

GINNY   Lay

GRANDPOP   Back
　　　Drink

POP   Cup

GINNY   Water

ELLIOT Hello? Stay calm. Put a beret on. Fall away. Drink a hot tub. Fuck. Stay with me, Ortiz. Big El going to be okay. Hello? Big El okay. Right?

POP Fast-forward pictures.

GINNY Mom

POP Pop

GRANDPOP Grandpop

POP Fast-forward.

GINNY Grandpop

GRANDPOP Pop

POP Mom

GINNY Rapid shutter motion.

GRANDPOP Frames with no sound.

GINNY Moving lips, no words.

ELLIOT Mom

POP Pop

GRANDPOP Grandpop

ELLIOT Stay calm. Lay back. Smoke a cigarette.
[*He pulls a cigarette out of his pocket.*]
Anyone got a light?
[*He smokes the unlit cigarette.*]

POP Instructions if wounded while alone.

GRANDPOP Call for help.

POP Signal commander.

GINNY Call for your corpsman.

POP Identify yourself.

ELLIOT Sarge! Waikiki! Big El down. Big El down.

POP   His blood congeals in the sand.

GRANDPOP   His fingertips are cool.

GINNY   He enters a euphoric state.

GRANDPOP   The boots,

ELLIOT   Beautiful.

POP   The barbed wire,

ELLIOT   Beautiful.

GINNY   The stars,

ELLIOT   Beautiful.

GINNY   In the event of extended blood loss.
　　　Reflect on a time you were happy.
　　　When have you felt a sensation of joy?

ELLIOT   Mom...
　　　Pop...

[ELLIOT *remains injured under...*
POP *enters and lays on a cot.*]

GRANDPOP   An evacuation hospital.
　　　Made of a Vietnamese monastery.
　　　Ancient windows with no glass.

GINNY   Through the window, views of Vietnam.
　　　That look like views of Puerto Rico.
　　　Mountains.

ELLIOT   Mountains.

GRANDPOP   Waterfalls.

ELLIOT   Waterfalls.

GINNY   All different colors of green.
　　　Rock formations.
　　　A few bald spots from the bombs.

GRANDPOP   The wood floor is covered with cement.

The cement is covered with water and blood.

The cement is cool.

The blood is cool.

ELLIOT   Cool.

[ELLIOT *nods off, going into shock.*]

GINNY   A woman enters.

[GINNY *enters, approaches* POP*'s cot.*]

Hey.

POP   Nurse Ginny. Still on duty?

GINNY   Shh. Don't wake the babies.

POP   Can't sleep?

GINNY   Yeah.

POP   Me too.

GINNY   Nightmares. Weird stuff, I kept seeing your leg. I thought I should check up on you.

POP   It itches, but you know. The guy next to me's got no left leg at all.

GINNY   I was thinking, a private physical therapy session.

POP   Sounds good.

GINNY   Clean you up.

[GINNY *lifts up his pant leg. There is a big gauze patch there. She slowly pulls back the gauze.*]

POP   That's as far back as it goes. The rest is stuck to the gauze.

GINNY   We're all out of anesthetic. I'll be gentle.

[*She works on his wound. He is clearly in physical pain.*]

Twenty-eight stitches.

Two diagonals.

The first time she touched the man's wound,

A pain pierced up through her index finger.

Through her knuckle.

Wrist.

Forearm.

Elbow.

Humerus.

Shoulder.

The pain jolted in her veins.

Exploded in her vital organs.

Pancreas, lungs, brains, spleen.

Planted itself between her legs.

She touched the blood on his skin and had the desire to make love to the wounded man.

POP Ay dios mio. Fuck.

GINNY Think of the time in life you were happiest.

POP Why?

GINNY You forget the pain.

POP It's not pain. It fucking itches!

GINNY Sorry.

POP Sorry.

[*Pause.* GINNY *covers the wound. She pulls down his pant leg. She sits on top him.*]

GINNY Is it too much weight?

POP Please, crush me to death.

GINNY There's too many bells and whistles in hospitals. To be a nurse is easy. Give a dog a bone.

POP Reach into my pocket.

GINNY Lance Corporal Ortiz.

POP Go ahead.

[*She puts her hand into his pocket. She feels around.*]

GINNY What am I looking for?

POP   You'll know when you find it.

> [*She removes her hand from his pocket. She's holding a joint.*]

> Medicine.

GINNY   Anesthetic.

[GINNY *lights the joint. They pass it back and forth. Between inhales, they touch each other.*]

GRANDPOP   Through the window, views of Vietnam.

> That look like views of Puerto Rico.

> Mountains.

> Green.

> Stars.

> Bamboo.

> Little huts up the mountainside.

POP   [*Stoned.*]

> I got one. I was a little boy in Puerto Rico. Bayamón. I had this ugly scrappy dog. We used to run around scaring my dad's roosters. One of the roosters got pissed and poked the dog's left eye out.

GINNY   What was his name?

POP   Jimmy.

GINNY   Jimmy? Jimmy!

[ELLIOT *shivers.*]

ELLIOT   Ugghhh . . .

POP   Shh. Did you hear something? The operating room.

GINNY   No, it's the monkeys. There's a whole family of them that live in the tree.

POP   They're not rock ape, are they?

GINNY   What's rock ape?

POP   Big, brown, and ugly.

GINNY Rock ape!

[*They laugh. She suddenly gets off of him and walks to a far corner of the room. She still has the joint.*]

GINNY Tonight you're going to do like Jesus did. You're going to get up and walk on water. Defy all the odds. And I'm going to do like a circus tamer. Like someone who trains dogs or exotic animals. If you're a good tiger and you do your trick and you don't bite, you get a reward. If you do your dolphin tricks, I give you a fish.

POP Seafood is my favorite.

GINNY Walk to me. See if you can make it.

POP Not even a hand out of bed?

GINNY If you want a taste of this ripe avocado, you got to pick it off the tree all by yourself.

[POP *struggles to get up. This is a difficult, painful process. He slowly makes his way across the room.*]

POP

Shrapnel.

In the ligaments.   **ELLIOT**

In the soft-hard knee cap.   Stay

In the spaces between stitches.

Shrapnel from a mortar bomb.   Back

Splinters that fragment within you.   Lay

Wobbling within your guts.

Creating ripples in your bloodstream.   Home

[POP *arrives at* GINNY. *He falls into her. They kiss.*]

Signal

Elliot Ortiz

[GINNY *and* POP *stop kissing.*]

POP Do you heal all your patients this way?

Elliot Ortiz.

GINNY Let's go outside and watch the monkeys.

POP No, really. You do this a lot?

Elliot Ortiz.

GINNY Think you can make it outside?

POP Give me a hand this time.

Ortiz.

GINNY There's a gorgeous view of the moon.

[*They exit, slowly, carefully, in each other's arms. They pass in front of* ELLIOT, *who is shivering.*]

ELLIOT Mom?

Pop?

··· 11/prelude ···

[*The empty space.* ELLIOT *wears big radio station headphones.*]

RADIO VOICE You're listening to WHYY, member-supported radio, welcome back. I'm having a conversation with Elliot Ortiz, a North Philadelphia native who graduated from Edison High in 2002. So, Elliot, you're seventeen years old, just finishing boot camp, and the President declares war. What was going through your mind?

ELLIOT I was like, okay then, let's do this.

RADIO VOICE You were ready. Is it exciting to be a marine?

ELLIOT People say, oh, it's like a video game. Oh, it's like the movies. Naw. Base is the most depressing place ever. You wake up, go outside, you see rocky sand mountains. That's it. Rocks. Sand. You gotta drive thirty minutes to find a Wal-Mart. I just mainly stay on base, rent a lot of movies.

RADIO VOICE But not base, let's talk about Iraq. Did you see a lot of action?

ELLIOT Yeah.

RADIO VOICE   Were there times you were scared?

ELLIOT   The first time I heard a mortar shell. That scared the crap out of me. Literally.

RADIO VOICE   And you were injured. Tell me about that.

ELLIOT   It's a long story.

RADIO VOICE   What sticks out in your mind? About the experience?

ELLIOT   I got two corrective surgeries. They'll send me back if I want.

RADIO VOICE   To Iraq? Will you go?

ELLIOT   I mean, my leg is still messed up but. I'm not trying to stay here and work at Subway Hoagies. "Pardon me, sir, you want some hot peppers with that roast beef?"

RADIO VOICE   What do the troops think about politics? Do they support the war?

ELLIOT   Politics? Nobody cares about that. People drink their sorrows away. You hear people running down the hallway like, "F this!" "F that!" "Kill raghead!"

RADIO VOICE   [*Slightly changed tone.*] Editor flag last remark. [*Back to interview.*] Both your father and grandfather served in the military.

ELLIOT   My pop was in Vietnam, marine corps. Three purple hearts.

RADIO VOICE   It must be something else to trade war stories with your father.

ELLIOT   He doesn't bring up that stuff too much.

RADIO VOICE   Some say there's a code of silence after returning home.

ELLIOT   My mom's got a box of his old letters, his uniform, dog tags. Our basement flooded and everything is in piles down there. But I was like, mom you gotta find that stuff.

RADIO VOICE   What about your grandfather?

ELLIOT   He was in Korea. He was a flute player. He'll be like, "I played Mozart in the north when everyone had frostbite." He's got two or three stories that he just tells them over and over. He's got old-timers.

RADIO VOICE Alzheimer's?

ELLIOT Right.

RADIO VOICE You must have felt a great deal of pressure to enlist.

ELLIOT Naw, I didn't even tell them. I just went one day and signed the papers.

RADIO VOICE Just like that.

ELLIOT Dad was actually kind of pissed, like, "The marines is no joke. The marines is going to mess with you."

RADIO VOICE So why go then?

[*No answer.*]

Why did you enlist?

ELLIOT I was like, dad was a marine. I want to be a marine. I really did it for him.

··· 12/prelude ···

[*The garden.* GINNY *holds a large yellow envelope stuffed full of papers. She pulls out one sheet at a time.*

GRANDPOP *appears separately, reading a letter.*

POP *appears separately. He is incredibly happy, slightly drunk.*]

POP April 4, '67

To my pop back in the Bronx aka "Little P.R.",
The evac hospital was like Disneyland. Real beds.

GRANDPOP Clean sheets.

POP Fresh pajamas. The women there? I met this one nurse, Ginny. Nurse Ginny. So let me ask you.

GINNY "Nurse Ginny."

POP How old were you when you fell for mom?

GRANDPOP   Did you know right away she was your woman?

POP   I'm serious, old man, I want answers. Got back to the platoon this morning. The guys were still alive, which is a good feeling. We had a big celebration.

GINNY   "Helmet stew."

POP   Hess's mom sent a package with wood alcohol. Stuff she made in the bathtub. Awful stuff.

GRANDPOP   We got drunk.

POP   Joe Bobb pulled out his guitar. I pulled out your flute. I made a big official speech, told them the whole story. You're a decorated veteran,

GINNY   "Bird watching."

POP   you served in Korea, back when they kept the Puerto Ricans separate.

How you played the same exact flute to your platoon. Then when I enlisted you handed me the flute and said,

GRANDPOP   "You're a man. Teach yourself how to play."

POP   Joe Bobb showed me a hillbilly song. I showed him a danzón. The keys are sticking, it's the swamp. Low D won't budge, two of the pads fell off. Here's my little plan I'm putting together.

GRANDPOP   Get home safe.

POP   Marry nurse Ginny.

GINNY   "C-rations."

POP   Have a son, give him the flute. One flute, three generations. Aw man, right now Joe Bobb is throwing up all over. The smell is bad. It's the wood alcohol.

GRANDPOP   Tell mom my leg is okay.

GINNY   "Date unknown."

POP   And sorry I didn't write for so long.

···13/prelude···

[*The garden, at night.* ELLIOT *stands in the garden.* POP'*s letters are on the ground.*]

ELLIOT   My little green Bible. Every soldier has something you take with you, no matter where you go, you take that thing. Waikiki had a tattoo of his mom. Mario had a gold cross his grandma had gave him. He wore it around his neck even though it was against the rules. I kept the Bible right inside my vest pocket. I had a picture of Stephanie in it, like a family portrait with all her cousins. My senior prom picture with all the guys. A picture of mom and pop. I looked at those pictures every day. Stared at those pictures. Daze off for like two hours at a time. [*Pause.*] The first guy I shot down, I kept his passport there.

One night, I don't know why, I was just going to kill my corporal. He was asleep. I put my rifle to the corporal's head and I was going to kill him. All I kept thinking was the bad stuff he made us do. He was the kind of guy who gets off on bringing down morale. Like making us run with trench foot. Trench foot is when your feet start rotting. Because of chemical and biological weapons, we didn't take our boots off for thirty-six days straight. When I finally took my boots off, I had to peel my socks from the skin. They were black, and the second they came off, they became instantly hard. Corporal made us run with trench foot. Run to get the water. Run to get the ammo. Everyone was asleep and I was ready to pull the trigger. Waikiki woke up and saw what I was doing. He kicked my arm like, "Eh, man, let's switch." So I looked at my pictures and slept, he went on watch. The next day me and Waikiki were running to get the water and he was like, "Eh, man, what were you doing last night?" I was like, "I don't know." He was like, "It's alright. We'll be out of here soon."

After I got injured, when my chopper landed in Spain. They pulled me out of there. They cut. My clothes were so disgusting they had to cut them off my body. My underwear was so black. The nurse had to cut it up the sides and take it off me like a pamper. The second she did that, it turned hard like a cast of plaster. You could see the shape of everything. Everything. It looked like an invisible man was wearing them. She threw it like a basketball in the trash. When the guys had finally found me, they had stuffed my leg full of cotton rags. The nurse counted one two three then ripped all the cotton out. I thought I was gonna die. I broke the metal railing right off the stretcher.

They didn't have underwear to put on me so they put a hospital gown instead. The kind that opens in the back and you can see the butt. I was still on the runway. The chopper took off, my gown flew up over my face, but my hands were tied down so I couldn't do nothing. I was butt naked in the middle of everybody. Next thing I know, someone pulled the gown away from my face and I saw this fine female looking down at me. When I saw her, it was like angels singing. [*He imitates angels singing.*] Like, *aaaaaah*. So what's the first thing that's gonna happen to a guy? She saw it. I was so embarrassed.

The sponge baths I got while I was over there? They give you a sponge bath every other day. The first time. Once again, it was another fine female. It was four months since I seen one. Most female officers, out in the field, they don't look like this one did. So something happened, you know what happened. She was sponging me down and saw it and was like, "You want me to leave the room?" After three days she got used to it. She would be chatting, changing the subject. When you catch a woody with an officer, who you have to see everyday in Spain? The day I left she was like, "Yo, take care of your friend."

When I first landed in Philly, Chucky and Buckweat met me at the airport. They came running up to the gate like, "Did you kill 'em? Did you kill 'em? Did you have a gun? Did you have a really big gun?" I was like, nah, don't you worry about none of that. Don't think about those things. I was trying to forget, but that's how they see me now. That's what I am. That's how Stephanie sees me. And the guys.

On the airplane flying home. All I could think was, I have to talk to Pop. Hear his stories. He used to tell stuff from the war but looking back, it was mostly jokes. Like he swallowed a thing of chewing tobacco and puked for three days. He took a leak off a

tank and a pretty Vietnamese lady saw him. He never sat me
down and told me what it was like, for real. The first night I got
here, I was like, pop, I need to hear it from your mouth. That
was Monday. He was like, we'll talk about it Tuesday. Wednesday
rolled around, I'm like, pop I'm only home a week. Did you have
nightmares, too? Every single night? Did you feel guilty, too?
When you shot a guy? Things he never opened up about. Finally
I got him real drunk, I'm like, now's the time. I was like, did you
shoot anyone up close? Did you shoot a civilian? Anything. He
threw the table at me. Threw his beer bottle on the steps.
Marched up the stairs, slammed the door.

Seeing mom, it takes so much stress off. She laid me down, and
worked on my leg in an old-fashioned way. Went to the herb store,
got all her magic potions. The gauze bandage, it hardly came off.
I could peel it back like a inch. The rest was infected, stuck to the
gauze. At night, it itched so bad I had to scream. Mom laid me
down in her garden, she told me to relax. Breathe in. Breathe out.
Breathe like a circle. She told me to close my eyes and imagine
the time I was happiest in my entire life. Then I felt her fingers
on my leg. That felt so good. Hands that love you touching your
worst place. I started to cry like a baby. I don't know why. It's just,
I forgot how that feels. Like home. The tears were just coming.
She put aloe and all sorts of stuff in there. I could tell she was
crying, too. She knows I been through a lot. She understands.

[GINNY *enters. She begins to braid vines around* ELLIOT's *body, from the garden.
She wraps his body in intricate, meticulous ways. She adds leaves and other flora. This
is a slow process. It lasts until the end of the scene.*]

It's a hard question. Of every second in your life, nail down the
best one. I started playing memories, like a movie in my mind.
The prom. Me all slicked out with the guys, in our silver suits.
Matching silver shoes. Hooking up with Stephanie. All the
different places me and Steph got freaky. In her mom's house. On
top of the roof for New Year's. This one time I took Sean fishing
down the Allegheny. He farted real loud. He ripped a nasty one.
All the white dudes, in their fisherman hats, they were like,
"Crazy Puerto Ricans. You scared the fish away."

The first time I ever went to Puerto Rico. With mom and pop. We drove around the island with the windows rolled down. I was like, damn, so this is where I come from. This is my roots. This one time we stopped at Luquillo Beach. The water was light light blue, and flat like a table, no waves. Mom was like, "Pull over, George, and teach me to swim." We swam in there like for five hours. Pop was holding mom on the surface of the water. He would hold on, like, "You ready? You ready?" She was like, "Ay! Hold on, papi! I'm gonna sink!" And he would let go and she would stay, floating, on the top. She was so happy. It looked like they were in love. Then you could see the moon in the water. It was still day but she floated on the moon. I could live in that day forever. See them like that every day.

After mom fixed my leg, she was like, "I got a gift for you. Something important." She gave me a fat yellow envelope. Crusty and old. She was like, "Burn this or read it. It's up to you." I sat out in the garden, started pulling letters out of the envelope. It was all of pop's letters from Vietnam.

[POP *enters the garden.*]

POP   Date unknown

ELLIOT   I read every one. All night, I didn't hardly move.

POP   Dad, I just want to say I'm sorry.

ELLIOT   I was like, pop, I fucking walked in your shoes.

POP   I threw your flute away.

ELLIOT   Pop, we lived the same fucking life.

POP   All these thoughts were going through my head, like thinking about the Bronx, you, mom.

ELLIOT   It's scary how much was the same. Killing a guy. Getting your leg scratched up. Falling in love.

POP   They got Hess and Joe Bobb.

ELLIOT   Nightmares. Meds. Infections. Letters to your father.

POP One instant. Their bodies were covered with dust. Tree bark. Their eyes.

ELLIOT Even ripping them up, taping them back together. It was like the feeling from Puerto Rico, but not a peaceful feeling.

POP It was like shoot someone, destroy something. I threw your flute in the river.

ELLIOT You see all the shit you can't erase. Like, here's who you are, Elliot, and you never even knew.

POP You can't sit around and feel sorry for yourself or you're gonna die. I had to do something, so that's what I did.

[POP's *letter is done.*]

ELLIOT Pop's up on the second floor, got the AC on, watching TV. Probably smoking weed. Probably doesn't even know I seen his letters. I know he won't even come to the airport tomorrow. He'll just be like:

[POP *speaks directly to* ELLIOT.]

POP Well, you chose it, so good luck with it. Don't do anything stupid.

[ELLIOT *is tangled in vines. Lights fade.*]

··· 14/fugue ···

[*The empty space.*
Three duffel bags are on the floor.]

GINNY A runway.

The Philadelphia airport tarmac.

July 2003 is dry and windy.

Two seagulls fly even though the ocean is miles away.

Luggage carts roll in one direction,

Taxiing planes in another.

The windows are sealed to airtight, noisetight.

People crowd around the departure monitors.

ELLIOT   A man enters.

[ELLIOT *enters.*]

Cologne is sprayed on his neck.

A clean shave.

[ELLIOT *looks at his watch.*]

0700 hours.

Thinking in military time again.

He fixes his short hair.

[ELLIOT *fixes his short hair.*]

Grabs his life.

[ELLIOT *picks up a duffel bag.*]

Inside his bag are two fatigues his mother ironed this morning.

Fresh sorullito from Grandmom.

Still warm, wrapped in two paper towels.

Grease-sealed in a plastic bag.

A naked photo from Stephanie.

In the photo she is smiling and holding in her stomach.

Her skin is brown.

The hair on her body is brown.

She is blinking, her eyes half closed.

GINNY   San Juan Bay.

A boarding ramp.

A transport ship to South Korea

Via Japan via Panama Canal.

September 1950 is mild.

The water is light light blue.

And flat like a table, no waves.

GRANDPOP   A boy enters.

[GRANDPOP *enters. He stands beside* ELLIOT *and picks up another duffel bag.* GRANDPOP *waves good-bye to his family, offstage.*]

Slacks pressed.

Hair combed.

Family standing at the rails.
His wife wears a cotton dress.
Sweat gathers in her brown curls.
On her hip, Little George.
His five-year-old son.

A boarding ramp.
Corrugated steel.
His first ride on the ocean.

[GRANDPOP *picks up his duffel and freezes.*]

GINNY A runway.
The Newark Airport tarmac.
August 1965 is unseasonably cool.

[POP *enters. He stands beside* ELLIOT *and picks up a duffel bag.*]

POP A boy enters.
[*He looks at his watch.*]
9:15 a.m.
He will never get used to military time.
He grabs his life.
At the bottom of his duffel, good luck charms.
A red handball glove.
A bottle of vodka from the Social Sevens.
Two pencils and paper.

A long corridor.
A gray carpeted ramp.
A plane to Parris Island
To a ship to Vietnam.

[POP *picks up his duffel and freezes.*]

ELLIOT The bag
The duffel
The photo

Stephanie

Teeth

Jazz

Calvin Klein

Fubu

Flute

Helmet

36 springs

Ink

Heliconia

Handwriting

[ELLIOT *grabs his duffel, steps forward.*]

He walks down the gray carpeted ramp.

Boards the plane to Camp Pendleton.

Where he will board his second ship to Kuwait.

Where he will cross the border north into Iraq.

Again.

Happy he has an aisle seat.

Going back to war.

The Rapture
of Mammon

Jules Tasca

Jules Tasca

Through I.U.P., Jules Tasca has taught playwriting at Oxford University in England and he has performed with a Commedia dell'arte group in central Italy. He is the author of over 125 full-length and one-act published plays that have been produced in numerous national theatres, from the Mark Taper Forum to the Bucks County Playhouse, as well as abroad in England, Ireland, Austria, Germany, South Africa, Canada, and Australia. He has also written for radio and television. He scripted *The Hal Linden TV Special*. His plays *La Llorona* and *Maria* were produced on National Public Radio. Other one-act pieces were broadcast in Los Angeles and abroad in Germany.

He was the national winner in New York's Performing Arts Repertory Theater Playwriting contest for his libretto *The Amazing Einstein*, which toured the country and played at the Kennedy Center in Washington, D.C. He has adapted the stories of Oscar Wilde, Guy de Maupassant, Mark Twain, Robert Louis Stevenson, and Saki and has modernized Aristophanes' *Ecclesiazusae* (Women in Congress). He has published new versions of Hamlet and Macbeth.

His libretto for C.S. Lewis' *The Lion, the Witch and the Wardrobe* had its world premiere in California and played in London and New York and is currently touring nationwide. For his play *Theater Trip*, he was the recipient of a Thespie Award for Best New Play, and *Old Goat Song* won a Drama Critic's Award in Los Angeles. His plays *The Spelling of Coynes*, *The Death of Bliss*, and *Deus-X* have been included in the *Best American Short Plays* anthology. His tragic piece *The Balkan Women* won the prestigious Barrymore Award for Best Play. His play *The Grand Christmas History of the Andy Landy Clan* was broadcast on forty-seven National Public Radio stations.

Mr. Tasca received a grant from the Pennsylvania Council of the Arts to develop a new theatrical form, the Eurhythmy, a system of movement of language, music, and sound. His tragedy *Judah's Daughter* received the Dorothy Silver International Playwriting Award. He won first prize in the Bucks County Writers' Club Screenwriting Contest. His piece *Live Drawing* is about the relationship between Leonard da Vinci and the *Mona Lisa* and has been published by the Dramatic Publishing Company. Mr. Tasca's play *The Mission* finished its run in May 2008 at the New Theatre in Miami and received the Theatre League of South Florida's Silver Palm Award for Outstanding New Work. The author is a member of New York's Dramatists Guild.

characters

UNCLE HENRY WALMONT, an old man
CLARENCE WALMONT, Henry's nephew
CIELIA WALMONT, Clarence's wife
CINDY ANNE DIBBS, a lap dancer

• • •

The setting is a black box with four swivel chairs on casters. The actors turn and stand and sit as they interact. Behind each chair are two chorus members who give us some of the thoughts of the characters.

CINDY   I'm Cindy. I'm a lap dancer.... That is ... I used to be ...

CINDY CHORUS   But now ... Jesus ... Now ...

CINDY   It's all changed.... This is Clarence Walmont, a big money lawyer...

CLARENCE   This is my wife, Cielia.... It happened this way.... Uncle Henry Walmont here was 87 and he really couldn't take care of himself anymore.

CIELIA   I always thought...

CIELIA CHORUS   If he had any human decency, he'd die.

CIELIA   He needed a caretaker.

HENRY   I'd lose my false teeth.

CLARENCE CHORUS   Klutz.

HENRY   I'd miss the commode and spritz the floor.

CIELIA CHORUS   Pig...

HENRY   I couldn't hear the phone ring, so when I didn't answer, my nephew, Clarence, thought...

CLARENCE CHORUS   Hoped...

HENRY   That I died.

CIELIA   We want to help you, Uncle Henry.

HENRY   I suppose I do need some help, because I hope to live a few more years . . .

CLARENCE   We hope you live to be a hundred, Uncle Henry.

CIELIA CHORUS   One Methuselah was enough.

HENRY CHORUS   That Cielia's got some body on her. Thou shalt not covet thy nephew's wife. Oh, Christ, covet, Henry. You're too old to commit sin . . .

CLARENCE   Cielia, it troubles me that the old bastard is worth more than the G.N.P. of some countries. We stand to inherit and yet . . .

CIELIA   He goes on and on and on . . . I know . . .

CLARENCE   People would say that I'm a high priced lawyer making a comfortable living . . .

CLARENCE CHORUS   But normal simian avarice pushes us . . .

CIELIA   It's only normal to want more, Clarence.

CIELIA CHORUS   If you say you don't want more, you're a liar or a wacko saint.

CINDY   As I got the story, it happened over a bottle of wine one night.

CLARENCE   Cielia, I'm almost drunk enough to admit it.

CLARENCE CHORUS   The old bastard's just using up oxygen for no reason.

CIELIA   I know what you're going to say, Clarence. The old bastard's overdoing living.

CLARENCE CHORUS   How I hate to hear her say what I'm thinking!

HENRY   Cielia . . . Clarence . . . I know you, my only living relatives, care for me and you want to make my life livable, so I admit it. Yes. You both were correct. I'm no longer self-sufficient. I'm going to need a housekeeper.

HENRY CHORUS   Goddammitt!

CIELIA   We're surprised, Uncle Henry.

CIELIA CHORUS   Why don't you just go quietly in your sleep?

CLARENCE   We know how you pride yourself on your independence.

HENRY CHORUS   God makes us old to punish our youth.

CIELIA   But beware, husband. With a caring, compassionate housekeeper he could live another ten years.

CLARENCE   Hmmmm . . . Hmmmm . . .

CLARENCE CHORUS   Hmmmm . . . Hmmmm . . .

CIELIA CHORUS   Hmmmm . . . Hmmmm . . .

CIELIA   Hmmmm . . . Hmmmm . . .

CLARENCE   I've got it, Cielia!

CIELIA   What? What is it?

CLARENCE   Well . . . you know what a ladies man he always was . . .

CIELIA   I do . . .

CIELIA CHORUS   When I first met him years ago, he fondled my breasts.

CIELIA   I poured Clarence another drink and then another before his feelings wriggled out onto his tongue. . . . What're you saying, Clarence?

CLARENCE   Suppose . . . Suppose . . . Suppose . . .

CIELIA   You want another drink?

CLARENCE   No. No more or I won't be able to connive.

CIELIA   It turns me on when a lawyer connives. It really does . . .

[*She kisses him.*]

CINDY   I'm to be part of the connive.

CLARENCE   You said it. He's always been a dirty minded old fellow.

CELIA   Did I say that?

CLARENCE   I don't know. Listen. Suppose we find the old bastard a housekeeper who . . . who is so sexy and attractive and sultry that . . .

CLARENCE CHORUS   Oh, say it for Christ's sake!

CLARENCE That he'll try to make love to her.

CIELIA CHORUS That'd kill him!

CIELIA Yes . . . It's a wonderful sentiment.

CLARENCE Perhaps it's a most pleasurable way to go.

CLARENCE CHORUS Watch what you're saying, Clarence!

CLARENCE You know, what they mean by a . . . a good death . . .

CIELIA One problem . . .

CIELIA CHORUS Sometimes one must be immoral to do what is right.

CLARENCE Well?

CIELIA Where would we get someone sexy and attractive and yet naïve enough not to catch on to what we're doing?

CLARENCE As a matter of fact, Cielia, there's this gentlemen's club.

CIELIA CHORUS How does he know about a . . .

CIELIA What gentlemen's club?

CLARENCE It's a place called Spells.

CIELIA Spells?

CLARENCE A gentlemen's club. Yes.

CLARENCE CHORUS See, Mr. Sagacity, how'd you explain your familiarity with Spells?

CLARENCE Some of the guys from the firm took me there for my bachelor party.

CIELIA Bachelor party?

CIELIA CHORUS I didn't know that.

CLARENCE I didn't really want to go but . . .

CIELIA CHORUS I'm upset, but I don't want to lose the course of action. No. Jesus. There's money involved here.

CIELIA I believe you, Clarence. You went to be a good sport.

CLARENCE CHORUS And to see the parade of pulchritude writhing on long phallic poles.

CIELIA Lawyers . . . with strip tease girls . . . It's so . . . so déclassé.

CIELIA CHORUS Redneck even.

CIELIA Tell me everything, Clarence, if you want understanding and forgiveness.

CLARENCE Well . . . Cielia . . .

CLARENCE CHORUS Tell her while we're tipsy up here. Tell her and be done with it.

CLARENCE You watched them dance. Some of them were quite accomplished.

CIELIA CHORUS Bimbos.

CLARENCE Later they would meet you—for a price—in a small room and give you a . . . a lap dance . . .

CINDY A slow turning and a rhythmic bounce. I so loved squeezing money from them.

CIELIA Are you trying to hurt me, Clarence?

CLARENCE No. I'm just trying to kill a beloved uncle whose money we'll inherit.

CLARENCE CHORUS Bimbos are a species necessary to men.

CLARENCE I married you, Cielia, because you are not a bimbo. I only bring up this . . . this lurid and regrettable incident in my life to tell you where we can get Uncle Henry a housekeeper who will break his back. . . . Spells . . .

CIELIA CHORUS I'm more greedy than I am jealous, so I'll let it go.

CIELIA We'll go to Spells together, Clarence.

CINDY Clarence Walmont came into Spells. His wife waited next door. He came in before opening and asked the manager for me.

CLARENCE I remember her name . . . Cindy. . . . She was a goddess with blue eyes . . . C-cup . . . legs so long that they went from the earth to the moon.

CINDY The manager said, oh, you want to see Cindy Anne Dibbs.

HENRY   Cindy Anne Dibbs . . . I called her Cin . . .

CINDY   I'm Cindy . . .

CLARENCE   I'm Clarence Walmont.

CLARENCE CHORUS   Her breasts take away my breath! I can't lust and breathe at the same time!

CINDY   And? Hello . . .

CLARENCE CHORUS   Get right to it.

CLARENCE   How'd you like to make some real money?

CINDY   I make real money here at Spells.

CLARENCE   I'll double whatever you make here a week.

CINDY   Double?

CLARENCE CHORUS   Jesus, she almost speared me with her tits!

CINDY CHORUS   Careful, Cindy Anne . . .

CINDY   What're you looking for? Kinky stuff?

HENRY   Kinky stuff adds years to your life.

CLARENCE   No. Not at all. Look, let's go next door to the coffee shop. I'd like you to meet my wife.

CINDY   Your wife?

CLARENCE   She'd never enter an emporium of lust like this.

CINDY   I don't know what an emporium is, but Spells is a classy place. Why, we even have lawyers who come here.

CLARENCE   I stand corrected.

CLARENCE CHORUS   She could raise the penis on a stone statue.

CIELIA   I'm happy to meet you, Cindy.

CINDY   Same here.

CINDY CHORUS   Look at the diamonds on this chick!

CIELIA CHORUS   The slut . . . I'll never forgive Clarence for remembering her!

CIELIA   Let us explain . . .

CIELIA CHORUS   Bitch built bimbo!

CLARENCE   You see I have an old uncle.

CIELIA   Uncle Henry Walmont.

CLARENCE CHORUS   Look how her body strains the fabrics! Jesus!

CLARENCE   And we love Uncle Henry more than anything in the world.

HENRY   Cindy . . . Cin . . . Cin, I called her.

CINDY   Where does Uncle Henry fit in with me?

CLARENCE CHORUS   Same place as any other man.

CLARENCE   Cindy, Uncle Henry loves . . . loves . . .

CIELIA   Has always loved women . . .

CIELIA CHORUS   Even someone cheap like you.

CLARENCE   We . . . We . . . We want to make his final days pleasurable for him by having someone . . .

CLARENCE CHORUS   Screamingly hot!

CLARENCE   Attractive to look after him.

CIELIA   Make him some tea.

CIELIA CHORUS   Induce him to start smoking again.

CIELIA   Pick him up if he stumbles . . .

CLARENCE   Answer the phone.

CINDY   Oh, sort of a companion like.

CLARENCE   Exactly.

CINDY CHORUS   These two must have some big bucks.

CINDY   Well, if the money's what you say it is and I see the first week in advance.

CIELIA CHORUS   The slut's agreed!

CIELIA   We'll pay the advance. Yes.

CLARENCE Of course...

CINDY CHORUS Clear the picture, Cindy.

CINDY Am I understanding right? Like, Uncle Henry's not into sex...

HENRY When I met Cin, I knew the question would have to be raised.

CLARENCE Good God, he's in his 80s.

CIELIA Docile... Dependent...

CIELIA CHORUS The old bastard.

CINDY For that money, I'll give it a try.

HENRY Even a blind man hath an eye for women...

CLARENCE Uncle Henry...

HENRY Well... Well... Well... Clarence and Cielia and...

CIELIA We found you a housekeeper, Uncle Henry.

HENRY She? Her?

CLARENCE Cindy Anne Dibbs, meet Henry Walmont.

HENRY CHORUS Am I hallucinating?

CINDY Pleased to meet you, Uncle Henry.

HENRY CHORUS Look at those jugs!!

[*We hear music made by horns, drums, and cymbals.*]

HENRY What's that music?

CIELIA What music, Uncle Henry?

HENRY CHORUS Even my ears are turned on!

CINDY I can put some music on for you if you show me where everything is.

CLARENCE I'll show you around.

CIELIA CHORUS No way.

CIELIA Why don't we leave and allow Uncle Henry to show her around.

CIELIA CHORUS And put his eyeballs back in his head!

CLARENCE CHORUS Damn!

CLARENCE I'll put your bags upstairs in the guest room.

HENRY CHORUS/CLARENCE CHORUS Look at her midriff!

[*We hear the music again.*]

HENRY What's all the music?

CIELIA CHORUS I don't think he'll make it through the week.

CIELIA You're just excited, Uncle Henry. Let us know how you're doing now and again, all right?

[HENRY *begins to growl.*]

CINDY Uncle Henry... Uncle Henry... are you okay? You're ... You're making a noise ...

HENRY Oh? Sorry, Cindy. It just came out.

HENRY CHORUS Did my eyesight improve or is it my imagination?

HENRY Cindy... May I call you Cin?

CINDY Cin? Sure. I don't mind.

CINDY CHORUS For the money I'm getting you can call me mortal Cin.

[HENRY *growls again.*]

HENRY Excuse these animal sounds, please. They can't be helped.

HENRY CHORUS Stop it, Henry! You sound like some animal in heat!

CINDY You make all the noises you need to, sir. I'll just like look over the house to see where everything is ...

HENRY Go ahead. I'll come with you ...

CLARENCE Cindy said the first day, he just followed her all over the house ...

CLARENCE CHORUS Lucky old bastard!

CIELIA In that tight skirt, what do you expect?

HENRY Her buttocks move like giant marshmallows ...

CIELIA Up and down the stairs, that'll blow out his ventricles.

CLARENCE   I hate doing this to him, God, Cielia . . .

CIELIA   We have no choice, Clarence. There's money involved.

CLARENCE CHORUS   I remember in Sunday school learning about the curse of Mammon. That silly old reverend didn't understand that a man can't fight nature . . .

HENRY   Cin, you've been here a week and a half.

CINDY   My, that long?

CINDY CHORUS   Seems like a month!

HENRY   And I . . . You see, I'm a sensitive man . . .

HENRY CHORUS   Oh, Christ, tell her, Henry!

HENRY   Don't think me unseemly . . .

CINDY   Oh, no, I won't . . .

CINDY CHORUS   I don't even know what the hell unseemly means.

HENRY   Last night . . . It's better you know, Cin. Last night . . . Watching you shower . . .

CIELIA   How'd he see her shower, Clarence?

CLARENCE   She called me and told me, he admitted peeping through the keyhole . . .

CINDY CHORUS   This fogey's still got game.

CINDY   You watched me shower?

HENRY   Cin . . . Cin . . . Listen to me. . . . Last night . . . I heard that music again and . . . and . . . Cin, my pecker moved off its perch on my leg and stuck its turtle head out of my boxer shorts.

CINDY   Uncle Henry Walmont!

CINDY CHORUS   How cute!

HENRY   In yesteryear they used to canonize people for such miracles.

CLARENCE   I told her if the old bastard makes a move on her and she's willing . . . well . . .

CIELIA CHORUS   How enthused Clarence is . . .

CLARENCE   I told her its her call. . . . But if she has to jump into bed
with him, I'll double her money.

CIELIA   Double?

CLARENCE   Hell, she's worth it . . . I mean . . .

CLARENCE CHORUS   Watch what you're saying!

CLARENCE   It could be a fatal blow . . . Her body's lethal . . . Believe
me . . .

CIELIA CHORUS   How vicariously he lives through this.

CIELIA   But doubling the money.

CLARENCE   Cielia, the old bastard's becoming harder than we thought.

CINDY   You're willing to double the money?!!

[*We hear the music.*]

CINDY CHORUS   That's a lot of money! How can I turn it down? I
can't!

HENRY   Cin . . . Cin . . . Cin . . . Where are you?

CINDY   Right here, Uncle Henry.

HENRY   I'll bet you thought me incapable . . .

CINDY   I . . . I honestly did, Henry.

CINDY CHORUS   Call the Guinness record book people!

HENRY   Damndest thing is . . . I feel good . . .

CIELIA   We're paying her a small fortune, Clarence.

CIELIA CHORUS   I feel like a pimp!

CLARENCE   We need to spend money to make money.

CLARENCE CHORUS   We thought once maybe . . .

CIELIA CHORUS   Twice maybe . . .

CIELIA CHORUS/CLARENCE CHORUS   And he'd be dead!

HENRY   Cin . . . Cin . . . Cin . . . Let's climb into the hot tub.

CLARENCE How long could he last, straining his body like this?

HENRY Cin, wear the red bra with the red panties and the garter belt.

CINDY Okay.

[*Music.*]

CIELIA Maybe she's being too gentle with him.

CIELIA CHORUS He needs wild sex to kill him.

CINDY Henry . . . Where'd you learn so much about screwing?

HENRY CHORUS Once in 1972, I had two women and a case of chocolate syrup.

HENRY I'm just a natural, Cin. Say, wear the black thong tonight, huh?

[*Music.*]

HENRY Cin, Jesus, no more chocolate syrup, will you? . . .

CINDY You're right. I think you're gaining weight.

CLARENCE It's beyond comprehension!

CIELIA What is it now, Clarence?

CLARENCE Doctor Fried took the old bastard off his heart meds!

CIELIA What?

[*We hear music.*]

CLARENCE CHORUS I can almost hear him getting it on with her!

CLARENCE Doctor Fried told me his heart rhythms have stabilized. The old bastard's gaining weight. His color's improved. His glucose intolerance is down. And his goddamned prostate's shrunk!

CIELIA This is not good.

CLARENCE CHORUS His pecker's working like a teenage cobra!

HENRY Cin . . . You know . . . I think behind my back, my nephew and his wife refer to me as the old bastard.

CINDY I never heard them talk that way.

HENRY Maybe not. My hearing's not as good as it used to be. Cin . . .

CINDY Henry...

CINDY CHORUS What the hell's the old bastard want now! Jesus!

HENRY I want to buy you a piece of jewelry.

CINDY Oh?

HENRY Money is no object.

CINDY It's not?

CINDY CHORUS Double dip, Cindy... Yeah...

CLARENCE More trouble, Cielia...

CIELIA What now?

CLARENCE This orgy of his has gone on so long that the lap dancer has figured out who Henry Walmont is...

HENRY I love you, Cin.

HENRY CHORUS When she puts her earrings on, to me it's a sex act.

CINDY You opened your heart to me, Henry.

CINDY CHORUS Better yet, you opened your books!

CINDY Jesus. Like, he's got mutual funds that have mutual funds. He owns parking lots. He has a library of bank books. His stocks scroll along the computer screen without end. How much does the old bastard own? I didn't go long enough in school to count that high. You'd need accountants to say how much! Jesus, I've been sitting on a goldmine and didn't know it!

[*Music. Then* CINDY *makes a growling sound.*]

HENRY Is that you growling, Cin...

CINDY Me? Was I... I dunno... I was just thinking of how rich you are.

CINDY CHORUS Yeah. And the nephew's screwing me over for pennies!

CINDY You're the oil guy.... You're that Henry Walmont?

HENRY Yes, I am, Cin. I make money the way most make saliva.

CINDY Wow! So to speak, I mean.

CINDY CHORUS   Start using your head, Cindy Anne!

CIELIA   Then we will have to give her more money.

CLARENCE   Or...Or...Maybe...

HENRY   Cin, tonight the chaps and the...

CINDY   The cowboy boots, the ten-gallon hat, I'm putting them on now, lover.

HENRY   Then gallop right on in here, pardner!

HENRY CHORUS   Yahooo!! Yahooo!! Yahooo!!

[*Music.*]

HENRY   Oh my, oh my, oh my...He who would see perfection should see your legs, Cindy.

CINDY   I used to be a dancer.

HENRY   Regardless of your indiscretions, I'm smitten, Cin.

CINDY CHORUS   Cindy Anne, you thinking what I'm thinking?! Hey! Heyyy!!

CINDY   I understand....Dear Henry...

HENRY CHORUS   Dear Henry?

CINDY   We've grown...Well...like, so close...

CLARENCE   Cindy, we've called this meeting to...to...to...

CIELIA CHORUS   Stop drooling over her and speak!

CLARENCE   How should I put it...

CIELIA   We're going to have to let you go.

CINDY   Let me...

CIELIA   Yes...

CINDY   Why?

CLARENCE   We decided that perhaps Uncle Henry needs a housekeeper with more domestic skills...

CINDY CHORUS   Liars!

CINDY   I dunno why. Your uncle's real happy.

CLARENCE CHORUS   How could he not be? Living a life of happy humping!

HENRY   Oh, I know I take a long time. . . . All right . . . a long, long time. . . . All right . . . a long, long, long, long, long, long time . . .

CINDY   You two never told me the old . . . That is to say . . . that Uncle Henry was the oil guy . . . the oil Walmont . . .

HENRY   All right . . . It takes me three hours . . .

CLARENCE   We don't refer to the sweet old guy as the oil Walmont . . .

CINDY CHORUS   I do understand these two-faced relations now.

CINDY   Be that as you say, I won't leave Henry unless he says so . . .

CIELIA CHORUS   That'll never happen!

CLARENCE CHORUS   What have we done for God's sake?!

CINDY   Also, too, I think there is more in this for me than meets your eye.

CLARENCE   We think we've been overly generous, Cindy . . .

CINDY   I don't see it that way. . . . No . . . no . . . I'm sorry . . .

HENRY   Cin, when I'm alone I think . . .

CINDY   What, dear?

HENRY CHORUS   About getting a dick transplant!

HENRY   About the fact that I can't afford to lose you . . .

HENRY CHORUS   Or your breasts or your legs or your . . .

CINDY   That's too bad, Henry dear, because I've been offered something that pays more than what your nephew gives me.

HENRY   What?

CINDY CHORUS   Play him, Cindy! Strum him like an old guitar!

CINDY   Yes. The New York Ballet has made me an offer.

HENRY   Screw the ballet! You're my Cin. I need you.

CINDY CHORUS   He needs me. Christ, it pays to be cute.

CLARENCE   Cielia, we're in huge trouble.

CIELIA   Why? What can the slut do?

CINDY   Yes, Henry dear . . .

CINDY CHORUS   Rub his head. . . . Make him feel loved . . .

HENRY   Hear me out . . .

CINDY   Why wouldn't I? . . .

CLARENCE   She's not educated, Cielia . . .

CLARENCE CHORUS   But who cares in bed?

CLARENCE   But where money's concerned, even the most ignorant human beings can negotiate as well as geniuses.

HENRY   You'll not leave me for any ballet. Never.

CINDY   But, Henry, I'm just a working girl.

CLARENCE   This Cindy Anne Dibbs knows the power of sexual rapture.

CIELIA CHORUS   You should know. She danced on your lap!!

CLARENCE CHORUS   Christ, I paid her 400 dollars that night in Spells!

CIELIA   Stop thinking of her.

CLARENCE   I'm not thinking of her. I'm thinking of . . .

CLARENCE CHORUS   Of her ass and the money!

CLARENCE   I'm thinking of how men's judgment—the old bastard's judgment . . . cripples up when faced with an overwhelming . . .

CLARENCE CHORUS   Luxury lay!

CLARENCE   Overwhelming temptation. That's all.

CIELIA   The old bastard should be dead by now . . .

CIELIA CHORUS   Instead . . .

HENRY   Cin, what I'm asking you is . . .

CINDY CHORUS   Keep rubbing his body, baby!

HENRY   I'm . . . I'm . . .

HENRY CHORUS   She'll laugh at you, Henry!

CINDY   Say it.... Say it ... Henry.... It's what I been waiting for ... waiting to hear ... because ...

CINDY CHORUS   Take him home, Cindy Anne!

CINDY   You old stud! I've fallen in love with you!

[CINDY *sits on his lap.*]

HENRY   You ... You ... You ...

CINDY   Yeah ... Yeah ... Yeah ...

HENRY CHORUS   Lord, give me another five years and I'll build you a church ... a cathedral ... I'll sponsor the second coming ...

HENRY   Marry me, Cin ... Marry me ...

CINDY CHORUS   Bingo! The old bastard's yours! Yeah!

CINDY   Oh, Henry ... Yes.... Yes, I will.... Like, all my life I've waited for a person like you.... Male ... Mature ... Loving ...

CINDY CHORUS   Rich!

CINDY   Experienced.

CINDY CHORUS   Richer than rich!

CINDY   Generous.

CINDY CHORUS   Sinfully rich! ...

CINDY   Sexy ...

CINDY CHORUS   So what if I go to hell! I'll be the richest bitch in hell! I'll have the Devil himself waiting on me! I'll tip him big, he'll keep the place cool!

CINDY   Caring ...

HENRY CHORUS   Christ, the way she tells it, I don't even recognize myself!

CINDY   Honest ... Modest ...

CINDY CHORUS   Don't overdo it. You've got him.

HENRY   I knew you cared for the real Henry Walmont.

CINDY CHORUS   I know doing this for his money is wrong . . . but . . . I can't help myself.

CIELIA   Clarence, she wouldn't . . . She couldn't . . .

CLARENCE   I actually went to a church, Cielia, and I prayed that this wouldn't happen . . .

HENRY   Cin, let's go upstairs to bed and celebrate our newly declared love . . .

CINDY CHORUS   Another three hour wait. . . . Christ, it's like waiting for a train during a strike.

HENRY   Cin . . . I was saying . . .

CINDY CHORUS   The screws now . . . not the screw.

HENRY CHORUS   Newly declared love! Come on, Henry. You sound Victorian. Try to sound younger, you old fart.

HENRY   Cin . . . what do you say? You wanna make it, baby? Right here on the living room floor? Huh?

CINDY   I do, Henry . . . And we will . . . Someday . . .

HENRY   Someday?!

HENRY CHORUS   There's no *someday* for a man my age!

HENRY   Cin, I live from hour to hour, girl.

CINDY   I understand. It's just, like, now that we're engaged, I wouldn't feel right doing anything until we're legally married.

HENRY   Huh?

CINDY   Until we get all the paperwork done. Marriage license . . . Change the name in the telephone book . . .

CINDY CHORUS   Your will . . .

CINDY   The deed to the house . . .

CINDY CHORUS   Your will . . .

CINDY   I mean, like, this is a big step in our life, Henry . . . dear. . . . Like, I know I'm changing my will and leaving everything to you . . .

HENRY You are?

CINDY CHORUS Yeah, all of thirty-nine cents!

HENRY CHORUS She really does love me.

CLARENCE We'll have to threaten the greedy bitch.

CIELIA Going after our money . . .

CLARENCE CHORUS I know what you're thinking, Cielia.

CIELIA CHORUS I regret that we didn't murder the old bastard in his sleep!

HENRY Let's go to City Hall right now and get a license.

CINDY It's Sunday night, dear.

HENRY You'd deny me your sacred nakedness, Cin?

CINDY Oh, Henry Walmont, City Hall opens in eight hours.

HENRY CHORUS We could start foreplay now, then I'd be ready for the honeymoon.

HENRY Well then . . . Let's go start the paperwork you spoke of. I want to change my will too, Cin.

CINDY Then you really do love me as much as I do you.

CINDY CHORUS Get the will changed before the geezer keels over!

HENRY And tomorrow, after we're married . . .

CINDY Yes, Henry . . .

HENRY You'll wear the tight satin outfit with the seven-inch high heel shoes.

CINDY I'll lay them out tonight on our wedding bed . . .

[*Music.*]

HENRY CHORUS God, I hope I live to see it!

CLARENCE Cindy, you can't do this!

CINDY CHORUS It's practically a done deal!

CINDY Uncle Henry loves me.

CIELIA How can you love decrepitude?

CINDY I see through the physical.

CINDY CHORUS/CIELIA CHORUS/CLARENCE CHORUS Right down to the goddamned money!

CLARENCE Cindy, we're not stupid.

CINDY You're saying, like, I don't love the old guy to pieces? I do. Nobody can do a thing when real love happens. Look at Romeo and Joliet.

CIELIA Juliet. Joliet's in Illinois.

CINDY I don't care where she lives.

CLARENCE He's 87 and you're 26!

CINDY So? I'm told Romeo was older than Joliet.

CIELIA That's just cynicism . . .

CLARENCE Expedience . . .

CLARENCE CHORUS/CIELIA CHORUS We're kin! The money's ours!

CINDY The old . . . guy proposed to me.

HENRY Satin pants . . . Tight ones . . .

CINDY You saying the old dear doesn't know what he's doing?

CIELIA Yes, we are.

CLARENCE Isn't it obvious?

HENRY/HENRY CHORUS And, Christ, seven-inch heels. I've got to live! I have a purpose!

CLARENCE Suppose we can show that the old bastard's out of his mind.

CINDY Because he wants me . . .

CLARENCE CHORUS No. That's the sane part of him!

CLARENCE Because he wants to turn his life and . . . and property over to . . . to . . . to . . .

CIELIA CHORUS A slut . . .

CLARENCE A virtual stranger.

CINDY Who you calling virtual?

CINDY CHORUS Besides I already thought you'd try to say the geezer's nuts.

CINDY Henry's psychiatrist . . .

CIELIA Doctor Fried?

CINDY Who is also to be the best man at our wedding.

CLARENCE Doctor Fried?

CLARENCE CHORUS I can see it. She did him too!

CINDY That's so. Doctor Fried will testify that Henry Walmont . . .

CIELIA CHORUS That crazy old bastard!

CINDY Is not crazy.

HENRY/HENRY CHORUS I would have her someday dress as a nun and I as a priest . . .

CIELIA You used your sexual wiles . . .

CLARENCE CHORUS Your considerable sexual wiles . . .

CIELIA To cloud his thinking.

CINDY I never touched his thinking. Even changing the will was his idea!

CIELIA/CLARENCE/CIELIA CHORUS/CLARENCE CHORUS HE CHANGED HIS WILL ALREADY?!!

HENRY When she struts around naked, my will is not my own.

CINDY He loves me.

CLARENCE Cindy . . . I am a lawyer and I can guarantee you this: we can tie up that will in probate for a lifetime. With you 26 and him to soon be 88, do you think a judge will rule against the original will?

CIELIA   Clarence is his own flesh and blood.

CLARENCE   The court'll see you as nothing but a thief . . .

CLARENCE CHORUS   Who can make men wet.

HENRY   It's been such a long time since anyone's loved me.

HENRY CHORUS   I'd like to see her in leather.

CINDY   Now that we're man and wife, love, I'll dress up in anything you want.

CINDY CHORUS   Love him to death, Cindy Anne! Even latex. Yeah, I could hug him and smother him in my outfit.

HENRY   I've never been happier, Cin.

CLARENCE   He went through with it!!!

CIELIA   Didn't invite us, because he knew we'd try to dissuade the old . . .

CINDY   It was just me and Henry and Doctor Fried and the J.P. Why, Henry told me I'm your aunt now, Clarence.

CLARENCE CHORUS   Now the bitch has me thinking incest!

CLARENCE   All right. What's done is done. The reason we came over . . .

CIELIA   Is the old bastard asleep?

CINDY   Oh, yeah. . . . He had a big night last night.

CINDY CHORUS   I felt sure when he orgasmed, he died.

CLARENCE   We . . . We talked it over and to . . . to . . . to avoid a court battle over the will . . .

CINDY   Oh?

CLARENCE   I . . . We . . . We're willing to make a deal . . .

CINDY CHORUS   Uh-oh.

CINDY   What deal?

CIELIA   You have the old bastard draw up a new will.

CINDY CHORUS   Watch it, Cindy Anne Dibbs.

CLARENCE   Seventy–thirty.

CINDY   Seventy–thirty what?

CIELIA   You get thirty percent of everything.

CLARENCE   And we'll get . . .

CINDY   Seventy percent?

CLARENCE   It's more than generous.

CINDY   I don't think so. No deal. I'll take my chances in court. I'm the wife here. Like, I'm Mrs. Walmont . . .

CIELIA CHORUS   Callow greedy bitch!

CLARENCE   Calm down, Cindy. Sixty–forty.

CINDY   I wouldn't gamble with my husband's money. I love him.

CINDY CHORUS   I bought Viagra, so I can kick him off faster.

CLARENCE   All right. . . . You're a sharp dealer, Cindy. Fifty–fifty. Cindy? Cindy? Cindy, let us back in!

CIELIA   She threw us out of the house!

HENRY   Cin, is that you slamming the door?

CINDY   You know . . .

CINDY CHORUS   They're right. A judge would, like, see me for the money grubber that I am. Look at me and look at him.

HENRY   Cin, you know what you did for me last night?

CINDY   What's that?

[*Music as* HENRY *speaks in mime.*]

CINDY   Well, thank you. I'm glad you liked it.

CINDY CHORUS   You know, Cindy Anne . . .

CINDY   No . . . No . . . No . . . I just couldn't . . .

HENRY   You talking to yourself, Cin?

HENRY CHORUS   Maybe all this screwing's driving her crazy . . .

CINDY   Well . . . It would be worth it.

CINDY CHORUS   It would be insurance . . .

CINDY   It would . . .

HENRY   What're you saying, Cin?

CINDY   Henry, listen up. . . . Henry stop looking at my legs and listen . . .

[*She grabs his ears.*]

HENRY   You want to start early today?

CINDY   How about this. Henry Walmont, I love you so much . . .

HENRY   Yes . . .

CINDY   So, so much . . . That I . . .

HENRY   Go on. . . . Go on, Cin . . .

CINDY   I want to bear your child.

CINDY CHORUS   It's a way to beat the courts!

HENRY   You want to . . . You want to . . .

HENRY CHORUS   I make women so hot for me . . .

CINDY   Yes.

HENRY   A child?

CINDY   Our child . . . our own flesh . . .

HENRY   Am I too old for a child?

CINDY   Oh, no. When the kid's ten you'll only be 98 . . . Henry . . . dear Henry . . .

HENRY CHORUS   Hmm. Hmm. Hmm.

HENRY   Get undressed, we'll try it.

[*Music.*]

CLARENCE CHORUS   It's brilliant . . .

CLARENCE   No court in the land would separate the old bastard's child from his father's wealth.

CIELIA CHORUS   How? His sperm don't swim. They just tread water!

CINDY   We plan to name the boy Henry Walmont the Second.

CLARENCE   Have the abortion and we'll go sixty–forty. We'll take the forty.

CINDY   I could never harm a child. I could never harm any living thing.

CIELIA CHORUS   I could!

CIELIA   Seventy–thirty. We'll take the thirty.

CINDY CHORUS   They're screwed now!

CINDY   No. I don't want to.

CLARENCE   Eighty–twenty?

CINDY   You people think about money too much. I promised Henry I'd keep his fortune for his son. Oh, look who's up from his nap . . .

CINDY CHORUS   My lap dancing days are over. I'm rich!

HENRY   Oh, Clarence . . . Cielia . . . I'm glad you're here. . . . It's long overdue that we talked. And I do owe all my present joy to you two. I know you never think of this but . . . Well . . . before I married Cin, you two were my sole heirs in line to inherit close to, well, a billion five . . .

CLARENCE CHORUS/CIELIA CHORUS   Don't remind us, you old bastard!

CIELIA   Uncle Henry, we have our own money.

HENRY   I know. But I decided . . .

CLARENCE CHORUS   Maybe she'll die in a car accident. Don't lose hope.

HENRY   I've decided and Cin agreed . . .

CINDY CHORUS   Just to keep the greedy suckers honest.

HENRY   To leave you two loving relations a couple of million.

CIELIA CHORUS   Damned pittance!

CIELIA   We don't need anything, Uncle . . .

CLARENCE CHORUS   We want everything!

CLARENCE   We don't. But how loving that you thought of us.

CINDY   Your uncle Henry and your aunt Cindy have another surprise for you.

CIELIA   Oh?

HENRY   Yes ... It was Cin's idea. We want you two to act as godparents to our boy ...

CLARENCE CHORUS   She ... She ...

CIELIA CHORUS   She wants *us* to ... to ... to ...

CLARENCE   Why, jeez, thank you Uncle ... and Cindy ...

HENRY   Aunt Cindy, please, Clarence.

CLARENCE   I'm sorry. Aunt Cindy. ... Yes ... we'd consider being godparents an honor, wouldn't we, Cielia?

CIELIA   Oh, God, yes ...

CIELIA CHORUS   I'd like to drown him in the baptismal font!

CIELIA   New life, Lord, what a treasure ...

[CINDY *turns with the baby in her arms.*]

HENRY   Let me hold him ... Mommy ...

CINDY CHORUS   Mommy? I'm not ... Did he call me ...

CINDY   Mommy?

[CINDY *freezes with a phony smile on her face.*]

HENRY   Mommy of Henry Walmont the Second!! Five pounds, fourteen ounces!!

[CLARENCE*'s and* CIELIA*'s faces freeze in the same factitious smile as* CINDY*'s.*]

CIELIA CHORUS/CLARENCE CHORUS   The little bastard!

HENRY   Is there anything richer than a loving family?

HENRY/HENRY CHORUS   Not for my money. ... No, sir ...

[*Music up as lights fade.*]

• • •

Kong

Pamela Sneed

Pamela Sneed

Pamela Sneed is a New York–based poet, performer, writer, and actress. She has been featured in the *New York Times Magazine*, the *New Yorker*, the *Source*, *Time Out*, *Bomb*, *Next*, *MetroSource*, *Blue*, *VIBE*, *HX*, Karl Lagerfeld's "Off the Record," on the cover of *New York Magazine*, and in the PBS documentary *Black Artists Changing America*. She is the author of *Imagine Being More Afraid of Freedom Than Slavery*, published by Henry Holt in April 1998. She has also performed original works for sold-out houses at Lincoln Center, Creative Time at the Brooklyn Anchorage, the Studio Museum, Exit Art, PS. 122, Ex-Teresa in Mexico City, the ICA London, the CCA in Glasgow, Scotland, the Green Room in Manchester, England, and Literatur Werkstat in Berlin. In 2001, 2002, and 2005, she headlined the New Work Now Festival at Joe's Pub/Public Theater and performed before sold-out houses. In 1998, she was nominated for a Lambda Literary Award. She is a recipient of the 2006 Baxten Award for Performance, a Franklin Furnace Award, two Joyce-Mertz Gilmore Commissions for P.S.122, and a six-week residency at the Corporation of Yaddo. In 2006, she wrote and performed the solo show *Kong* at LIU's Kumble Theater. *Kong* was also performed in 2007, at UC Santa Barbara, Babson College, the PS13 Conference at NYU, and, in 2008, at the Ryan Repertory Company at the Harry Warren Theatre. In 2007, Sneed also headlined the Late Night series at the Pillsbury House Theater in Minneapolis, and directed students in a LIU campus production of her one-woman show *America Ain't Ready*. In 2008, she premiered an excerpt of the thesis work and solo show *Right to Return* at the Kumble Theater. She is a professor of speech and theatre at Long Island University. In 2004, 2005, and 2006, she became the television voice-over spokesperson for Merck and IBM's Linux and On Demand campaigns. Her current publications include work in *Downtown Brooklyn*; *To Be Left with the Body*; *110 Stories, New York Writes After September 11*; *Brown Sugar, an Anthology of Black Erotica*; *Role Call*; and *Voices Rising, The Other Countries Journal*. She is the author of the forthcoming book of her one-woman show *America Ain't Ready* and a novel, *Motherland or Chitlin Chimichanga*.

···Kong—Part 1···

Hands folded
Head down
Shoulders slouched
which I've told my students in the University to never do
but that was at a time when I earnestly believed
and I now I stand here wearing big Dumbo ears
a pig snout
carrying shards of a broken heart
looking like a cartoon character in a medieval play
because I earnestly believed
but before I go there
I want to talk about that last *Star Wars* movie which
they promised was a final installment
But we'll see
all I can say is it really sucked
except for the part near the end
where you see the transformation of Luke Skywalker
into the evil Darth Vader
His innocence destroyed
crawling through some molten lava—limbless
He looked like a soldier
or something out of a war movie
one of those battered survivors
who has left his child self behind him
But, I earnestly believed
And now all I can do is carry myself/battle scarred
to some semblance of safety
All I can do is hold on like a survivor of the tsunami
tidal wave
Hold on to a tree, a pipe, anything, my papers from an

old life
verifying who I am
wait for the storm to pass
a shoulder to lean on/anything
But I earnestly believed.
You know when I left my parents house
the small town for a big city
and experienced all accoutrements of a counter culture
I earnestly believed
queer boys
queer nations
nose rings
dread locks
muscle shirts on girls
dykes with nipple rings
punk rockers
were all some semblance of an alternative
I believed poet Glen James
who called us the sissified warriors
I believed when Marlon Riggs premiered the groundbreaking film
for Black Gay Men, *Tongues Untied*.
I believed Audre Lorde when she said in synopsis if we
don't do our work
One day women's blood will congeal upon a dead planet.
I believed poet Assoto Saint in all 6ft 4 of his cross
dressing self
I believed when he stood up at the funeral of Donald
Woods
and said in essence we must tell the truth about who
we really are.
I believed Black lesbian writer Pat Parker when she declared

straights are OK, but why must they be so blatant
I earnestly believed when my child eyes almost twenty
years ago
first saw bisexual poet June Jordan
and the first thing she said was this country needs a
revolution.
I believed when I first read Chrystos, the lesbian Native American author
of *Not Vanishing* and *Dream On*
when she wrote of AIM, the American Indian Movement, and said
"when I first heard you'd surrendered you don't know how much
I needed for you to go on."
I believed ten–fifteen years ago when the Hetrick Martin
Institute for queer youth
was still just a one- or two-room shack
located on the Westside Highway across from the piers
and no one invested in our lives
I believed even as an almost child working in that
agency
when many of us who pioneered were like slaves,
singularly doing the work
of twenty, thirty people
I believed in Nelson and Winnie premiering even at the
height of apartheid with their fists
and heads held high
I believed before Jennifer, Jessica whatever her name
is on *The L Word*.
I believed even after they found Angel my student at
Hetrick Martin murdered
a handsome boy chopped into pieces
Yeah when they were still pulling queers out of the
river there downtown

Dead from queer bashings and suicide
And then Kiki another bright young black queer
was murdered in the Meat District
Before him was Marsha P. Johnson, a drag queen and
neighborhood fixture
bashed and thrown into those waters
Even after they buried brethren artists and poets,
Essex, Rory, Don, Donald, Craig, Alan
And cancer got Audre, June and Pat Parker
I kept on believing change was possible.
I read the literature
had hope
I lived in America after all.
I've sort of joined the middle class.
I believed when I first saw a woman's silhouette in
5 a.m. light.
I believed kissing her nakedness
there'd be honor there.
I earnestly believed.
You know this is an aside but
I'm tired of the previews for that latest *King Kong*
movie
Tired of all the actors looking to the sky with that
same
perplexed look,
That over the top awesome
because King Kong is computer generated
they can't see him
so they're really acting
and you know King is a thin veil for a Black man
America assuaging it's racial fears.

Still, I'll pay ten, or twelve or twenty with popcorn
to see it.
There was a time too when I earnestly believed in
theatre
in performance
Believed I'd be a great big over night success
that courage, innovation, tenacity would be recognized.
I earnestly believed
And I know there are those who will say I'm bitter
mislabel me
say I spew hatred
am raining down on their parade
That I lack optimism
when I try to say there is another America
when I try to say things are not equal
when I try telling them there are crimes
being carried out with doctors
many of them are modern criminals
who don't deserve white coats
There's another final solution that's occurring
right under our noses
and it's gonna get tougher and tougher
and tougher and tougher to hide the bodies
I earnestly believed
Saddam Hussein has been tried and convicted
but maybe its just my secret silly wish
I keep wanting them to try George Bush
I keep wanting those feared 30,000 Iraqi soldiers dead
I want their bodies to rise up
walk to the White House
speak against this senseless war

For them to matter
to someone besides their mothers
I want those countless Americans killed little Black and Latino boys
I want all their lovers
Both women and men to tell what they've lost.
I want to see something like the truth and
reconciliation
hearings after apartheid
where this country must admit to committing atrocities
I want those millions of Americans living without health care
after working an entire lifetime . . .
I want seniors who can't afford their prescriptions
I want my parents to go
I want America's poor
ones who know about when hospitals and doctors
pull the plug on those who can't pay
I want the family of that little Black girl in New
Orleans
whose body was found floating facedown
still wearing pink short shorts and a pink squeegee in
hear hair.
Again, in New Orleans, I want the son whose mother
died during the floods
waiting for governmental help,
I want everyone to see the eyes of my student,
a black girl whose family is from the Ninth Ward in New Orleans
and how she looked the day in class when she said
they won't give us back our houses
want everyone to hear my friend when she said Bush
got up in the middle of the night to sign papers to help Terry Schivo
but did nothing to help the people of New Orleans

I want every year for those gays and lesbians in New York
during Gay Pride
to stop dancing on the piers and form a political movement
I want all those voiceless people we're turning our
backs on
right now in the Darfur region of Africa to speak
And thank you Oprah, Thank you Bono, Thank you Jon Bon Jovi
for your generous donations
but the system has to change
Yes, there was a time when I earnestly believed
People get so defensive when I try telling them
what's happening systemically
when I say under this regime censorship has increased.
Artists no longer have spaces to work
nor money
and it's not just all about personal will
pulling oneself up by a bootstrap
There is marginalization and silencing
occurring across the board more than in other eras
perhaps this is a return to.
I honestly believed once that there were people more
enlightened
that competition and jealousy couldn't destroy our
world.
I believed helping a neighbor
was more important than money
I earnestly believed
Yes, by now I'm probably like someone in a horror film
who gets killed off easy
wasn't careful enough
Kept running toward instead of away

from the monster
The one who stayed in haunted house
you know who goes into an attic or a basement
to investigate what's going on
when they should have been long gone, the one who
stays in an abusive cycle
believes the partner will change
The one who hasn't read all the signals
walks into a thieves den
like on the old 42nd St.
with money hanging out of their pockets.
I earnestly believed like Anne Frank in human good.
I believed the slogans I read in kindergarten
that policemen help you across the street
will return lost children to their parents.
Maybe I'm as naïve as MLK
when he said he had a dream of what America could
become
Maybe he isn't here to witness
just how tough things have become
Integration is now only a small step or
small slice of what we need.
Yesterday I sat down in the sun
and let it beam across my face
I prayed like Martin Luther King
I could live one day in freedom
One day not racked by pain or injustice.
I felt like Harriet who lived in slavery
Just one day wanting to feel freedom's kiss
And caress.

···Kong—Part 2···

I have to go back in my mind
Because I saw that Kong movie last night
It was spectacular
except for the first hour which dragged on
and I almost walked out when the crew got to
Skull Island aka Africa
where Kong comes from
and I saw all those white oil painted actors playing natives
when everyone knows lots of Black actors need jobs
but the movie might have been even more offensive
if they'd cast them
Anyway, this Kong was an alpha if I've ever seen one—
He was like the Zulu warriors handling his business in
the jungle
Directed by the same guy who directed the Lord of the Rings trilogy
this Kong gets medieval
There's a part where he snaps the neck and jaw of another animal
then thrusts it aside
leaves the carcass
I mean this computer generated you could never guess was a cartoon Kong
was so fierce
The American government could use him in their war to
fight Iraq
He could help them find looming terrorist at large
Osama Bin Laden
They could send him to change history
He could be like Rambo and try again to singlehandedly
win the Vietnam War—
Like Donald Trump, Charles Brosnan, and Rambo rolled

into one
This Kong's got dominion
He's Shaft, a '70s icon
A private dick/ex-cop dispensing his own brand of
street justice
This Kong is like a Dominican warlord, not at all to be fucked with
I mean this Kong had that Fay Wray bitch climbing into
his hand
Excuse me, Naomi Watts
no argument, minimum screaming
What is it about sex or attraction to a good woman
that makes you want to beat your chest, go all
illiterate, yell oonga fucking boonga,
jump from the bushes, tie her up, dance with wolves,
unleash your inner self
Well this Kong is pure and unadulterated
He's some straight-up niggah, no rocks, no chaser
He's got a little of the fucked-up wild haired Ike
who told Tina
Don't you ever try to leave me
He's like Samuel Jackson on a bad day
Have you ever noticed how Sam Jackson, talented actor
that he is
plays the same character in every movie
He's perpetually angry
and excuse me for asking but what was he doing in the
Star Wars movie
He was like speaking Ebonics in space
You know how every syllable is over exaggerated and
drawn out
Like M-A-S-T-E-R S-O-L-O

I saw Sam's latest movie last night
Provocatively titled *Freedomland*.
All the acting screamed this is an important film
discussing race in America.
It's typical Hollywood fare
where complex human emotions
complex characters get reduced down to broad sketches
and caricature
not to mention everyone knows in 2007
parts of America are no better than Soweto during apartheid.
I mean come on I saw that new movie *Hustle and Flow*
sitting in the all-black audience
It was like back to days of segregated cinema/produced by MTV films
about a ne'er-do-well pimp/who just happens to also be
a rapper
trying to make it in America
The theme song just won an Academy Award called
It's hard out here for a pimp,
but everyone knows it's hos who built America
slave labor.
I'll tell you this if you think I'm lying—
Stretching about this King Kong, Black man link
One of the white racist cops yells out to Samuel
Jackson's character
who is also a cop, You're supposed to be lord of the
jungle—
and then he points to a young black kid standing by
and says "So,
why aren't you handling this monkey?"
You've probably asked by now what's her investment
Why does she even care

and this is gonna get pretty painful
because I don't want to say
There were times right here in America
when I needed simple things like friendship,
health care, love, resources
And I was made to live like an animal
Less than
Caged in
Speaking of pimps and hos
Can any of us ever forget the way Tina Turner was
treated by Ike
She was actually beaten with the heel of his shoe
Games, betrayals, sabotage, competition
Conscious and unconscious
Anything he could do to destroy her spirit
Not let her use that powerful beautiful voice she had
Except as a way for him to make money
I mean real moments where I've felt like this is
Cambodia 1975
And these are killing fields/like in the movie/the
story of
that skinny war-torn reporter who gets left behind
while everyone else escapes
And all he tries to do every day is just survive
and I'm not the only one
with the way things are going
there will be more and more who'll one day
have to choose between their breakfast cereal
and taking their own lungs out
and if we don't watch out/this is the fall
the end of a once great civilization

a crumbling empire
I read recently in the paper
They found one of the Black men, a government official
dead in a ditch—
He was one of many who helped orchestrate the
Rwandan massacre
We all remember 1994 right
½ million dead
Black tribes in Africa warring against each other
And I can't believe I'm saying this about another
human being,
But I'm glad they killed that motherfucker
I'm glad he's dead
I have to go back again because I feel guilty that
earlier I mentioned Cambodia and killing fields and
the nature of that extermination
was so huge actually an estimated 1.7 million
but just today I read in the paper about a measure
being discussed in the Senate
on how to rid the United States of 12 million illegal
immigrants
and the language they used was rid.
The thing about this *King Kong* which differs from the
classic
is you can see what a great warrior he is
but a monster too
he's kind of human/contemplative
He actually manages in ape talk to sign the word
beauty
when they take him down/chloroform him
it's human beings/white people who look barbaric

when they put him on display
and you see his great paws
you know there isn't a theatre big enough to contain
him
and the chains around his wrists represent all of our
greatness
both blacks and whites wrapped up in human bondage
all of our potential that's been lasso'd, corralled
Yeah, the only difference is when this Kong
Climbs on top of the Empire State Building to escape
Instead of seeing him shot down
Broken in captivity
This one, unlike the classic/that unruly inhumane
beast
This Kong—you want to be free

··· Kong—Part 3 ···

It wasn't until I put posters up
handed out flyers of me, a 6ft 2 black woman
presiding over the city in a bra
while an image of King Kong lurked in the background
did I realize how long people had waited to see images of Kong usurped—
to see images we could laugh at/point fingers at/subvert.
It wasn't until then I realized how long King Kong had been lurking
in our cultural history/in our shadows/our shame.
Most of us know where he came from
from that birth of a nation era
born in 1933 from that great depression
where the Klu Klux Klan held dominance
not more that fifty years out of slavery

he was the story of slaves/a savage
brought here in chains/driven by his desire for a white woman.
He is the myth/the fear
just two years after the Scottsboro boys/twelve Black men
were accused of raping a white woman.
We continue to see him over and over in our movies
He is the subject of *To Kill a Mockingbird*
and the film just cause
he is the recent real-life story of a garbage man accused of raping and
murdering a white woman in a upper-middle-class neighborhood
as her five-year-old daughter stood by
he is the accused wilding wolf pack that went after
a Central Park jogger
And you wouldn't believe the responses I got
from people who weren't even followers of performance art
who weren't black clad
with purple hair or shaved heads
like the black security guard a LIU where I teach
who never gets involved in anything
saw the poster and said to me you go girl
Miss Foxy Brown, Cleopatra Jones
and then gives me a hug
and then the young black boy who works behind the counter
in the school cafeteria
who recognizes me from the poster
He says, Your piece looks interesting
and asks if I'm going to be playing King Kong or Fay Wray
and then the secretary in the school where I work
actually pulls notes she wrote out of her desk drawer she wrote
after seeing the Kong poster and says
I think he's a gentle giant.

And to her he is a symbol of good.
The there are the more radical/expected/unexpected responses
like from the genteel black screenplay writer on my block
whom after I tell him casually I'm doing a piece on Kong
his face breaks into a disdain and grimace
as if he'd gone to the cinema and been betrayed
I brought my niece to see that new Kong film
I was so angry after I left/I wrote the producers a letter
which reminds me of another black man on my block/an investment banker
whom I've only ever seen planting flowers on the street
in boxes that aren't even his
he is genteel and middle class
and I thought to ask him what he thought
about what happened to blacks during the floods in New Orleans
and his face breaks into a Rubik's Cube I've never seen before
suddenly he thrusts his hands into the sky and starts to yell
It was wrong what they did to those people/it was wrong!
And all of this is coming from people
who would consider themselves to be ordinary people
not the lefties or revolutionaries
Even Donald Trump said the other day on television
President Bush has grossly mismanaged this country
and they found no weapons of mass destruction
and it all reminds me/shows me how under this regime
years of living under it has made a lot of us, everyday people
into heroes.
But the flower guy reminds me of something Audre Lorde said
in the book *Our Dead Behind Us*
She like the flower guy is gardening
but thinking of the violent deaths of black people in America
and then in her lover's country which is South Africa,

And she says,
My hand comes down like a brown vice over the marigolds
reckless through despair
we were two black women touching our flame
and we left our dead behind us.
Someone else sends me an article
about King Kong written by a man with my father's name James Snead
Someone else, a young white girl when she hears me recite *King Kong*
says excitedly and angrily
You should talk about how the FBI was an organization
built primarily to destroy radical movements.
Look what they did to the Panthers.
Someone else calls Peter Jackson a fascist
and I'm actually afraid to tell him I like the Lord of the Rings trilogy.
Someone else says you mentioned *Top Model*
will you talk about that
and I say I do in another piece
and then I try to prod people as gently as I can
and say these are your stories to tell now.
I simply pressed buttons, opened a door
but then something else comes to mind
that's unexpected after all is said and done.
Something that still haunts
I keep telling everyone who works on *Kong*
the video person and poster designer
make sure there's a skyline
we need images of the skyline it's important
since 9/11 I say the skyline/the city Kong stomped over
has changed
I'm aware now whether it's shown or not in pictures
something in our skyline is missing

Poet Sekou Sundiata said America lost her innocence
and it's true
it's like a jack-o'-lantern
someone took a knife and gauged out
a huge hunk of who we are
gone is our candyland
our jungle gym/our slide/our Tarzan-like swing
our playground of yesteryear
Poet Sekou Sundiata said America lost her innocence
and it's true.
And all I can say revisiting *Kong* trouncing through
all of the footage
suddenly the image of a great goliath
being taken down by tiny planes
has entirely new and different meaning.

• • •

The Courier

Carol K. Mack

Carol Mack

Carol K. Mack's recently completed play *The Visitor* was a recipient of a 2005 grant from the Foundation for Jewish Culture. Premieres include: *In Her Sight* and *After*, Humana Festival, Actors Theatre of Louisville; *The Accident*, American Repertory Theatre; *Without a Trace*, Tron, Glasgow, and tour of Scotland, 2002; *A Safe Place*, the Berkshire Theatre Festival in Association with the Kennedy Center; *Territorial Rights*, The Women's Project. Her awards include the Julie Harris/Beverly Hills Theatre Guild Award, the Stanley Drama Award, and a Rockefeller Foundation Fellowship at the Center for Study in Bellagio. Her one-acts appear in three separate editions of Best Short American Plays. Other publications include *A Field Guide to Demons, Fairies, Fallen Angels & Other Subversive Spirits*, written with Dinah Mack, published by Arcade, and Henry Holt, paperback, published by Profilebooks, London, October 2008.

cast

(Two actors)

OLDER MAN, Professor Ahrensky (a trace European accent under
    speech)

Recruiter (a Texan background)

Doctor

YOUNG MAN, Courier

Policeman/Interrogator

set

The play takes place in an unidentified location where the PROFESSOR is
being held and in the remembered moments in the PROFESSOR's consciousness. There are two chairs. Lights shift to change moments.

• • •

[*Lights up. A man sits on a chair. An* INTERROGATOR *stands upstage of him.*]

INTERROGATOR   . . . Go on.

PROFESSOR   So. I'm walking along through the park, my hands clasped
behind my back. Habit. A scholar's walk? My wife, she always
teases me about it. "Save it for Prague!" she says. "It's hazardous
on hikes." Right. She should talk . . . Being an artist, you see
[*Remembering.*] she . . . she gets distracted by a branch, a butterfly, a
rock. . . .

INTERROGATOR   That happened in the park?

PROFESSOR   So . . . I'm walking along when it begins to rain . . . just
then I see a man lying on a bench. I stop to see if he is all right,
just sleeping it off, or . . .

INTERROGATOR   And then?

PROFESSOR   . . . then he opens his eyes. Wide. Looks terrified. I say, it's
O.K., I'm just walking by . . . And he grabs my arm. He says,
PLEASE. That's all. Please. Stops me cold, that *desperate* sound in

his voice. So. I can't then just walk on . . . he pulls himself up on my arm. He feels so light. Weighs no more than a ghost. His face is unshaven. He sits and looks right through me, and then he looks around, all round, and so do I, as if somehow we're in something together now—something that feels . . . dangerous. There's nobody anywhere. Empty paths, vacant benches . . . and I hear him say, "Let me tell you." Then he stops dead as if he hasn't talked to anyone in a long time and his own voice shocks him. I say, like you would to a child, 'It's O.K., what is it? What's wrong?' He says, "Let me tell you how I got here." Then he tells me the story I've already *told* you.

INTERROGATOR   You didn't recognize him?

PROFESSOR   What?! I told you—

INTERROGATOR   You were supposed to meet him there. You arranged it? Think!

PROFESSOR   I never saw him before! [*Think!*] How many times must I—

INTERROGATOR   You're the only people in the whole park, huh?

PROFESSOR   That's right. Fate. Call it what you will. Why am I *here*? . . . [*As* INTERROGATOR *turns away.*] What is this place?! [*As* INTERROGATOR *exits.*] Where is "here"?! [*Calling to offstage.*] Was that too fucking existential for you?! [*Beat.*] . . . Whatever. "Whatever," as my students say.

[*Angrily to offstage.*]

You'll have to let me out soon! They're looking for me! They're all . . . they must all be . . .

[*To himself, bitterly, fighting to remain himself.*]

I will not forget the story! I will make notes every day. I will pad myself with them. I won't forget. I'll write it all down bit by bit and when they let me out I'll shed the pieces. All of them. I'll give them to my wife. Oh, Rachel! . . . [*Very upset.*] You'll send them to the newspapers. In case I . . . am silenced, in case I come home unable to speak or. . . . *You'll* find them. *You'll* know what to do. Oh . . . my dear. I'll say I've forgotten. I'll wait. But I'll remember every single word. How he told me he was "chosen." Chosen! I looked at him like he was crazy.

YOUNG MAN   [*Linking to remembered moment, on bench as lights shift, urgently.*]

But it's true! Honest. That's how it started. I was chosen, see? out of hundreds of candidates. I was secretly tested. Before the interview. They never said where or how. I mean, all they said was: "You've been selected for the job."

RECRUITER VOICEOVER   Now, son, we have conducted a thorough search and you have been chosen out of hundreds of potential candidates as most trustworthy. Most reliable. Total trust must be upheld on both ends at all times ...

[*The* PROFESSOR *reappears as the* RECRUITER *in the remembered scene.*]

RECRUITER   At all times! Understand? We picked you outta hundreds of candidates. We had profiles covered this whole wall here. This is one real important job, son. We need somebody trustworthy, loyal, and smart. All potential candidates were secretly tested over months on all the above and out of this thorough search we selected you. Now, son, this is one of the most important secret government jobs you could ever hope to do. This is about *total trust* in your country, O.K.? This takes a pledge that is way beyond allegiance. A pledge that only a few could begin to understand. This is about faith. That's what we're dealing with here. See that package, son? *That* package and every package must be delivered under *any* circumstances. This is no "storm, no dark of night" here like your old job. This is deliver under attack, under fire. You run with that package and you get it there. You never ever ask questions. And, son, if necessary you give your life for your country. Now what does this take? It takes a hero. It takes dedication and *faith*. Got it? And you walk ALONE. Outside this room? Anybody asks what you do for a living, you say you're a parking attendant, limo driver, whatever. You say you're a part-time whatever but you do NOT say "courier." You do NOT say you carry a package from someplace to anywhere. It could get you killed, son. Got it? [*At nod, he pushes a note across desk.*]

These are your instructions. When. Where. How. Memorize it. . . . Good. There's your first mission. Good luck.

YOUNG MAN   Thank you, sir.

RECRUITER   For what?

YOUNG MAN   Choosing me.

RECRUITER   What's that you said?

YOUNG MAN   Choosing me?

RECRUITER   For what?

YOUNG MAN   The job?

RECRUITER   What job?

YOUNG MAN   . . . I . . . can't say.

RECRUITER   Why not?

YOUNG MAN   'Cause I don't know?

RECRUITER   Don't know what?

YOUNG MAN   . . . Don't know anything, sir.

RECRUITER   About what? Anything about what?!

YOUNG MAN   Nothing.

RECRUITER   [*As he exits.*]
  Good!

YOUNG MAN   The packages. They were all sealed. And every day there was a new one. I was taking them to a lab. All these boxes, sealed red boxes. Shiny. Nothing could leak out but . . . all going from Central to this lab, see? After a coupla months I wonder who's it going to? And what's in the boxes? He never said nothing about that. I think maybe it's O.K. if I know what's inside-a-them? I mean, it don't make no difference. I'd always do my job. Do my best! Like he said. All I did was take off the label. Not even get the tape off. Just the label. No name. Some kind of bar code label. I just start to take it off with my penknife—

[*Very odd mechanical noise.* YOUNG MAN *startled, stands.*]

And before I know it these guys show up, see? Then I get arrested for possession of lethal materials. They accuse me of planning a terrorist attack. They say the box contains a biological weapon. I say that's not possible. They say, "Who do you work for?" I tell them I take the package from Central to the lab. I tell them that's my job. They tell me there IS no lab. They tell me there IS no central nothing. That they don't exist and they never have. Then I figure O.K., O.K., this has gotta be some kinda test. Right? Maybe they test you every month. So then they say, "Who do you work for?" and I say, "What"? And they say, "Who do you work for?" and I say, "I . . . I used to work for the U.S. post office and I don't work for *nobody* now," and they say, "Then who told you to do it?" [*Breaking down, in tears.*] And I say, "Do *what*?" Do WHAT? For chrissakes! I trusted them. I BELIEVED in them. I was selected for this job and now they turn against me for WHAT.

DOCTOR [*Appears standing with case file, listening, then assured, clinical.*] I see . . . Do you know where you are? . . . [*At the nod "no."*] . . . You're in a hospital.

YOUNG MAN . . . Why?

DOCTOR So you can get better.

YOUNG MAN [*Looking at* DOCTOR *a beat, then . . .*] You look like him.

DOCTOR Who do I look like?

YOUNG MAN . . . That guy. Who hired me?

DOCTOR The man you say "selected" you?

YOUNG MAN That's right. Yeah. You look kinda like him.

DOCTOR The man who "betrayed" you. From what you call the "Central Office"?

YOUNG MAN . . . Right.

DOCTOR Well, that's to be expected in a case like yours. I have your file here. And your diagnoses. But we *are* going to *cure* you. You'll be all right.

YOUNG MAN   Then do I get out of here? I mean, if I get better?

DOCTOR   Yes. Of course. Absolutely.

YOUNG MAN   How'd they find me? I mean, after I ran away? Does it say in the file?

DOCTOR   Who are "they," these people who "found you"?

YOUNG MAN   I don't know, but they musta thought I was dangerous 'cause they tried to kill me. I got away and I was hiding out in this other city and they . . . I could see how they thought maybe I'd talk about the lab? Where I took the stuff? I could—

DOCTOR   Listen, try to hear me out. There is no lab. There is no what you call "Central Office." There is no "package." We know how real these things are to you but they are *not* real, and when you can understand this, you'll feel much better.

YOUNG MAN   So why don't you believe me?

DOCTOR   I do believe that you believe. [*Exiting.*] Now, I'm going to arrange some medication—

YOUNG MAN   . . . I trusted them. I had faith. I trusted my *life* to them. Why?!

[*Light shift.*]

PROFESSOR   [*Alone on chair, remembering, as he was earlier, making a note.*] And by the time he finishes, his face is wet with tears and rain and he starts coughing, then choking and I put my arm around him. . . . He twists round and his jacket opens. . . . There's a wound. Dark, blackened blood. He twists violently *once* more, then collapses. I take his hand, his wrist. There's no pulse. . . . People must die like this every day. Alone. Shot by criminals. Perhaps criminals themselves but, he seemed, so . . . *innocent.* I don't know what to think. His story seems incredible. A fantasy. And yet, they were his last words . . . his last story. Either he's died sane or not. I must call the police . . . and my wife. She'll worry . . . Oh my God. If I hadn't stopped. If I hadn't heard . . . Rachel!? What is happening *now* out there to *you*?

[*Thinking.*]

I didn't believe his claim that they could track him. After he escaped the hospital . . . To be *that* . . . able to find him in another city and then to be so near when he tells a stranger his story. Of course I don't know who "they" are. . . . But suddenly there's a man in uniform . . . a policeman.

POLICEMAN [*Enters, looking at offstage body and then back at* PROFESSOR.] You found him like that?

PROFESSOR No, I . . . he just started *choking*, then all this blood—

POLICEMAN Hands up. Keep them up.

[*Frisking* PROFESSOR, *takes his wallet out, looks at I.D.*]

You were just walking by here, huh?

PROFESSOR Yes!

POLICEMAN You do it a lot? Walk in the rain?

PROFESSOR It wasn't raining when I started out.

POLICEMAN So you stop by here and he's lying there bleeding?

PROFESSOR No! Yes, I mean. I, I didn't, I didn't see the *wound* until—

POLICEMAN And what's your name?

PROFESSOR Dr. Ahrensky, I teach at Columbia—

POLICEMAN Ahrensky [*Inspecting wallet.*] What's the origin of this name?

PROFESSOR What?!

POLICEMAN The name. Where's it from?

PROFESSOR Ellis Island.

POLICEMAN What's that supposed to mean?

PROFESSOR It was longer before. The *name*, it was—

POLICEMAN What *was* it? The name, before?

PROFESSOR How far back? Russia? Aramaic? What are you?—

POLICEMAN Look, you got *blood* on your hands. That guy's dead.

PROFESSOR   What's that got to do with my name—

POLICEMAN   I'm looking for motive, relationship. Whatever.

PROFESSOR   Whatever.

POLICEMAN   "Professor," you're gonna have to answer questions. That guy? You say you never seen him before?

PROFESSOR   No. I—

POLICEMAN   He talk to you? Did he *approach* you?

PROFESSOR   No, I . . . I walk by, see he's bleeding, I see *blood*, I see he's been shot.

POLICEMAN   That right? But you said, uh, "I didn't see the wound at first."

PROFESSOR   Did I? I'm . . . I'm quite upset. I need to wash my hands. All this blood. I must call my wife, I—

POLICEMAN   I'm trying to get the story straight. Now can you *identify* this guy or not?

PROFESSOR   Only as a fellow human being.

POLICEMAN   Uh-huh. So did this guy say anything at all to you that might be helpful to us?

PROFESSOR   "Helpful" how?

POLICEMAN   Look, we've got a *homicide* here—

PROFESSOR   Are you accusing me of something? If so, I believe you have to read me my rights.

POLICEMAN   You're wrong on that one, "professor," O.K.? Now, how about I do *my* job, you stick to yours. What exactly is your field, professor?

PROFESSOR   Ethics.

POLICEMAN   "Ethics." Look, I gotta know exactly what happened here. How you got involved. We got a dead body. There's blood on your hands. First you say you didn't see the wound. Then you say you did. You say you don't know this person but you're *here*, right?

PROFESSOR [*At his chair as at top of play.*]

Rachel! I should've run then. I should've had my cell phone, like you . . . But it's Central Park! On Poet's Walk. That's where I was! That's . . . I was in shock. And I *assumed* he was just a cop . . . I assumed the world was a different world. . . . I know. I know I'm naive, but then, weren't we all?

[*Pause. Then passionately.*]

I find it impossible to believe that it has all come to this "life being nasty, brutish and short" and all people against each other like driven mad animals.

[*Pause.*]

That policeman. I thought he was "only doing his job." He believed that *I* could kill another human being . . . in the park. In the rain. In some world that . . . Had I known we'd come to *this*. HERE?!

POLICEMAN So he tells you that whole story?

PROFESSOR Yes . . . Yes he did.

POLICEMAN Incredible.

PROFESSOR Yes. But, officer, somebody shot him—

POLICEMAN Drugs. Probably drugs. Gangs. But that story—

PROFESSOR Yes! I know. Officer, I . . . I *do* need to make a phone call. My wife will be—

POLICEMAN Sounds to me like he made up the whole nine yards.

PROFESSOR Perhaps. Are we finished here? Do you need me? You have my number—

POLICEMAN So you don't buy it either, huh? The story.

PROFESSOR . . . I don't know. Poor kid, he seemed so, *lost*, so . . . Yes, I think I *do*.

[POLICEMAN *exits.*]

Yes. I *do* . . . Wedding vows. Commitment. Yes, I *do*. Magic words. And the world changed, in less than a glance away, a branch, a rock . . . The towers fell, and the ivory tower tumbled invisibly and in the rubble, from there to here we fell into another world where I am taken unaware. Yes, I DO! Assertion in the face of some local cop with an attitude baiting me? . . . I don't know why I said it. But, Rachel, who *am* I?! Just some . . . why would anybody *care* even if I told the story? I am just an old professor. . . . And what do I know?! That the boy worked for some . . . *what*? Secret government organization somewhere? Some lab, but *where*? I don't even know *where*! Is it still in operation? What does it *do* that's worth killing for? Worth removing anybody who knows it *exists*. It is impossible to believe that. . . . OH God, Rachel, now I put you in danger! If you make too much noise. "Yes, I do." Then they put me in a car and bring me here. Poor kid. The "courier" . . . It must be much more complicated to vanish someone with a family . . . Unless you were to take the whole family. Oh, Rachel, please don't do anything foolish! . . . What are you thinking? I vanished? Where to? Why? I was not unhappy. I was not "political," not according to my noisier, contentious colleagues. . . . *Please* be careful. Watch what you say. The more you say, the more publicity, the less likely it is I can get out . . . from here. Now that I'm here.

[*Pause.*]

But where *is* here? Where are we?

[INTERROGATOR *enters and raises his gun.* BLACKOUT. *Shot in dark.*]

• • •

Props

Michael Roderick

Michael Roderick

Michael Roderick started Small Pond Entertainment five years ago, when he found that it was virtually impossible for an artist to be at their best when they also had to produce. He developed a system for the advancement of a producing organization to be the umbrella for shows that lacked producers. Over the years Small Pond has become a major name in the New York City theatre community, having presented shows in numerous venues and with hundreds of different artists. As artistic director, Michael has produced over thirty shows since his arrival in New York in September 2002. He has also been the organizer of networking events that have included representatives from the New York Musical Theatre Festival, Fractured Atlas, and RWS Casting and Associates. He holds a BA in secondary education English and theatre performance from Rhode Island College, and an MA from NYU in educational theatre colleges and communities. Michael also teaches English at LaSalle Academy, where he is the head of the drama program. He has written fifteen plays, and his play *I'll Do It Tomorrow* was published in the *2004–2005 Best American Short Plays*, published by Applause Books. He also plans on eventually publishing a book about his first year teaching, called *Stage Fright*, as well as a young adult novel titled *Norin's Quest: Beyond the Gates of Lavender*.

cast

ANDREW, a young man
SUSAN, his girlfriend
KERRI, his perfect woman
DENISE, his first love
MELISSA, his best friend

• • •

··· scene one ···

[*The stage is in complete darkness. There can be a few chairs and perhaps a table. The locations change quickly and can be done through suggestion rather then elaborate set pieces. ANDREW stands center stage and the rest of the cast are at one of the four corners. KERRI sits with her back to the audience, SUSAN sits facing the audience, MELISSA stands in the upstage right corner, while DENISE stands in the upstage left corner. Whenever one speaks they light a match and let it burn out.*]

ANDREW Love.

SUSAN I . . .

DENISE Don't!

ANDREW Love . . .

MELISSA You . . .

[*Flame goes out and we are left in darkness for a moment. The soft sound of crackling fire is heard. Then we hear KERRI softly crying, it lingers for a moment and then stops. The lights slowly fade up and the cast is still standing onstage. During this next piece, no one looks at each other. Everything said is delivered straight out to the audience.*]

ANDREW Love. Love. I thought that's what I had, what I felt, but I don't know what's happening to me. I mean, do we connect? Am I worth anything to you? Or is this another one of your famous silent moments. The time when you hold back so you won't hurt me?

SUSAN I . . . I'm going. I can't do this.

ANDREW   Well, it hurts more when you don't say anything! When you leave me alone with the silence and my own mind. Don't give me time to think.

DENISE   Don't think about me, Andrew. Don't dream about me. Not now.

SUSAN   Why can't you just let me walk away and regain my composure and then I'll come back and we'll talk about this? We'll talk about why I said what I said—

DENISE   Not now. When we had a chance you threw it away and now I'm happy. I've moved on. You need to stop thinking about me and move on.

ANDREW   I'm begging you! The worst thing in the world is to give me time to think. I would never do this to you! I would at least try to talk. Can't you at least try? Please? God . . . I

SUSAN   I love you, Andrew. . . . But you drive me frigging crazy sometimes

MELISSA   You don't deserve this. You're one of the kindest and sweetest people I know and any girl would be more than happy to love you. There's so much within you. So much to give and you shouldn't be with someone who only takes.

DENISE   Please replace me and stop torturing yourself. I'm smoke, Andrew. You know all about smoke. It's what remains after the fire. There's only you now . . . only you.

SUSAN   Why can't *you* just let me walk away and regain my composure and then I'll come back and we'll talk about this?

MELISSA   I don't want to hear about what she's done for you either. All you do is defend her. As if she *made* you or something. You just have to tell yourself that you're more, that you deserve more.

DENISE   There's only you now . . . only you.

ANDREW   I would never do this to you! I would at least try to talk. Can't you at least try? Please? God . . . I

SUSAN Andrew

MELISSA You don't deserve this.

DENISE I wish you nothing but happiness . . .

SUSAN I'm sorry.

ANDREW It hurts more when you don't say anything

MELISSA You shouldn't be with someone who only takes . . .

SUSAN Let's talk.

DENISE Replace me, Andrew. It's not hard.

MELISSA All you do is defend her.

DENISE I'm smoke, Andrew. You know all about smoke. It's
what remains after the fire. There's only you now . . . only
you.

SUSAN I love you.

DENISE Only you.

MELISSA You just have to tell yourself that you're more, that you
deserve more.

ANDREW Love.

DENISE Stop torturing yourself!

SUSAN Let's talk . . .

ANDREW Say anything . . .

MELISSA You just have to tell yourself—

SUSAN I love you

MELISSA Any girl would . . .

ANDREW I

MELISSA Would be more than happy to . . .

ANDREW love you too.

[*Blackout.*]

[*Lights fade up on* ANDREW *sitting in a chair directly across from* KERRI. *Her back is still to the audience. He appears to be putting makeup on her.*]

ANDREW   I'm not sure why I talk to you. I think maybe it's because I feel safe with you. At home somehow. I'm not sure what I'm going to do about all of this. There is no clear-cut answer to this sort of thing. I mean, how do you let go of something that you know is bad for you but has been your life? How is it that you can ignore it when someone says things to you that really hurt? How can you just accept that pain and hope things will change? [*Laughs.*] Why am I asking *you* all these questions? It's not like you can answer. [*Looks at his watch.*] It's three o'clock in the morning and I'm still working. Well, I guess that's the price one pays for perfection, right? Shit, I need some sleep. [*Moves over to her and puts his hands on her shoulders. She slumps over against his chest.*] Whoa. Don't get fresh now. [*As he props her up, it now becomes clear to those watching that* KERRI *is a puppet.*] Why would anybody ever ask someone to create a replica of another human being, huh? When I signed on for this job, I thought they just wanted a mannequin, but no. They asked me for the most life-like prop I could make and that my dear is how you were born. God, I'm tired. Who talks to inanimate objects in the middle of the night? [*Puts up his hand with a slight giggle.*] Guilty. Seriously, though, I really must be going. Thanks again for listening to my woes and soon enough you'll be ready to go onstage and you won't have to listen to my boring stories anymore. [*Pause.*] Wow. This is really sad. I almost looked at you as a real person there for a minute. I guess it's because I talk to you. Maybe I need help. Oh, I don't know. [*Sits back down.*] Or maybe I'm just looking for an excuse not to go home to an empty bed. That's so terrible. I shouldn't try to stay at work all night, just because I can't face being alone. I'm such a loser. [*Laughs.*] That would be why I'm still in the woodshop at this time of morning. Oh well. Good night, Kerri. You debut in a few days. [ANDREW *sits in the chair looking at his creation. His eyes grow heavy until he falls asleep.*]

[*Slow fade down.*]

··· scene two ···

[*Soft piano music plays as the lights slowly come up. The entire cast is onstage again.* ANDREW *moves to* SUSAN *and kisses her. They dance around the stage in a soft waltz.* ANDREW *closes his eyes and* SUSAN *fades out of his arms and exits.* MELISSA *replaces her and slowly dances and hugs* ANDREW. ANDREW *opens his eyes to smile for a second and then closes them again.* DENISE *taps* MELISSA *on the shoulder and cuts in as* MELISSA *exits.* ANDREW *and* DENISE *kiss passionately as they dance around the space. The music begins to deteriorate and the passion leaves the dance.* DENISE *looks up at* ANDREW *with tears in her eyes and kisses him and exits.* ANDREW *remains frozen, holding on to that kiss, as* KERRI *rises from her chair. She still retains her puppet-like features and moves a little clumsily at first. She eventually moves over to* ANDREW *and allows her arms to envelop him. Their lips touch and* ANDREW *opens his eyes for a moment. He is in a state of disbelief, but cannot stop the kiss from overtaking him. The music swells back up to a fever pitch and ends on a loud chord. The lights come up very harsh.*]

ANDREW What?

KERRI Shhh. Don't say anything. [*Kisses him again.*]

ANDREW You're . . .

KERRI Yes.

ANDREW How?

KERRI Shhhhhhh. It's OK.

[ANDREW *melts into* KERRI's *embrace to the point of near collapse. She tenderly rubs his back and kisses his tear-stained cheeks. Soft piano music plays in the background as the lights fade to black.*]

··· scene three ···

[*The lights come up and it is clear that it is morning.* KERRI *is back to her original position and* ANDREW *is passed out in the chair. He wakes up and looks around the room suspiciously. He spots* KERRI *and moves towards her very cautiously. He taps her and there's no response. He looks relieved. Just to be sure, he taps her again.* DENISE *enters.*]

DENISE Andrew, what are you doing here?

ANDREW What are *you* doing here?

DENISE You first.

ANDREW Well, *I* was working and I guess it must have gotten late. I guess I fell asleep in the chair.

DENISE You guess you fell asleep in the woodshop? Andrew, do you even remember last night?

ANDREW Last night?

DENISE You called me at four in the morning saying something about losing your mind and you kept mentioning the name Kerri. Who is Kerri anyway?

ANDREW [*Looking at* KERRI *as* DENISE *surveys the room.*] Kerri? Um, I'm not sure. I must have been high on that Krylon spray. You know I always forget to use the hood. I'm surprised I don't remember any of this.

DENISE So you don't remember the other things you said either. Are you sure? Or are you just afraid to admit to saying that?

ANDREW Denise, honestly, I don't remember a thing. I remember working on Kerri. . . .

DENISE What do you mean "working on"? How does one work on someone, and I thought you said you didn't know what I was talking about, and now this Kerri appears in the conversation again. What is it that you're doing here, Andrew? This place looks like you've been in here for a week. It's kind of creepy, like Frankenstein's lab or something. Anyway, who is Kerri?

ANDREW This is a little awkward. [*With a slight gesture in the direction of the chair.*] That's Kerri.

DENISE Um, that's not real. Why did you give it a name? More importantly, why were you talking about it last night? Come to think of it, why did you just try to say you didn't know *her*? How much time did you spend on her? Is she the only thing you've been working on? This is unhealthy. [*Pause.*] I think maybe we should talk. There was something else you said last night, besides all the talk about the puppet. You still don't remember?

ANDREW No.

DENISE You brought up the past again. Those . . . times . . . You seriously don't remember any of it?

ANDREW I wish I could remember. The truth is last night is so unclear. I remember working late and falling asleep and I seriously don't remember anything else. I don't even remember calling you.

DENISE Well, you did and what you said to me got me all confused. It was like I was hearing the you I fell . . . Damn. Please, don't think about me, Andrew. Don't dream about me. Not now. When we had a chance you threw it away and now I'm happy. I've moved on. You need to stop thinking about me and move on. Replace me, Andrew. It's not hard. You're a wonderful guy and I wish you nothing but happiness, but please replace me and stop torturing yourself. I'm smoke, Andrew. You know all about smoke. It's what remains after the fire. There's only you now. . . . Only you. Timing was never our strong suit. You were pining for someone when all I wanted was you and I fell in love when all you wanted was me. I think that we need to spend some time away from each other. I think that you need to get out of this shop and stop talking to toys. I think you need to talk to Susan because it's obvious you're not over her.

ANDREW Now that's not fair. Who are you to tell me—

DENISE I don't want to be the one to bring this up, but you chose Susan over me, remember? I would have waited for you, but she took you away from me. We didn't talk for an entire year. Do you know what that's like? Having a best friend and losing him for a year? Having the person who you value more than anything turn their back on you? I had to find some comfort, Andrew, and I did. It's not with you. I'm sorry. Talk to Susan and stop obsessing over this job. I worry about you all the time. You've been working nonstop for the entire week. You actually gave the puppet a name and refer to it as her. Look at me. I know you need a friend, but you can't test the boundaries of our friendship. I can only be your friend, Andrew. No matter how much you're willing to give. I can't give the same.

ANDREW You can't even try?

DENISE I'm sorry. No. Replace me. I have to go. You should too. [*She hugs him.*] Good-bye. [*She exits.*]

[ANDREW *sits in the chair and stares long at* KERRI. KERRI *just stares right back. There is another knock at the door and this time it's* MELISSA.]

MELISSA Hey.

ANDREW Hey. What's up?

MELISSA Been here long?

ANDREW Kind of haven't left yet. So I guess it would be hard to say how long I've been here.

MELISSA You've been working a lot these past couple of days. [*Looking at* KERRI.] She looks good.

ANDREW I'm trying.

MELISSA What's the matter, Andrew?

ANDREW Nothing.

MELISSA Remember who you're talking to. Is it Susan?

ANDREW Why bring her up? We broke up. I'm alone. There's nothing left to say about it.

MELISSA I think there's plenty left to say. You made the right choice, Andrew. She was hurting you.

ANDREW But at least I wasn't alone. At least I could roll over in the morning and know she was there. Now I can't even face that bed. It looks so empty. It's like finding a shell on the beach. You know there was once something in it, but you also know that whatever it is, is gone. Maybe I was too harsh. I mean, she did love me, she just... showed it in a different way. I mean, maybe she just was having one of her moments and I took it too harshly. Maybe I overreacted and she had a point in what she said. I just feel so... empty. Like that shell. There was something in me for somebody to love and now it's just . . . dried out. . . . I'm hollow. I'm hollow without her.

MELISSA   I'm not going to try and say that this is easy, but this is the healthiest thing for you. You don't deserve this. You're one of the kindest and sweetest people I know and any girl would be more than happy to love you. There's so much within you. So much to give and you shouldn't be with someone who only takes. I don't want to hear about what she's done for you either. All you do is defend her. As if she *made* you or something. You just have to tell yourself that you're more, that you deserve more.

ANDREW   I know. I just miss her. I can't be alone. It's killing me to be alone.

MELISSA   That's the worst reason for wanting something back. You have to ask yourself what is the price of filling a void? This is why people stay in horrible relationships! They have this fear of being alone. I was alone for a long time before I found Christian and it was good for me. Sometimes it's a good thing to spend time with yourself and decide who you really are.

ANDREW   That's the scariest thing. I really don't know. It's like I've identified myself as a part of her. Like she was this film that enveloped me and now I have to peel all of that off and find me. I don't even feel like I remember who I am.

MELISSA   Don't be silly. You are my best friend, Andrew. You love poetry and making things. You're a great props master who makes incredible works of art. You're caring, intelligent, and talented and deep down you know exactly who you are. You need to stop thinking about who you were so you can find the person you are.

ANDREW   It's hard.

MELISSA   No one ever said life was easy. You've just got to roll with the punches. There are hills and valleys and right now you're in a valley. You'll get out. I have faith in you.

ANDREW   I'm glad one person does.

MELISSA   Enough of this depressing talk. Let's get some nachos!

ANDREW   Yeah. Let's get out of here.

[MELISSA *exits as* ANDREW *moves towards the desk lamp and shuts it off. He looks over at* KERRI, *who is still looking straight ahead. He takes a moment to look at her and then shuts off the lights.*]

[*Blackout.*]

··· scene four ···

[*It is about four hours later. The last bits of sunlight are poking through the window of the shop.* ANDREW *looks more tired than ever as he rummages through various spray cans and other bits and pieces of makeup and garments. He's lost in his world of trying to reorganize the shop as* SUSAN *enters. She is tall, statuesque and strong-looking. She surveys the scene in front of her before speaking.*]

SUSAN   You've been busy.

ANDREW   [*Not looking up.*] Yeah.

SUSAN   You haven't been answering your phone.

ANDREW   I haven't been home in a while.

SUSAN   I miss you.

[ANDREW *looks at her.*]

　　　Can we talk?

ANDREW   We're talking now, aren't we?

SUSAN   I mean, can you stop cleaning and look at me for more than a second and we can have a conversation?

ANDREW   Why did you come here?

SUSAN   I wanted to see you. I told you I miss you. I just want to talk about this. It's not easy for me. To tell you the truth, I never thought *you'd* be the one to do this.

ANDREW   It's not like you gave me a choice. I thought you loved me.

SUSAN   I still do!

ANDREW   Then why hurt me like that? Treat me like I was some sort of toy that you can just break at will and get Daddy to buy you a new one. I have feelings, Susan. You stepped on that. You destroyed that. You've been wearing on that from the day I met you. Everything you said was discounting the things that I held dear. If you think for a second that is something to forgive and forget, then I feel sorry for you because you have no idea how the world works. YOU HURT ME! And *I* can't let that go.

SUSAN   How many times do I have to tell you I'm sorry? I lost my head. I never should have . . .

ANDREW   What's the matter? You can't say it? The thing is it would have meant so much to me if you could have just admitted you were wrong, but no you held on to even that. You acted as if I pushed you to it.

SUSAN   But you did push me to it. That's what you do! You push and push and sometimes I snap. Sometimes I get angry.

ANDREW   Why were you so angry, Susan? What did I do? Just answer me. If you want to talk, then here we are we're talking. Tell me why you got so angry with me; what it was that I did that caused you to say what you said? That's all I'm asking for. If you can just justify it, then maybe I can find a reason to forgive—

SUSAN   Stop! I . . . I'm going. I can't do this. Why can't you just let me walk away and regain my composure and then I'll come back and we'll talk about this. We'll talk about why I said what I said. I love you, Andrew. . . . But you drive me friggin crazy sometimes. If you can just look beyond that one moment and look at our love—

ANDREW   Love? Love! Susan, I thought that's what I had, what I felt, but I don't know what's happening to me. I mean, do we connect? Am I worth anything to you? Or is this another one of your famous silent moments? The time when you hold back so you won't hurt me? Well, it hurts more when you don't say anything! When you leave me alone with the silence and my own mind. Don't give me time to think, Susan. I'm begging you! The worst thing in the world is to give me time to think. I would never do this to you! I would at least try to talk. Can't you at least try? Please? God . . . Fine. Don't say anything. You know exactly what you said to me and why I'm so hurt and you know exactly why I left you. You can't say it for yourself, and you know what? That gives me hope. It means that maybe somewhere you have some semblance of a conscience about all of this. I miss you more than I can stand, Susan. I wake up in the morning and bury my head in the pillow until I can stop coughing up tears and face the day. I walk through the streets looking at every girl who looks even remotely like you. I taste your kisses in the food I eat, but I cannot get beyond what you've done. You screwed up! Not me! You can't admit to it but you screwed up! It tears at every waking moment I spend on this earth but I need to rip you out of my life. As messed up as that is I WILL NOT PLAY THIS FUCKING ROLE ANYMORE! I do not belong to you! I'm learning what it's like to stop loving you. And until you can admit to what you've done, you do not belong in this shop or in my life.

SUSAN   You want me to say it again, Andrew? It hurt you so bad the first time, what makes you think the second will be better? I am sorry for what I said, but I also remember you provoking it. You asked me to tell you what was wrong and I refused. You pushed me and you pushed me until I finally told you why I was so upset. I told you how I felt at that moment. It had nothing to do with how I truly feel about you. I got caught up in the moment. I was so angry with you I just said those things. I never meant them. I don't see why we can't get past all of this. Why you can't just come back to me. [*She moves towards him.*] You know you belong with me. Why push me away? I said I'm sorry. I miss you. Please. [*Her arms are now around him and she kisses his neck.*] I can change. I'll never say anything that horrible again. I promise. Come home with me. Come to bed. You don't have to wake up alone tomorrow, Andrew. It can all be so much better. Come on [*She unbuttons her top.*] don't you miss me?

[SUSAN *begins to kiss* ANDREW *as light yet harsh chords play on the piano. She takes his shirt off and the music builds again. They begin to get more and more passionate and finally fall onto one of the chairs. The music builds to a point where it is so loud it is deafening and suddenly there is a crash of keys. The piano stops abruptly.* ANDREW *pushes* SUSAN *off and begins to put his clothes back on. She looks truly hurt but gathers her top as well.*]

SUSAN   I guess that means we're done.

ANDREW   I guess so.

SUSAN   Andrew...

ANDREW   Don't. Just go.

SUSAN   We don't have to end it like this. I scared you. You can come home. We can talk.

ANDREW   It's not home anymore.

SUSAN   What are you talking about?

ANDREW   We broke up, remember? My home is not your home anymore.

SUSAN   I just thought.

ANDREW   Don't.

SUSAN   Andrew, you're throwing something wonderful away. I've made some mistakes, but things can change. I felt the way you kissed me. You haven't given up on us yet. You still want this as much as I do. I'm asking you to not turn me away.

ANDREW   It's the only thing I can think of doing right now.

SUSAN   Stop thinking so much and just allow yourself to feel! I know you still feel me.

ANDREW   Good-bye, Susan.

SUSAN   Andrew.

ANDREW   Good-bye.

SUSAN   Fine. I'll call you.

ANDREW   I won't be home. I've got a lot to do here.

SUSAN   Of course.

ANDREW   Now what's that supposed to mean?

SUSAN Nothing. Good-bye.

ANDREW No wait. What did you mean by "of course?"

SUSAN Oh, come on, Andrew. It's no secret where your heart lies. It's always with your work. Why do you think this has been so tough for us? Because you always put this place before me. There is no us when there's this.

ANDREW That's not fair. I always made time for you.

SUSAN But your heart was always in this room. Listen, I've gotta go.

ANDREW No, let's talk about this. What do you mean—

SUSAN I'M TIRED OF TALKING! Good night.

[SUSAN *exits and with her the last specks of daylight.* ANDREW *sits down and buries his face in his hands.* KERRI *seems to move slightly as if she's looking at him and we can see a tear run down her cheek. Lights fade and we see both* DENISE *and* MELISSA *illuminated downstage of the scene. It is clear that they are in another room but the shop remains as the main playing space. Throughout this scene we see* ANDREW *working on* KERRI. *He sometimes applies makeup, sometimes paints, polishes, etc. He pays careful attention to every detail and seems to be enjoying it. He loses some of the sadness from the previous scene as he does this. Light piano plays underneath this.*]

··· scene five ···

[MELISSA *and* DENISE *are sitting in what appears to be a common room of some sort. Two chairs and some soft drinks complete the suggestion of this.*]

MELISSA So what do we say to him?

DENISE You know Andrew. He always gets into any project he works on. This will pass just like the others.

MELISSA I know, but I'm still worried about him.

DENISE Why?

MELISSA He's been working in the shop for three days now. He hasn't gone home. I'm not sure if he's even eaten. We were on the way to get nachos and he bailed before we got there. Said he had to go back to the shop and clean.

DENISE I saw some Chinese food, so I think he's eating. He said something kind of strange though last night.

MELISSA What?

DENISE He called me and told me he loved me.

MELISSA Shit.

DENISE I told him to calm down and to get some rest and he started talking about Kerri.

MELISSA Wait a sec. You mean the puppet?

DENISE He talks to it, Melissa. I think he thinks it's real. He's losing his mind and we need to do something about it.

MELISSA Are you sure he's talking to her? I mean, he could just be referring to her as if she's a person. People do that to cars and nobody thinks they're crazy.

DENISE I think it goes further than that. I think he might really believe that she's real.

MELISSA I really doubt that. He may be a little bit out there, but he's not that wacky. Maybe he just talked about the puppet so that you'd worry about him and go there to comfort him. He's taking the whole breakup with Susan pretty hard.

DENISE Well, if my boyfriend one day came out and said those kinds of things, I think I'd take it pretty hard too. I don't think, however, that I would start talking to a puppet.

MELISSA I think that you're being a little extreme.

DENISE Fine. Can we at least agree that we're both worried about him and need to talk to him?

MELISSA Maybe we should go see him now.

DENISE No, it's late. We'll stop by the shop tomorrow.

MELISSA Yeah, I have an early morning class, so it shouldn't be a problem. I can meet you at the theatre?

DENISE Sure. When is she due on stage anyway?

MELISSA Another couple of days. I hope that he gets over this. He doesn't seem himself.

DENISE You can say that again.

[*Both girls freeze as* ANDREW *goes over to* KERRI *and touches her lightly on the cheek. We watch as she slowly melts into his hand and kisses it.* KERRI *then stands and wraps her arms around* ANDREW *as they begin to dance. Soft waltz music plays as the lights come up on* SUSAN, *who is doing her hair in a mirror. The effect is created by a wooden square that is propped in front of her that will turn as the action on the stage continues. It begins by facing out so that she is facing us. She talks to the mirror as if she is talking to herself.*]

SUSAN Andrew, Andrew. What has come over you? I don't understand you at all. If you don't want to see me, who are you seeing?

[*She turns the mirror in the direction of the two waltzing and the music builds. She is now in profile watching herself in the mirror, but simultaneously watching the two of them dance.* MELISSA *and* DENISE *unfreeze as the waltz between the two overtakes the stage.*]

MELISSA When he looks at the girl he's making who do you think he sees?

DENISE Maybe me. Maybe Susan. Maybe someone completely different.

[KERRI *and* ANDREW *freeze in the middle of the step and the piano stops abruptly.*]

DENISE [*Looking in his direction.*] Who does he see?

MELISSA [*Looking in his direction.*] Who do you think he sees?

SUSAN [*Looking straight in the mirror directly at the two.*] Andrew, Andrew, Andrew . . . Who are you seeing?

[*Blackout.*]

··· **scene six** ···

[*The lights come up to discover* KERRI *and* ANDREW *lying on the floor with a sheet covering them. There are various supplies strewn throughout the shop and all over the floor. The chair that* KERRI *was on is overturned. She appears to have lost some of her puppet-like appearance. The two kiss passionately.*]

ANDREW Am I dreaming?

KERRI No. It's morning.

ANDREW Then how?

KERRI Love. The work you put in to make me, Andrew. That's love. You spent hours and hours. I heard everything you said, but couldn't find the right moment until the other night.

ANDREW So that wasn't a dream either? I really did call Denise and tell her about you?

KERRI You look so worried. It's OK. Relax. It'll all be fine.

ANDREW This doesn't make any sense. Am I losing it? You're not real. I made you. I *made* . . . I put . . .

KERRI All your pain and hurt went into me, the way you looked at me told me you loved me. Told me that I was real. I didn't need anyone to tell me I was alive. I just was. You made that happen.

ANDREW I need to wake up. This is getting scary. I mean, you can't be alive. I'm dreaming you. I'm creating you. This is—

KERRI Stop it! You created me. You told me last night that I was all you ever wanted. Susan came and tried to take you back and you turned her down. You looked right at me when you did it. You have to remember that.

ANDREW I don't know what I remember right now. I mean, I think that I'm talking to you but I could just be talking to myself. There's no one else here, so you could be something that my mind has created. But you seem so real and that's what makes me question it.

KERRI Stop questioning it! Is it so hard to believe that we can make something real? What is reality besides something that is molded by us like clay? What am I? Am I alive? Do I exist, or do I just believe that I exist? What do you want, Andrew?

ANDREW I want you to exist. You're . . . You're perfect and I want to stop hurting. I want to feel like I exist and I . . . I want you to exist.

KERRI So why can't I?

ANDREW   There is no reason why you can't. [*Smiles.*] I make it happen. Maybe I am crazy. What does that mean anyway? Somebody else tells me that I'm not supposed to believe in what makes *me* happy, and that means *I'm* not sane? It doesn't matter. *We* matter. I found you and you matter. I made you and my love brought you to life. My love, no one else's. That's beautiful. But what do I do when they came to take you away? You were made for this show. They'll be asking for you soon. What am I suppose to tell them?

KERRI   Tell them I'm not done. [*Starts to get dressed.*] Tell them you still have to work on me. Maybe there's a joint problem or something. Tell them you need to replace a part that was broken.

ANDREW   What are they going to say when they find out? They're all asking me a lot of questions about why I spend so much time here.

KERRI   I know why you do. You don't want to be alone. You don't have to be. [*Kisses him.*] I'm here.

[*Both of them are now partially dressed when* DENISE *and* MELISSA *walk in.* KERRI *freezes.*]

DENISE   What is going on here?

ANDREW   I still had painting to finish up on.

DENISE   Who were you talking to just now? I heard you talking to someone.

ANDREW   I had the radio on.

MELISSA   Andrew, we've already established that you're a terrible liar. Tell me what's really going on. Maybe we can help you.

ANDREW   I don't need help! I need to be left alone.

DENISE   I think that's the last thing you need.

MELISSA   Andrew, we're worried about you. You've closed yourself off from the rest of the world. You never leave the shop. You talk about her as if she's real. I know it's been hard for you after . . . We just want you to think about maybe going outside for a little while. Get some fresh air.

ANDREW   She's real.

DENISE Oh geez. Andrew, this is crazy even for you.

ANDREW I'm not joking. She is. [*He looks at* KERRI, *who stays frozen.*]

MELISSA I know that it's been a rough couple of days, Andrew, and that you haven't gotten a lot of sleep. Do you think that maybe, this might be something that you're dreaming or making up?

ANDREW Melissa, I swear to you that she is real. I'm not sure why she's not speaking now, but she's real. Kerri? It's OK. Show them. Show them. Tell them about what my love did. Tell them how it brought you to life. [*Cracking.*] Tell them about . . . us. Kerri? Why won't you tell them? I . . . I . . . [*Sinks to his knees.*] I think maybe I need to go home.

DENISE That may be a good idea.

MELISSA [*Throws a sheet over* KERRI.] Come on. Let's go.

ANDREW It all seemed so real. . . .

DENISE It's OK. It'll be OK.

MELISSA Come on, it's time to rest. . . .

ANDREW So real . . .

[*The three exit the shop, leaving* KERRI *with the sheet on her. As the lights slowly fade we see the sheet fall off of her.* KERRI *moves towards the back of the shop and looks at the place the three just exited from. She turns the chair over and sits as the lights dim. Just as we reach complete darkness, we see her resume her puppet-like pose.*]

··· scene seven ···

[*The lights come up on what appears to be* ANDREW's *apartment. The startling thing is that his apartment looks a lot like the woodshop. In fact the only thing that clues us in to the fact that this is his apartment is the absence of* KERRI. *We see* ANDREW *sitting in a chair coming out of a stupor as* DENISE *sits across from him padding his face with a face cloth.*]

DENISE Wake up, Andrew.

ANDREW Where am I?

DENISE You're home. You had a fever. You were delusional. You were talking to the props in your shop.

ANDREW   Kerri!

DENISE   Don't worry. She's fine. Nothing happened to her.

ANDREW   [*Tries to get up.*] I have to see her. I have to go back.

DENISE   Shhhhhh. It's OK. You're running a fever. You haven't slept in days. The puppet is still there. It will be there when you get back. Just rest now.

ANDREW   What happened to Melissa?

DENISE   She went home. We've both been up all night with you. She needed to get some rest.

ANDREW   Why are you still here?

DENISE   I just don't think that you should be alone right now. [*Touches his forehead.*]

ANDREW   Why not?

DENISE   Well, you're sick. I don't want to leave until you're all better. [*Smiles.*]

ANDREW   And what about your boyfriend?

DENISE   Let's not talk about that.

ANDREW   Well, I don't think he'd approve. So what about him? What is he going to have to say when you tell him you spent the night here?

DENISE   I don't think . . . I don't think he's going to care.

ANDREW   Why wouldn't he—

DENISE   Because it's over.

ANDREW   What? I thought you said you were happy. You told me to replace you. . . .

DENISE   I know, I know. Don't remind me. I just didn't want you to think. I don't know. You still don't remember any of what you said in that phone call?

ANDREW   No! What did I say?

DENISE   You told me you loved me again, Andrew. You talked about the time at the beach when I was drawing circles in the mud with my feet. When we sat there watching the waves wash away the circles and I tried to make them again. When your mom bought us slushes and you had that stupid thing about walking everywhere barefoot because your feet were so tough. You remembered every detail like it was yesterday and we were twelve. Then you talked about wanting to kiss me at that stupid dance we went to, and how you wanted to kiss me on New Year's Eve but you chickened out and kissed my cheek. Why did you bring those things up? It was like I could see it all again. You in your goofy glasses with that stupid-looking mullet of yours. Why ask me to see that again? Why ask me to remember that? The reason I said those things in the shop, the reason I told you to forget me was I didn't want you to think that. To know that . . .

ANDREW   What?

DENISE   That I still had feelings for you! He knew it. He saw me after I got off the phone with you. He asked me about the call and he could see what I was thinking before I even spoke. He told me he knew that part of me was still with you on the sand at that beach. He couldn't accept that and I couldn't blame him. I can only blame . . . myself . . .

ANDREW   You still . . .

DENISE   Yes.

ANDREW   And you . . .

DENISE   [*Moving towards him.*] Yes.

ANDREW   Why now?

DENISE   [*Getting closer.*] Why not?

ANDREW   You mean?

DENISE   [*Moving even closer.*] Yes.

ANDREW   Now?

DENISE   Yes. [*Goes to kiss him.*]

ANDREW   No! [*Pushes away.*]

DENISE   What?

ANDREW   The other day I pour my heart out to you and you tell me that we can never work. Then all of a sudden you want me again? You'll have to excuse me if I'm a little doubtful.

DENISE   So people can't change their minds?

ANDREW   Not this quickly.

DENISE   If you . . .

ANDREW   WHAT?!

DENISE   You'll regret it

ANDREW   Will I? Or will I feel like I have control over my own life? Over my own emotions.

DENISE   THIS FROM A FREAK OBSESSED WITH A PUPPET!!!!!

ANDREW   Leave.

DENISE   Oh my God . . . I'm so sorry. I didn't mean . . .

ANDREW   Leave.

DENISE   Don't do this . . . .

ANDREW   Leave.

DENISE   Don't . . .

ANDREW   [*Grabbing the face cloth and throwing it at her.*] Leave! Leave! Leave! Get the FUCK OUT!!!!!!!!!!!

DENISE   I'm going. But I just want you to think about what you're letting go. I am not coming back once I walk through that door, Andrew. All the history, all the times that you think I've forgotten, they're still here. I'm giving you one last chance to say that you lost your head and that this is all a result of the fever. I am standing here hoping that I am making a dent in whatever wall it is that you're putting up. If I suddenly mean nothing to you, then I'll walk right now. But I don't believe that. I believe there is a part of you that is praying I won't leave this room. I'll bet there is a part of you that believes you still love me. It's the same part of you that kissed me two nights ago. If there's anything left for me, you'll say it right now.

[*Long silence.*]

Fine. Good-bye, Andrew. [*She exits.*]

[ANDREW *stoops to pick up the face cloth and falls to his knees. He hugs himself and begins to silently cry. His head slowly sinks and connects with the floor. A soft piano melody begins again. He remains like this for a few moments until* MELISSA *enters. As she walks into the room there are a few harsh chords struck and then it is silent. The silence sits for a moment while* MELISSA *takes in the picture.*]

MELISSA Andrew?

ANDREW Leave me alone. [*Sits up.*] Nobody will leave me alone today.

MELISSA You're sick. We're all just trying to help you get better. You've been running a fever since we took you home.

ANDREW A fever?

MELISSA Yes. You've been burning up. We found you at the shop delirious. Where's Denise?

ANDREW Gone.

MELISSA Where did she go? What did you say?

ANDREW It doesn't matter.

MELISSA Well, you're awfully cryptic. Is she coming back?

ANDREW I don't think so.

MELISSA WHY?!

ANDREW Will you forget it? It's not important. How long have I been here?

MELISSA What do you mean it's not important? Did you two fight? I told her not to bring up—

ANDREW [*Violently.*] How long have I been here!?

MELISSA I don't know, about ten hours maybe?

ANDREW   [*Now gathering things from around the room.*] What time is it?

MELISSA   Two o'clock. Why?

ANDREW   I gotta go.

MELISSA   Andrew, you're still running a fever. Why do you have to go? Where do you have to go?

ANDREW   Back to the shop.

MELISSA   What for?

ANDREW   Kerri.

MELISSA   Stop it! Kerri can wait. You're health is more important than this stupid project. Do you think it's easy watching your best friend disintegrate? I know that you take your projects seriously, but even the most amazing artists took a break every once in a while.

ANDREW   THAT'S WHERE YOU'RE WRONG! Newton spent days inside of his lab while his servants sent him food that piled up at his door because he never ate it. A great artist suffers for what he creates. The physical self is a hurdle that only those who have control can overleap. It's the weak who allow themselves the luxury of sleep and food and relaxation, who spend their entire lives being complete failures. THE ART IS YOUR BREATH! THE LOVE IS YOUR BLOOD! THE DREAM IS YOUR ONLY SUSTENANCE AND YOU MUST NOT WEAKEN! WITHOUT THE PASSION, YOU MIGHT AS WELL BE MADE OF WOOD!

MELISSA   LISTEN TO YOURSELF! You sound like a madman. Like some deranged scientist. It's like Jekyll and Hyde. As your friend I am trying to tell you that you've gone too far. That this puppet is not worth—

ANDREW   STOP CALLING HER A PUPPET! I LOVE HER!

[*Silence.*]

MELISSA   Andrew. Take a second to think about this, OK? She's not real. You made her for a show. She is beautiful, but she's artificial. You have to accept that before you can move on.

ANDREW   You don't understand. . . .

MELISSA   Is this what you were arguing with Denise about? Listen, I know that breaking up with Susan was hard for you, but you have friends. We're all here to support you. You don't have to make people up—

ANDREW   I'm not making her up. If you could just see.

MELISSA   I see a prop, Andrew. I also see someone who is very sad and very disturbed right now. I see someone who I want to help, who I'm truly worried about. Please, let's talk. Don't go to the shop. She'll be there tomorrow. Let's talk about this. [*She hugs him.*]

ANDREW   I'm sorry.

MELISSA   It's OK. It's going to be OK. We'll talk about this. Just have a seat, get some sleep, and we'll talk tomorrow.

ANDREW   OK.

[ANDREW *sits.* MELISSA *sits opposite of him and pads his forehead with the face cloth. The soft piano starts up again as the lights begin to fade.* ANDREW *starts to drift off to sleep and* MELISSA *does the same. The lights change slowly until there is an eerie glow around the entire stage. It becomes clear to us that we have stepped into a dream world.* SUSAN *enters upper stage right,* MELISSA *moves downstage right,* DENISE *enters upper stage left, and* KERRI *enters upper stage left.* ANDREW *stands and* MELISSA *begins to dance with him. It is the same dance as in the first act, but the music has changed. It seems darker and harsher. His dance with* MELISSA *has more passion to it now. They are closer, as if they could melt into one another. Suddenly, there is a drop in key and* MELISSA *goes limp in his arms. He tries to continue dancing with her but she stops completely. He eventually lets her down onto the floor. When he looks up* DENISE *is standing there waiting for him. They begin to dance and the music picks up again. They kiss slowly and there is another slight key change as* SUSAN *appears behind* DENISE. *She touches her neck and* DENISE *goes limp in his arms.* ANDREW *again tries to dance with her but eventually must lay her down on the ground as well.* SUSAN *takes over and it is clear that she is leading the dance, the music becomes loud and discordant.* KERRI *walks over and taps* SUSAN *on the shoulder to cut in.* SUSAN *looks at her and all freeze. The music stops abruptly. All the women rise and go back to their original place. The lights go back to black. In the darkness, as each one speaks, a match is lit and burns out.*]

SUSAN   I.

DENISE   Want.

MELISSA   Don't!

KERRI   Love.

SUSAN   Don't!

DENISE   Love.

MELISSA   I.

SUSAN   DON'T.

DENISE   Want.

KERRI   LOVE.

SUSAN   DON'T!

DENISE   Leave.

KERRI   LOVE!

SUSAN   Don't! DON'T DON'T DON'T DON'T. [*Overlap.*]

MELISSA   Leave LEAVE LEAVE LEAVE. [*Overlap.*]

KERRI   Love. LOVE LOVE LOVE. [*Overlap.*]

[*Piano intensifies as* ANDREW *moves back to his seat and closes his eyes. The lights change multiple colors as the overlap continues until blackout. When the lights come back up, it's clear that it is late night. The only ones onstage are* ANDREW *and* MELISSA. ANDREW *wakes up and notices that* MELISSA *is still asleep. He kisses her on the forehead and begins to gather his things. He looks back for a second and shuts off the light. Lights fade down to black.*]

··· scene eight ···

[*The lights come up to discover the shop, where* KERRI *is still looking out the window for* ANDREW. *It appears as if she hasn't moved from that spot the entire time that he has been gone.* ANDREW *enters.*]

ANDREW   [*Hugs her.*] I want you to exist.

KERRI   Then I'm here.

ANDREW   Everyone is saying that I'm crazy.

KERRI   You're not. I love you.

[ANDREW *goes and looks out the window.*]

What is it? Why are you so worried?

ANDREW   They'll take you away from me.

KERRI   It's going to be OK. Don't worry. We'll get out of here. We'll go somewhere else.

ANDREW   I made you *for* someone, remember?

KERRI   That's right, the show.

ANDREW   They'll be expecting you any day now.

KERRI   What are we going to do?

ANDREW   I'm going to get some stuff together and we are going to get out of here.

KERRI   When?

ANDREW   As soon as possible.

[*The piano starts in again very slowly and the two freeze. This time we see* SUSAN *upstage with the mirror from the first act, but now there is* DENISE *with the exact same mirror on the other side of the stage.* MELISSA *slowly wakes up and realizes what is going on. She stands and freezes as well. All are frozen during this sequence except* DENISE *and* SUSAN.]

DENISE   [*While undoing her hair.*] What are you seeing right now, Andrew? Who are you seeing?

SUSAN   Who do you see, Andrew? Who is this girl keeping you from me?

MELISSA   [*Turning towards center.*] Where are you, Andrew?

[DENISE *and* SUSAN *step away from the mirror and the music begins to pick up.* ANDREW *and* KERRI *become reanimated and start packing to leave.* DENISE *and* SUSAN *move towards center stage so that they are directly opposite of* ANDREW *and one behind the other.* MELISSA *is the last to fall into place as the chords again begin to fall apart.* ANDREW *looks up for a second from his work and drops everything. He* stares at the three figures standing in front of him. It's as if he's looking into a mirror that just keeps repeating itself. He is completely silent.]

KERRI What is it, Andrew?

[ANDREW *turns away for a second and staggers a few steps. He takes a moment, then turns back around.*]

SUSAN Have you forgotten me, Andrew? [*Overlap.*]

DENISE What are you seeing, Andrew? Who are you seeing, Andrew? WHO DO YOU SEE, ANDREW? [*Overlap.*]

MELISSA Where are you, Andrew? ANDREW, WHERE DID YOU GO? WHO ARE YOU, ANDREW? WHO'S SHE, ANDREW? WHO AM I, ANDREW ANDREW ANDREW!!!! [*Overlap.*]

KERRI Andrew! Andrew! ANDREW!!!!!!!!!!!
[*Silence . . .*]
What's the matter? [*Looking behind her.*] What are you seeing?

SUSAN WHO DO YOU SEE, ANDREW?

MELISSA WHO DO YOU SEE, ANDREW?

DENISE WHO DO YOU SEE, ANDREW?

[*They all begin to crowd around him as the music becomes scarier than it's ever become. Eventually, during the next bit of dialogue, they all envelop him completely.*]

SUSAN I LOVE YOU, ANDREW. I LOVED YOU. [*Overlap.*]

DENISE REPLACE ME, ANDREW. REPLACE ME. [*Overlap.*]

MELISSA I just want to help, tell me, WHAT'S WRONG? [*Overlap.*]

[*The stage goes completely dark. We hear the voices continue to overlap and then ANDREW screams. It is the deepest most guttural cry that can come out of a human being. It causes fear and pathos all in the same second. The voices stop. The lights slowly come up and ANDREW is on his knees while KERRI crouches over him. He looks like a wounded animal. She places her hands on his shoulders and sinks down next to him. He turns to her.*]

ANDREW I need you to exist.

KERRI [*Hugs him tighter.*] I'm here.

ANDREW   You have to exist.

KERRI   Shhhh. I'm here. It's OK. I'll make it—

ANDREW   Don't. Just be here. I need you to—

KERRI   Exist. I know. I'm here. I love you.

ANDREW   [*Turning towards her, shaking.*] Help me. . . .

KERRI   Shhhhhh. It's OK. Rest now. Rest. . . .

[*We hear knocking. It's SUSAN.*]

SUSAN   Andrew? Andrew, are you in there? Andrew?

[*The lights slowly fade down as the music becomes a soft suggestion. The last of the lights fade out as the last notes play against the silence and the knocking continues.*]

··· scene nine ···

[*The sounds of knocking and SUSAN calling for ANDREW are heard in the darkness as the lights slowly creep up. KERRI sits on the floor with ANDREW, who now appears to be close to unconscious. She continues to brush the hair from his face and hold him as the knocking continues.*]

SUSAN   Andrew! Let me in.

KERRI   Just ignore her, Andrew. It's going to be fine. *We're* going to be fine.

ANDREW   I have to get up.

KERRI   No, Andrew. Just rest now. You look so tired. Just rest.

SUSAN   Andrew!

ANDREW   I have to get up.

SUSAN   ANDREW!

ANDREW   [*Gets up.*] I'm coming.

[KERRI *moves to her chair and takes her frozen pose.* ANDREW *lets* SUSAN *in.*]

SUSAN   What is the matter with you?

ANDREW   What do you want?

SUSAN [*She puts her hand to his cheek.*] Why so cold?

ANDREW Leave me alone.

SUSAN I don't think that's really what you want. Come here.

ANDREW No!

SUSAN COME HERE.

ANDREW NO!

SUSAN I don't understand what's gotten into you lately.

ANDREW I . . .

SUSAN What?

ANDREW I . . .

SUSAN Whatever it is, say it, Andrew.

ANDREW I don't love you anymore. [*Looks at* KERRI.]

SUSAN [*Laughs.*] Are you serious? She's not real! Look at her!

ANDREW She is real.

SUSAN Prove it.

ANDREW Kerri? [*He moves towards her.*] Kerri, tell her [KERRI *doesn't move.*]

SUSAN Can we end this game now, please? Why don't you just come back? You don't need to sink to this.

ANDREW Kerri! Kerri! [*She still doesn't move.*]

SUSAN Andrew, come on. Forget about it.

ANDREW No! Kerri! Please, Kerri? Wake up! Please! [*Goes closer to her and touches her. She still does not move.*]

SUSAN Andrew . . .

ANDREW SHUT UP! Kerri? Please . . . I love you. . . .

SUSAN WHAT?!

ANDREW I want you to exist. . . . I . . . Need you to exist . . . Kerri.

[*He puts his arms around her and* KERRI *unfreezes. She turns to him and kisses him. They both stand in front of* SUSAN.]

SUSAN What?

ANDREW I brought her to life, Susan. My love gave her life. Every time you hurt me, I came here and cried to her. I told her all of my stories and she sat and she listened and eventually came to be real. No one believed me, but here she is. It was all a result of *my* love. I made her and she loves me. She can love me in a way that you never could. She'll respect me and treat me how I was meant to be treated. I could never be happy with you and it took me so long to realize that. *My* love brought her to life. This is something *you* never could understand.

SUSAN [*Nearing tears.*] Oh, I think I could.

ANDREW What?

SUSAN I think I can understand it quite well. . . .

ANDREW Wait, what?—

SUSAN Where are you from, Andrew?

ANDREW New York City. I don't see how this has—

SUSAN And what's your favorite food?

ANDREW I don't see where you're going with this I—

SUSAN Where were you born?

ANDREW I don't remember. I told you I only remember bits and pieces of my past. But why ask—

SUSAN Think about this one, Andrew. Put the pieces together. WHERE WERE YOU BORN?

ANDREW I told you I don't remember! Why is it so important to know—

SUSAN Look around you, Andrew!

ANDREW I HAVE NO IDEA WHAT YOU'RE— [*Thunderstruck.*] Oh. Oh God.

SUSAN Did something just click, Andrew? Did you just have a memory?

ANDREW   No. No.

KERRI   What is it, Andrew? What's wrong?

SUSAN   Look around, Andrew. Where were you born? WHERE were you born?

ANDREW   No. This is another dream. This is—

SUSAN   How dare you say that I would never understand!

KERRI   Andrew, I'm scared. What's going on. What's this—

SUSAN   Tell her, Andrew. Tell her where you're from.

KERRI   Andrew, what is she talking about?

ANDREW   No no no. No. No.

SUSAN   TELL HER, ANDREW! YOU REMEMBER NOW! TELL HER.

KERRI   Andrew! Please, what's happening?

ANDREW   This is not happening. . . .

[*Soft piano music begins again and* DENISE *and* MELISSA *come onstage. They appear much less human now. Almost robotic. They repeat phrases they said in the play and each one hits* ANDREW *like a bullet in the chest. He moves around the stage trying to steady himself and staggering back and forth between* SUSAN, KERRI, DENISE, *and* MELISSA.]

DENISE   Replace me, Andrew, it's not hard.

SUSAN   Where are you from, Andrew? Where were you born?

MELISSA   All you do is defend her. As if she *made* you or something.

KERRI   Andrew!

DENISE   I'm smoke, Andrew. You know all about smoke. It's what remains after the fire. There's only you now . . . only you.

[ANDREW *falls center stage and put his head in his hands. He is assaulted by millions of images that tear at his very being.*]

SUSAN   No, Andrew. How could I ever know what it's like to bring something to life through love? Look around the room! Look around this shop! It's here that *you* were born. I worked on you here for months and months. Carving those fine features that you've used against me again and again. Gluing those joints that you call your own. Polishing that pristine face of yours. I'm your fairy godmother, dear. You're my real boy. I made you to love *me*! That was *your* purpose! *My* love brought *you* to life and you go and make someone else yourself? How dare you? I gave you everything! I gave you life and you threw it in my face! You fuck! Yes, I may have taken advantage of our time together, but I always loved you. I never stopped loving you. You were mine. You are still mine and this will all be over very soon. [*Begins to cry.*] You really convinced yourself that you existed?

ANDREW   No. This isn't true. I exist! I am human. Denise and Melissa are human beings. They live outside of me. They—

SUSAN   Are nothing more than creations of your mind. You are the most advanced puppet ever. You actually have created this entire world for yourself. I never expected you to create her, though.

KERRI   Andrew, I'm scared.

SUSAN   Don't be. This will all be over soon. I spent years on you, Andrew. I wanted you to feel like you had a life. All of the others before you were too obsessed with *my* life. They wanted to follow me everywhere. My goal was to create someone who could be entirely independent. So I made you an artist with real goals in life. I provided you with a history and a degree. Select memories from your childhood that would fuel an individualistic spirit were implanted. I gave you a first love. Denise worked well and the stuff about her drawing circles in the mud with her foot was very cute. I then allowed you to create your own world. You chose to make Melissa, who was an excellent best friend, but the flaw with her was that she was against me. In fact, she's one of the reasons that you broke up with me. The one thing I never counted on, though, was that you wouldn't come back. I had no idea that you were making her. I knew that you were moving away from me but I thought it was just one of the other two. They posed no threat, because they could never actually love you while I was around. I hadn't planned on you being able to turn me down, though. I guess that comes with making you such an individual. In essence, making you believe that you existed. You're a puppet, Andrew. A prop. And I still to this day haven't been able to make you real. What makes you think that you can do that for her? And more importantly, what makes you think that I'll let you try? It ends here. I love you. But you are a failed experiment and there is only one thing to do with a failed experiment. Good-bye.

[*The stage goes completely dark and we see* SUSAN *light a single match. All of a sudden we see the match go out as if something has snuffed it. The lights fade back up to discover* ANDREW *standing directly across from* SUSAN.]

ANDREW   No.

SUSAN   What?

ANDREW   This is no longer about you and what you want. . . .

SUSAN   How dare you . . . You—

ANDREW   SHUT UP, SUSAN! I am not a failed experiment. I was able to create all of this myself? I don't consider that failure. As long as I can remember I have wanted to do things for others. Help others! Maybe it's part of this programming you've been describing or maybe it's something else, but I have never once thought about *myself*. I have had this constant need to make sure someone else was happy. Namely, *you* Susan. I made you happy and I refuse to believe that I didn't. There's a difference between my love and yours. You wanted to make something for *yourself* that would serve only you and then toss it aside when you were done. That's not love, that's greed. You created the piece but had no respect for the piece itself! I am the artist. I have respect for the entire process, including the raw material and whatever I create. . . . I accept. If you don't respect your work, it will turn on you. When you sculpt clay on a wheel, if you push too hard, the entire thing folds and you have to start over. Is it the clay's fault? Or is it that the artist didn't understand how delicate it was? Was it that the artist had no respect for the clay and tried to make it do something it didn't want to do? I clung to you for so long, because I thought you would eventually come to respect me and that one day you would be an artist instead of a goddamn carpenter. I am your clay, but it is *not* my fault that this fell apart, it's yours. You've never, ever been able to admit that YOU ARE WRONG! THIS IS WRONG! I DO NOT NEED YOU TO EXIST! I EXIST! I EXIST! And I am no longer yours. You say you made *me*? You say you created *me*? You're *my* fairy godmother? You put the pieces together and left! You just expected the pieces, this fucking prop, to find love and being real on his own. And I've finally found love and it is in the things I create. It is not with the person who I was never good enough for! I am the best clay, and you are a lousy artist!!!!!!! I don't need to replace you because I will not become you. I love myself and there is nothing you can do about it. You can light the match again! You can destroy everything in this shop including me and I will still exist. There is nothing that says that *you* are not a construct of *my* mind. There's nothing that says that *you* are not the failed experiment. That *my* love, no matter how good it was, could ever make *you* real. It's over, Susan, and whether you want to accept this or not, I EXIST!

[*There is a blinding flash of light and the entire stage is illuminated. Then it becomes completely dark. As the lights come back up we discover* SUSAN *frozen It is clear to us now that she is no longer human and that she has taken on the same qualities as* KERRI *in the beginning of the play.* ANDREW *stands onstage and it is very clear that he is now human. He moves to* KERRI *and kisses her.*]

KERRI   Andrew, what happened?

ANDREW   I don't know [*Puts his arms around her.*]

KERRI   Andrew, your heart I can feel it. . . . It's beating . . . you're—

ANDREW   Real.

KERRI   It's wonderful. It's . . . what I hoped for . . . it's . . . [*She begins to freeze again.*]

ANDREW   Kerri? Kerri?

KERRI   [*Smiles.*] Shhhhhh. This is what I hoped for. . . . It's why I came to life.

ANDREW   Kerri, what's happening?

KERRI   I have to go now, Andrew. . . . I . . .

ANDREW   Wait. What do you mean go? I told you I'll take you away from here. They won't take you to the show. . . . You'll be here . . . safe.

KERRI   You found love, Andrew. You didn't have to create it. I'll never forget you.

[KERRI *kisses* ANDREW *softly and as the kiss progresses she begins to slowly freeze. Eventually, she freezes completely and* ANDREW *moves his lips away. He looks at her, realizing for the first time why this has happened and smiles.*]

ANDREW   I'll never forget you, Kerri. [*He kisses her forehead.*]

[ANDREW *steps away and looks at both* SUSAN *and* KERRI *now frozen on opposite sides of the shop. He moves towards the door and opens it. The light from outside shines in as the lights fade down. He takes one last look as soft piano music plays.*]

ANDREW   [*With a smile.*] Good-bye.

[*He smiles one last time and exits. When he shuts the door, all we can see is* SUSAN *and* KERRI *in the dim light that is coming through the window. It appears as if* KERRI *has a smile on her face.*]

[*Blackout.*]

• • •

Come Rain or Come Shine

Jeni Mahoney

Jeni Mahoney

Jeni Mahoney is a playwright, teacher, and producer. Her plays, including *The Feast of the Flying Cow . . . and Other Stories of War*, *The Martyrdom of Washington Booth*, *Mercy Falls*, and *Light*, have been presented at the National Playwrights Conference at the O'Neill Center, InterAct Theater (Philadelphia), Greenwich Playhouse/Grey Light Productions (London), And Toto Too (Denver), L.A. Theater Center, Mid-West New Play Festival (Chicago), Lark Theater's Playwrights Week, Rattlestick Productions, NYU's hotINK Festival, Village Rep, and Chicago Womens Theater Alliance, among others. *Throw of the Moon* (written with Ben Sahl) and *American Eyes*, commissioned and produced by Gorilla Rep, can be found in *Plays and Playwrights 2001* (NY Theatre Experience). Excerpts from her plays can be found in numerous monologue and scene books. Jeni teaches playwriting at Playwrights Horizons Theater School, a studio school of New York University's Tisch School of the Arts. She is the co-artistic director of id Theatre Company and artistic director of Seven Devils Playwrights Conference in McCall, Idaho, which has developed more than sixty new plays since its inception in 2001. Jeni is a member of the Dramatists Guild of America.

characters

> MOM, 40s
> LUKE, her son, 20s
> CHRIS, Luke's friend, 20s

place

Mom's house

• • •

[MOM, *a 40-ish woman, urban hippie, comfy in her casual clothes and middle-aged body, cleans (hides the mess) and talks on the phone. Liza Minelli sings "Come Rain or Come Shine" in the background. She is on the phone.*]

MOM   No, you're right. No, I don't know what I was thinking.

> [MOM *reaches for a stack of new CDs still in the plastic wrap and sorts through them.*]

Um . . . *Sara Brightman, Best of Broadway, Les Mis*. Too much, right? No, I'll return 'em. Hey, what about *Rent*—that's something I might actually be listening to, right?

> [*She makes a face, obviously not the response she wanted.* MOM *opens a nearby drawer and drops the CDs in.*]

I know. I just want to be supportive. As long as he's happy, right? That's all any mother can ask for.

> [MOM *spots someone walking up to the driveway.*]

Oh! There they are! What? Yeah, nice-looking, in a sort of corporate way. Okay. Bye.

[*She hangs up the phone, puts it down—any old place, not in the charger, and sits on the couch and picks up a magazine—trying to look casual. The door opens slightly.* LUKE, *20s, young, impeccably neat, much more conservative than his mother, peeks in. Shy by nature, he hesitates at the door before entering.*]

LUKE   Mom—?

MOM   [*Pretending casual surprise.*]
      Boo-key!

[*She goes to him warmly and hugs him. A second figure lingers behind* LUKE.]
Lukey, Boo-key. My gosh, is it three already?

LUKE We're a little early.

MOM Of course you are. Always punctual. Oh, I missed you so much!

LUKE Good to see you too, Mom.

MOM Well, come in already, you big goof!

[LUKE *indicates his friend.*]

LUKE Mom, this Chris. Chris, my Mom.

[CHRIS *leans into the room. Like* LUKE, *he is dressed conservatively, obviously particular about his appearance and more well-practiced socially than* LUKE. CHRIS *reaches out a hand to* MOM.]

CHRIS Pleased to meet you, Mrs. Wilson.

MOM Chris.

[*She stares at him meaningfully, then confides playfully—*]

MOM It's Ms., actually—but you can just call me Mom.

CHRIS Thanks, that's very . . . friendly, Ms. Wilson.

MOM Yes. Well. Come in. Sit down. Tell me all about the drive!

[*The two men sit on the couch.*]

LUKE Are you alright, Mom?

MOM No, I'm not "alright," I'm thrilled! My long-lost Lukey Boo-key is here with his friend. Chris. See? Isn't this nice?

LUKE 'Cause you might want to cut down on the caffeine. . . .

MOM Drinks! You boys must be parched. What can I get you? Would you like a Cosmopolitan?

LUKE A what???

MOM I hear they're all the rage.

LUKE When did you start drinking?

MOM Me? No. I just thought you and Chris might want a drink.

CHRIS No thanks, Ms. Wilson. I don't drink.

[MOM *smiles warmly.*]

MOM Good for you, Chris. I can't tell you how glad I am to hear that. Really. Knowing that you respect your body, makes me respect you that much more.

CHRIS Thank you, Ms. Wilson.

MOM Oh, Luke. I like your friend very much.

LUKE You know, I think I'll take that drink—Como, Commie, whatever-you-call-it.

CHRIS Luke, do you think that's a good idea?

LUKE Oh . . . yes.

MOM Okay, then.

[MOM *flits—as best she can—to the kitchen. As soon as she is gone,* LUKE *makes a bee line for the front door.*]

CHRIS Hey!

LUKE I can't do this.

CHRIS It's just cold feet.

[CHRIS *goes to* LUKE *and puts his arm around him and turns him back toward the room.* LUKE *hyperventilates.*]

LUKE I . . . can't . . . breathe . . .

CHRIS That's totally normal. Luke, your mom seems very sweet.

LUKE You don't understand. THAT is not my mom! I don't know who that charming lady is. I've never, EVER heard my mom offer anybody a mixed drink that didn't include wheat germ and flax seed oil.

CHRIS She's nervous, Luke, just like you. It's clear she misses you. She wants to be a part of your life. That's a great start. Hey, maybe offering you a drink is just her way of treating you like a grown-up.

LUKE You think?

[CHRIS *nods. A loud crash and a curse from the kitchen*—LUKE *smiles: of course* CHRIS *is right.*]

LUKE   Everything okay—?

MOM   Fine, fine! Just . . . ah, why don't you put on some music! There are some CDs in the junk drawer!

[*Before* LUKE *can get to the CD drawer,* CHRIS *stops him.*]

CHRIS   Remember what we talked about, Luke: you gotta be who you are and be proud of it.

[LUKE *nods in agreement.*]

How many of us there are, hiding the shadows—afraid to tell our parents, our bosses, our friends? Afraid of what? This is America. We have as much right to be here as they do. More! And it's about time we stood up and got counted.

[MOM *enters proudly with a pink Cosmo in a martini glass. She hands it to* LUKE. *He puts it down without drinking it.*]

MOM   Aren't you going to try it?

LUKE   Mom. Look.

[LUKE *is stuck.* CHRIS *jumps in.*]

CHRIS   Why don't you have a seat, Mrs. Wilson. I think Luke has something he wants to say.

[MOM *sits.*]

MOM   Of course. What did you want to say, Luke?

LUKE   Mom, I . . .

MOM   I love you, Luke. You can tell me anything. Don't you know that by now?

LUKE   It's just that . . . I've been afraid that—

MOM   Afraid? Of me?

LUKE   You gotta admit you're acting a bit . . . strange.

MOM   Maybe I did go a bit overboard. I just wanted you to know that I support you—whatever choices you make for your self and your life. Haven't I always lived a life of tolerance and acceptance—why should my son be any different?

CHRIS I know that is a comfort for Luke. He was a little nervous about coming here today.

MOM And seeing you here with Chris . . . well, I just couldn't be happier. You're a lovely man, Chris—just the kind of partner I would pick for my son.

LUKE What?

MOM He obviously loves you, Luke.

CHRIS Well, I—

LUKE Mom! Chris is not my lover!

CHRIS Your what???

MOM It's alright, Luke—

LUKE I can't believe you—

CHRIS Are you implying that I'm—?

LUKE You think I'm gay!

MOM I love you no matter what you are.

LUKE I'm not gay! Why would you—? I can't believe— That's why you told Chris to call you Mom, isn't it? Isn't it! You think he's your new son-in-law!

MOM Well, then who the hell is he??

LUKE He's my roommate, Mom.

CHRIS Housemate—we're not—we don't—we don't share a *room*.

MOM So . . . then . . . what's this all about?

LUKE Have a seat, Mom.

MOM Are you okay, Lukey?

LUKE Just sit, Mom.

[MOM *sits nervously.*]

MOM Now you're scaring me.

CHRIS You'll be laughing in few minutes. Trust me. We all will.

LUKE Don't you get it? She wants me to be gay. *That* she could accept. She could be the proud "out" mother of her "I'm queer, I'm here" son—she could buy T-shirts, and join parent groups and march on Washington . . .

[*To* MOM.]

But I'm not gay, Mom. I'm not. I'm sorry. I'm . . . a Republican.

[*Beat.* MOM *laughs, but her laughter quickly shifts from disbelief to shock. She searches* LUKE's *eyes for any sign.*]

MOM You're—?

LUKE Republican. Come on, Mom. John Kerry? I just couldn't do it any more. He was . . . a weasel, Mom. I'm sorry.

MOM A . . . a . . . weasel?? John Kerry is a weasel? Compared to Bush?

LUKE He's leader, Mom. And that's the long and short of it. He's got convictions, he knows what they are and he's not afraid to stand up for what he believes in.

MOM I—I can't believe what I'm hearing.

CHRIS We're at war, Mrs. Wilson, in case you hadn't noticed. You don't change doctors in the middle of an operation.

MOM You do if the doctor is killing you!

LUKE But you don't replace the doctor with a philosophy professor.

MOM You're both . . .

CHRIS . . . Republican . . .

[*She looks at* LUKE. *He is a stranger to her. She gets up and crosses to the kitchen as if to leave.*]

LUKE Mom—!

[CHRIS *goes to* MOM. *Takes her arm to stop her.* MOM *looks at* CHRIS *pointedly— he releases her. She spots the Cosmo on the table and decides to take it.*]

MOM Okay, I'm going to need some time to sit with this.

[*She is about to exit when*—]

CHRIS Hold up—

[MOM *turns to face* CHRIS *and* LUKE. LUKE *stares dejectedly at his feet.*]

Let me get this straight—you would accept Luke being gay, but you can't accept him being a Republican?

MOM You're not born Republican. Luke was raised with solid LIBERAL values. He was raised to have a complex and nuanced understanding of national and international policy. We took him on Peace Corp vacations, spent holidays working soup kitchens! I poured my life and soul into this boy—what did I do wrong, Luke? Is it me? Is it my fault?

LUKE It's nobody's fault, Mom. It's just what I am.

MOM It is not "what you are!" It's a choice—a choice, I might add, that is going to kill your father, Luke, KILL HIM—

CHRIS Now, Ms. Wilson, we all know that's an exaggeration—

MOM Do you know where your father is right now, Luke? Do you know where he is? He is out protesting the reclassification of farmed salmon to inflate the administration's so-called environmental policy!

CHRIS Why should farmed salmon be prejudiced against?

[MOM *looks at* CHRIS *as if he's an idiot.*]

MOM And to think, just moments ago you looked so smart.

LUKE Mom, lay off him.

MOM Tell me, Luke, is this the kind of thinking you aspire to? Is this what you think? Is global warming a myth? Is Alaskan oil going to save the SUV? I knew we never should have let you go to college in the Midwest!

LUKE Mom! Did you ever stop to think that maybe . . . just maybe . . . if everyone disagrees with you, you might be wrong?

MOM Everybody does not disagree with me.

LUKE Okay. Let's say 4 million more people agree with me.

MOM Luke, those people are—

LUKE What? Stupid? Is that what you were going to call "those people"? Is that what you're calling me?

MOM I was going to say... reactionaries.

CHRIS Do you know why people voted in droves this year, Mrs. Wilson? To put an end once and for all to this nonsense about the Democratic Party being the "silent majority." It's not. THAT is the lesson here. THAT is why people like Luke and myself have to come out of the shadows and make our voices heard. Welcome to the real America, Mrs. Wilson. This is it.

MOM You don't know me. How dare you come into my house and lecture me about the "real" America.

CHRIS So much for tolerance, right?

MOM I think you should go now.

CHRIS I was just leaving anyway, can't stand the smell of hypocrisy. Come on—

[CHRIS *nods to* LUKE *and heads out the door, but* LUKE *holds his ground.*]

LUKE Well, what about it, Mom? Should I go too?

[MOM *stands frozen. Miserable. There is nothing more to say.* LUKE *turns to* CHRIS, *who disappears out the door, leaving it open.* LUKE *goes to the door, and takes the handle as if to shut the door behind* CHRIS. *He turns to* MOM. *She smiles: maybe he'll stay.*]

LUKE I'm not stupid, Mom.

[LUKE *exits, leaving the door open behind him.* MOM *remains frozen, Cosmo untouched in her hand.*]

[*"Come Rain or Come Shine" plays as the lights fade to black.*]

• • •

Beautiful American Soldier

Dano Madden

Dano Madden

Dano Madden is from Boise, Idaho. In 2007, he was named "One of 50 Playwrights to Watch" by the *Dramatist*, the magazine of the Dramatists Guild of America. His play *In the Sawtooths* was the winner of the Kennedy Center's 2007 National Student Playwriting Award and it is currently being published by Samuel French, Inc. Mr. Madden's plays have received readings at the Seven Devil's Playwrights Conference, the Northwest Playwright's Alliance, the Last Frontier Theatre Conference, Boise Contemporary Theater, and Woolly Mammoth Theatre Company. Mr. Madden's play *Beautiful American Soldier* was recently awarded the Kennedy Center's Quest for Peace Playwriting Award. His writing credits include: *The Wealthy Life of Sam Tyler* (The National New Play Network's University Playwright's Workshop); *The Save* (Mile Square Theatre); *Ella; Billy's Suitcase; Caravaggio Called* (Rutgers University); *Yo-yo* (State Theater in Olympia, Washington); *The Raccoon* (Idaho Theatre for Youth); *Forecast* (Honorable Mention, University of Idaho's One-Page Play Festival); *The New* (Actors Theatre of Louisville); *The Soft Sand* (Idaho Governor's Awards in the Arts); *Drop* (Samuel French, Inc]. *Drop* was the winner of the Kennedy Center's 1997 National Short-Play Award. Mr. Madden was the recipient of the 2001 Idaho Commission on the Arts Fellowship in Playwriting. He received his MFA in playwriting from Rutgers University and his BA in theatre arts from Boise State University. He lives in Hoboken, New Jersey, with the love of his life, Lauren.

···production note···

Beautiful American Soldier was first produced by the Mason Gross School of the Arts at Rutgers University in the Jameson Studio Theatre on April 25, 2006. It was directed by Charles Goforth; the setting was designed by Jonathan Wentz; the costumes were designed by Rebecca Ming; the lighting was designed by Ben Hagen; the stage manager was A. J. Stevenson. The cast was as follows:

LAMIYA, Sarah Rebekah Himmelstein
ULA, June Patterson
BAHLOOL, Ted Coluca Jr.

Beautiful American Soldier has received the following awards:

The Kennedy Center's 2008 Quest for Peace Playwriting Award
Second place, University of Tulsa's 2007 New Works for Young Women
Winner of the 2006 New Works of Merit Playwriting Contest, New York City

Acknowledgments: Susan Barrett, Michole Biancosino, Lee Blessing, Eric Brooks, Jessica Elliott, Sharon Farrell, Demetra Kareman, Alicia Anne Lees, Michael Lindsay, John Madden, Jerry Madden, Alice Madden, Kristyn McDaniel, Shannon Miles, Sarah Kate O'Haver, Isaac Perelson, Katie Pietrzak, Jason Pietrzak, Nicholas Pietrzak, Allie Pietrzak, Amit Prakash, Joe Novak, Sheri Novak, Nick Garcia, Gregg Henry, Karlena Riggs, Lia Romeo, Amy Saltz, Lauren Walsh Singerman, Lane Smith, Addie Walsh, Samuel Brett Williams, Bryan Willis, Crista Wolfe, Michael Wright.

characters

LAMIYA, awkward, clumsy, beautiful and in love, 20
ULA, her sister, 29
BAHLOOL, in search of treasure, 26

location

Somewhere in Iraq

time

Not so long ago

A note about the text: The monologues in the play, especially the longer ones by Lamiya and Ula, are laid out on the page in a way that is contrary to the traditional "block" format. This is in an attempt to indicate changes in idea, rhythm, or to emphasize a specific word or phrase. The space in between lines is not specifically there to indicate a beat or a pause.

• • •

[*The lights rise on a dirt road. A large tree in full bloom sits just off the road. It is a beautiful, sunny afternoon. ULA, 29, sits beneath the tree. LAMIYA, 20, moves about restlessly.*]

LAMIYA   English. I'm going to learn English.

I'm going to go to a university in America. Probably in New York or California. And I'm going to learn beautiful English.

Are you listening to me? You've no right to be angry. Do you want to know why I'm going to learn English? Because I'm in love. I am. I'm in love with an American soldier. Don't tell Mama or Papa.

[*Beat.*]

I met him at a checkpoint. The American soldier, the one I'm in love with. There were a lot of soldiers. They were checking us for guns and bombs.

I admit, it wasn't love at first sight. At first sight I just wanted my American soldier. His hair was cut so close to his head. His face was freshly shaven. It was a hot day and I could see little beads of sweat on his forehead. He was yelling, motioning for me to come to him. So I walked over to this soldier. He wasn't as large as some of the others—but his muscles were smooth and strong.

[*Beat.*]

Ula? I know you hate this kind of talk. You have to listen, though. You have to listen if you're just going to sit there. We can still make it. You're the one giving up.

[*Beat.*]

I tried to see his eyes, but they were hidden behind his sunglasses. I looked down to the ground and I noticed, beneath all of his weapons and his belts—I noticed him bulging, through his pants. And he started to check me. Feeling me. Up my sides. In between my legs. So gentle. Feeling me all over—searching me, trying to find a weapon or a bomb. I felt his breath on my neck. I imagined the bulge in his pants pressing up against me.

I began to wish that I did have explosives strapped on—all over my body. How wonderful if my soldier had discovered a bomb on me. He'd take me away to a tent. And he'd carefully start to take my clothes off until all that was left was the bomb and the tape holding it on—over my naked body. I'm certain that my soldier is very skilled and he would remove the bomb and all of its pieces safely, one by one. He would remove pieces from my arms and my back and my stomach and my chest. Slowly. Until my body was completely bare. The bulge in his pants growing, in spite of his concentration. His mouth so near my neck, my chest. His breathing getting heavier. The bomb completely removed, but his hands continuing to gently search my body. Both of us sweating from the heat of the midday sun—his breath all over my chest, his lips so near my mouth, my back arched and—

He'd take me. Right there in the dusty tent. Pieces of the bomb all around us.

[*Beat.*]

Ula! You're so boring! Just yell at me if you're angry. We still have time. The reception has only just begun.

[*Beat.*]

The soldier finished checking me and—

I love him.

Do you want to know why? All you have to do is ask me.

[*Beat.*]

I could leave without you. I'm sure I could find the way. Our sister is married by now, but the best part—the singing, the dancing, the eating. We can still make it.

[*Beat.*]

I can play this game too you know. I can. And I'll win.

[LAMIYA *sits down dramatically on the opposite side of the tree, demonstrating her ability to "not talk" to her sister. Pause.*]

How about a new game? Yes? Okay. I have a little journal here. Lately I've been writing about the American soldier I'm in love with. Here. Blank pages. Now. You write, on this page, write why you're angry at me. I can't imagine what I've done wrong. Nonetheless, you write. For example: "I am angry because we are late for our sister's wedding and I think it's Lamiya's fault." Or . . .

"I am angry because it turns Lamiya on when soldiers check her for bombs."

Or...

"I'm angry. Just angry. Because that's my personality."

[*Beat.*]

You can write now.

Please.

[*Beat.*]

Come on! Ula! We're wasting time!

You used to be my favorite sister. Yesterday I would've said Khaireya was the biggest pain. Always flirting with everyone. Makes me crazy. But this, this, whatever this is. Moodiness. Stubborness. Forget it. You are no longer my favorite. You are a pain. Just like Khaireya. Congratulations.

[*Pause.*]

I know why you're angry.

You're angry because all of your sisters have a husband. Except me. But—

I am the youngest and the prettiest. I have time.

As of... oh... about forty-five minutes ago, Shilan is married. And that leaves only the two of us who have no husband. The youngest and the oldest. That's why you refuse to go with me to the reception.

[*Beat.*]

That's stupid, you know. The reason you haven't married yet is because Papa adores you. The way he talks about you, the way he tells his friends how smart you are, how funny. I think, in Papa's eyes, there are no suitable men for you. None worthy.

[*Beat.*]

So don't be angry that Shilan is getting... well... is married by now.

We all want to be Papa's favorite.

But you are. Only you. Lucky you. Be happy.

[*Beat.*]

Come on. Tell me to shut up. Tell me why it is inappropriate to fall in love with an American soldier. Tell me in great detail why it is my fault we are lost. Or let's talk futbol. Even Mama cannot make you shut up. Speak speak speak speak.

Please.

[*Beat.*]

Aren't you hungry at least? Aren't you? I'm starving. Can we at least go for the food? Please? Even if, even if you hate it. Even if you're angry that nearly all of your sisters are married. We can't miss out on the food. The sweets. The sweets are so succulent at weddings.

[*Beat.*]

So it's official?

You're not going to speak to me? Or move from under that tree? Can you signal me in someway?

[*Beat.*]

Alright. I'm going to find my way to the wedding alone.

[*Beat.*]

Okay. Hmmmmm . . . This road leads in two directions. Hmmm . . .

[LAMIYA *looks in one direction.*]

West. Hmmm . . . or is that east? Do you . . . ? Oh, that's right. Forget it.

[LAMIYA *looks in the other direction.*]

There's that way.

[LAMIYA *looks in the other direction.*]

And that way.

We came from that way. We've traveled to this point and have not found the wedding.

Could you perhaps point if you feel strongly about a particular direction? What about that way?

[LAMIYA *points.*]

Or, or . . . that way?

[LAMIYA *points the other way.*]

We came from that way. I think.

[*Beat.*]

Fine. I will choose. Good-bye.

[LAMIYA *doesn't move.*]

Aaugh! Ula! Come on!

[*Singing in the distance. Singing and clanging.* LAMIYA *looks down the road.*]

Ah-ha! You see that! Look. Coming this way! A man! Perhaps he'll know the way to the wedding. Maybe he's a guest, one of Papa's friends.

[*Singing and clanging grows louder.*]

[BAHLOOL *enters. He is covered in dust and has clearly not seen a bath or a shower in weeks. He carries several large bags filled with a wide variety of items. Some items, such as pots and toys, hang from the outside of his bag.* ULA *and* LAMIYA *watch* BAHLOOL *cautiously.*]

LAMIYA   Good afternoon.

BAHLOOL   Afternoon.

LAMIYA   I don't suppose you know—

BAHLOOL   Wait. Hold on. One moment—

[BAHLOOL *digs through one of his bags.*]

LAMIYA   Yes. My sister and I, she's over there—

BAHLOOL   One moment.

LAMIYA   That's my sister—well, one of them—and her name is Ula. I'm Lamiya and somewhere we got turned around—

BAHLOOL   Just. Stop. Stop talking for a moment.

[BAHLOOL *continues to dig through one of his bags. He pulls out a portable radio/CD player, which is covered by dirt. He dusts it off.*]

Take a look.

LAMIYA   We . . . I would like—

BAHLOOL   Sssssshhh . . . sshh . . . Look. Nearly perfect condition. Everyone needs a little music. Right?

LAMIYA   Of course. Yes. I think so.

BAHLOOL Take a look.

LAMIYA I'm not—

BAHLOOL Ssshh... sshh... just take a look. I wish... well... let me see. There's obviously, there's no way to power up. I... I don't seem to have a cord. Not that you could plug it in anywhere if I did. I can offer you a small discount. Because the power cord is missing.

LAMIYA You're not—

BAHLOOL Hold this. I know I have... for a small charge. If you want the music box, I will throw in—

LAMIYA Do you know this road? We—

[BAHLOOL *digs through his bags and begins pulling out CDs with no cases. They appear to be scratched and battered.*]

BAHLOOL Here! Some music. CDs. We have, here's some... I don't know who this is. You like pop music? Okay, something in English, does either of you speak, well, it doesn't matter. I have quite a bit of American music. Quite a few CDs. I can of course guarantee their quality.

[LAMIYA *fumbles the boom box, almost dropping it. She inadvertently flips on a switch. The sound of static comes from the radio.*]

LAMIYA Oops, I... oh—

BAHLOOL What the...? Let me see that for a second—

[BAHLOOL *inspects the radio.*]

BAHLOOL Ah-ha! Batteries! Perfect. I'll throw in the batteries. For a tiny additional charge.

LAMIYA It's nice—

BAHLOOL It is in amazing condition. And. AND. I will throw in as many CDs as you want for a small fee. Do any of these interest you?

LAMIYA I... my sister and I—

BAHLOOL Your sister?

LAMIYA Yes—

BAHLOOL   She looks bored. What are you two doing out here? How 'bout some entertainment? Something to pass the time. You've seen the music. What about . . . here . . .

[BAHLOOL *pulls out a beat-up soccer ball.*]

BAHLOOL   Nothing like a little game of futbol. To pass the time. Right? No one's too old for a little game of kick . . .

[BAHLOOL *looks at* ULA.]

>   Well. She might be too old.

>   Regardless. Cheap. Nice futbol . . . I will practically give it to you.

[BAHLOOL *throws the ball to* LAMIYA. *She tries to catch it, but it bounces off of her head.*]

LAMIYA   Ouch. Oh. Ummm, we're actually late for—

BAHLOOL   I accept cash or food as payment. One small piece of fruit would buy that futbol.

LAMIYA   If you would just listen—

BAHLOOL   Perhaps. She looks very bored. Do you like books?

>   Hello?

>   She's quiet. Does she like books? We have . . .

>   [BAHLOOL *begins pulling books out of one of his bags.*]

>   Lots and lots of books. So many. Lots of these are . . . let's see, English. Shoot. Lots of these are in English. I don't really read English. A few in . . . does either of you speak Farsi? Ah, here we are. Arabic. Lovely Arabic. I love, do you know what I love? I love to sit beneath a nice tree, just like this one, and read a good book.

>   [BAHLOOL *demonstrates.*]

>   Ah. Especially on a day like today. What a beautiful sunny day. It's not too hot. Can you believe that? We must take advantage of a day like today. Choose a book.

LAMIYA   You said . . . you have books in English?

BAHLOOL   Yes! Lots! Do you speak English?

LAMIYA   Well—

BAHLOOL   Because I do, as I mentioned, I do have books in English.

LAMIYA   I don't . . . I don't speak English.

BAHLOOL   Oh.

LAMIYA   But I am hoping . . . planning to learn.

BAHLOOL   Okay . . . okay . . .

LAMIYA   Do you have any books that will teach me English?

BAHLOOL   Yes.

LAMIYA   Really?

[BAHLOOL *begins to search through the books.*]

BAHLOOL   I don't . . . my English is very poor . . . but . . . I know . . . okay. This one. This one is a book of English words. Here.

[BAHLOOL *pulls an English dictionary out of his bag.*]

Here. I think this might be exactly what you're looking for.

LAMIYA   Can I see it?

BAHLOOL   Of course.

[LAMIYA *flips through the pages of the book.*]

LAMIYA   Is there . . . does it say what the words mean in Arabic?

BAHLOOL   Certainly. Of course. The book is yours for one piece of pita bread. Or an apple. Do you have a piece of fruit? Fruit sounds so good right now. Doesn't it?

LAMIYA   I don't think there are Arabic translations in here. It's just. I think the words are only in English—

BAHLOOL   You gotta start somewhere. If you want to learn. This is the book for you. Guaranteed.

LAMIYA   I doubt it.

BAHLOOL   You might find it helpful. And how can you say no at such an inexpensive price?

LAMIYA   I'm afraid this won't help me—

BAHLOOL   What do you need to learn English for?

[*Beat.*]

LAMIYA   Oh . . . it's . . . it doesn't matter—

BAHLOOL   I know a few phrases. I've picked up a few. It's necessary. Makes it easier for me to get through the checkpoints. Used to take several hours. Twice I've been taken away for days because the Americans were suspicious of me. All the bags. Could be a bomb. So, in an effort to more efficiently travel, I have picked up a little English. What do you need to know?

LAMIYA   Oh, I don't know.

BAHLOOL   Come on. If I know, I'll tell you. Free of charge. Free after you give me a piece of fruit.

LAMIYA   Okay.
[*Beat.*]
I love you.

BAHLOOL   Excuse me?

LAMIYA   I want, I wish to learn how to say "I love you." In English.
To begin. I of course wish to someday speak fluent English. Fluency will be a necessity. But to start, "I love you."

[*Beat.*]

BAHLOOL   "I love you"?

LAMIYA   Yes.

BAHLOOL   "I love you"?

LAMIYA   Yes. Forget it. Do you know or not? Forget it.

BAHLOOL   Why on earth would you want to say that? In English?

LAMIYA   I don't. Forget it.

BAHLOOL   If you can tell me why, I might be able—

LAMIYA   It doesn't matter.

BAHLOOL   I know other phrases, that might be more useful. Why does it have to be—

LAMIYA   Please. It's not important. I—

BAHLOOL   Wait. Wait. I know. Let me guess. Let me guess. You've fallen in love with an American soldier.

[*Beat.*]

Am I right?

LAMIYA   It doesn't matter.

BAHLOOL   I'm right. I know your type. Young and beautiful. Attracted to men in uniform. Men who speak a foreign language. Especially English.

LAMIYA   Is something wrong with it? If I am in love with an American soldier?

BAHLOOL   "I love you" might be a little much. I recommend you start slowly. Be practical. "I have no weapons." "Hot out today, isn't it, sir?"—

LAMIYA   You don't understand—

BAHLOOL   I do. You can't be that forward.

LAMIYA   You don't know my soldier.

BAHLOOL   Yes. Unfortunately I do. You know one soldier, you know 'em all.

LAMIYA   You don't like the Americans?

BAHLOOL   I've come to terms with the Americans.

LAMIYA   What does that mean?

BAHLOOL   I used to hate them. But now I see it differently. The Americans are my business partners.

LAMIYA   Your business partners?

BAHLOOL   Yes.

LAMIYA   You're not making any sense.

BAHLOOL   It's not really appropriate to fall in love with an American.

LAMIYA   Why?

BAHLOOL   Your parents won't like it.

LAMIYA It's not my parents' business who I fall in love with—

BAHLOOL You're wasting your time.

LAMIYA I should be allowed to marry whoever I want. Besides, he loves me too.

BAHLOOL He does not love you. If an American soldier expresses interest in you, he is only interested in one thing.

LAMIYA You're wrong.

BAHLOOL I have traveled all over this country since the Americans arrived. You know what? They all have wives and girlfriends in America. They're not here to fall in love with a young girl like you.

LAMIYA How do you know? That proves nothing. My soldier loves me.

BAHLOOL Congratulations.

LAMIYA You're just jealous because no one loves you.

[*Pause.*]

BAHLOOL Do you think . . . are you or your sister going to buy anything? Do you want the book of English words?

LAMIYA I have no money.

BAHLOOL Great.
      [*Beat.*]
      I don't suppose . . . do you have any food you could spare?

LAMIYA No food.

BAHLOOL Not even a stale pita? Or a half-eaten piece of fruit? Please.

LAMIYA I'm sorry. No.

[*Beat.*]

BAHLOOL Send me an invitation to your wedding.

[BAHLOOL *begins to leave.*]

LAMIYA Wait.
      [BAHLOOL *continues walking.*]
      Please.

[BAHLOOL *stops.*]

LAMIYA   My sister and I are lost. I didn't mean to be rude. We're late for our sister's wedding. Can you help us?

BAHLOOL   Someone does love me.

[*Beat.*]

Just so you know.

LAMIYA   I'm sorry I said that. I don't even know you.

BAHLOOL   No. You don't.

LAMIYA   I'm sorry.

BAHLOOL   And I'm not just saying that. Someone loves me very much.

LAMIYA   I believe you.

BAHLOOL   You need something.

LAMIYA   I believe you. I do.

BAHLOOL   What do you need?

LAMIYA   We. My sister and I, Ula . . . she's right there. We, we . . . we're late for our sister's wedding. We . . . of, it's all my fault. I, it doesn't matter. We're late because of me and she's angry and . . .

[*Whispering.*]

I think angry because all of her younger sisters are now married. Well, four of them. All of her younger sisters except me. I'm the youngest. There's six in all. So, she, she doesn't care if we go to the wedding or not. You see—

BAHLOOL   What do you want from me?

LAMIYA   Can you please help me find the wedding? Maybe you passed it on your way here? I am really so thankful that you came along.

BAHLOOL   How is it possible that I would know the way? I don't know you—

LAMIYA   It's just, maybe you passed the wedding or possibly you can help us?

BAHLOOL   I don't know. I could probably help you determine which direction to travel.

LAMIYA   Oh! Thank you. Oh, I would really appreciate it.

BAHLOOL   But I must have payment.

LAMIYA   I . . . I told you before, I have no money. Or food.

BAHLOOL   I can't. If you have no way to pay me—

LAMIYA   The reception!

BAHLOOL   What?

LAMIYA   We . . . I'm certain we've missed the wedding. But if you come with me, if you help me find the wedding, there will be food. So much food—

BAHLOOL   Yes?

LAMIYA   Of course—

BAHLOOL   I can go to the reception?

LAMIYA   Of course. Of course. My parents will welcome you with open arms. They will thank you for escorting their daughters. You will be allowed to join my father in the men's reception tent. And eat and eat!

BAHLOOL   Okay! Yes! Agreed! Let's see . . . we need a map.

[BAHLOOL *begins to search through his bags.*]

LAMIYA   My favorite are the sweets. My Mother's baklava. At weddings. I've been to many weddings—three of my sisters are already married—

BAHLOOL   Let me see here, let me see—

LAMIYA   I guess I should say four. Four of my sisters are now married—

BAHLOOL   I know I must have a map here somewhere—
   [BAHLOOL *pulls out a torn poster with a woman on it.*]
   Okay. Not a map.

LAMIYA   Where are you from?

BAHLOOL   Baghdad.

LAMIYA   Oh! Baghdad! I've always wanted to live in Baghdad! So beautiful, I hear—

BAHLOOL   It used to be.

LAMIYA   I know I'd love the big city.

BAHLOOL   I know I have a map here somewhere.

LAMIYA   How do you know where you're going? If you don't have a map?

BAHLOOL   Instinct. I have a good natural sense of direction. Or, I just follow the explosions.

LAMIYA   Why would you do that?
[*Beat.*]
Wait. You're a looter?

BAHLOOL   Treasure hunter. I am a treasure hunter.

LAMIYA   So all of these things are stolen.

BAHLOOL   They—these things are not stolen—

LAMIYA   Are they yours?

BAHLOOL   Yes.

LAMIYA   But you stole them.

BAHLOOL   Do you want my help or not?

LAMIYA   Yes. I'm just saying it's . . . odd to steal things. To take these things. It's against the law—

BAHLOOL   Everything was stolen from me. I owned a restaurant in Baghdad, with my father and . . . when the bombings began the entire neighborhood became rubble. Except for our restaurant— until the looters came and took all the food, all of the money. And I was left with nothing.

LAMIYA   Oh.

BAHLOOL   So, I don't cry about the loss. I'm in business now with the Americans and the suicide bombers—anyone who blows things up. They blow them up and I salvage what I can. Is that okay with you?

[*Beat.*]

Now, do you want my help or not?

[LAMIYA *nods.*]

I know I have maps. . . . Don't just stand there. Look through this bag—see if you can find my maps.

[LAMIYA *begins to search the bag. She begins pulling out dirty clothes. She stops and stares at them.*]

LAMIYA   Are these? . . . Oh God, oh my God . . .

BAHLOOL   Those are from a fine clothing store in Baghdad.

LAMIYA   So they aren't from . . .

BAHLOOL   Do you think I'm some kind of monster? Look at the quality. Brand-new.

LAMIYA   Of course . . . yes . . . A clothing store! Wow! Beautiful clothes. So many beautiful clothes. Maybe I should put something on for the reception.

BAHLOOL   Hey! Hey, you said you didn't have any money! You have to pay—

LAMIYA   I'm just trying a few things on. . . . Do I look pretty?

BAHLOOL   There's no time. Won't the food get cold? Won't it be gone?

LAMIYA   My parents will feed you. Don't worry.

BAHLOOL   A book of maps! Yes! Now!

LAMIYA   I feel beautiful! I wish my soldier was going to be at the wedding—

BAHLOOL   If I can figure out generally where we are . . .

LAMIYA   The dancing is my favorite part. I mean—I am hungry and I always love the food. Do you like kabobs?

BAHLOOL   Yes! Makes my stomach hurt to think of it. We have to figure out where we are—

LAMIYA Let me . . . I want to practice my dancing. I—

[LAMIYA *trips over a rock.*]

You see. I have always been the most awkward of my sisters. Clumsy. Never able to find the rhythm.

BAHLOOL I'm just trying to find the correct map. Do you have some sort of invitation? I feel pretty certain we're . . . here.

[BAHLOOL *points to the map.*]

LAMIYA Ooo . . . wait . . . quickly, before we go, let me turn on some music, so I can practice my dancing. I've . . . I've fallen all over myself at every one of my sister's weddings. So, just . . .

BAHLOOL Wait. This map was upside down. Okay . . . if you can—my God, I'm hungry.

[LAMIYA *turns some music on.*]

LAMIYA Oh no . . . too fast. We need some, some sort of music you can dance to. Something pretty, to match these clothes.

BAHLOOL If you can remember the name of the village. Where is your sister's wedding?

[LAMIYA *has turned on music that is pretty and danceable.*]

LAMIYA Look at me! Maybe I can do this! Oh, I wish the men and women were allowed in the same tent! Then I could dance with my American soldier! Maybe I will sneak outside and dance with him!

BAHLOOL I think I know where we are. I just need the name of the village. Do you have an invitation?

LAMIYA I don't remember having an invitation. But I'm always losing everything. Look! Look at me! What is this music?

BAHLOOL I think I know precisely where we are. But . . . I don't know which direction to go in—

LAMIYA That's exactly the problem I was having. Do we go—

[LAMIYA *does a dance move followed by a gesture.*]

That way!

Or,

[LAMIYA, *dance dance dance, followed by a gesture.*]

That way!

BAHLOOL   Do you have any idea of the village? Even a nearby village? Come on, stop fooling around.

[BAHLOOL *turns off the music.*]

Please. I can't help you if I don't know where we're going.

LAMIYA   Ask her. I was just following her, to be honest.

BAHLOOL   She hasn't said—

LAMIYA   Maybe she'll talk to you.

[*Pause.*]

BAHLOOL   Excuse me. I . . . we're trying to get to your sister's wedding, do you know the name of the village? Do you—can you speak?

[*Beat.*]

Do you know the address?

[*Pause.*]

Fine.

[BAHLOOL *begins to gather his things up.*]

ULA   I know.

LAMIYA   Ha! I told you!

[LAMIYA *turns the music back on. The music should be appropriate in tone for both* LAMIYA's *dancing and* ULA's *story.* LAMIYA *continues to dance throughout all of the following. Her dancing becomes more graceful and beautiful as Ula gets further into her story.*]

BAHLOOL   You do?

ULA   Yes.

BAHLOOL   You know where your sister's wedding is?

ULA   Yes.

BAHLOOL   What's the name of the village?

[BAHLOOL *looks at a map.*]

ULA   You don't need a map.

BAHLOOL   I . . . but you're . . . she says you're—

ULA   We're not lost.

BAHLOOL   But you're late for your sister's wedding.

ULA   The wedding was three days ago.

BAHLOOL   I . . . I don't . . .

ULA   The wedding was three days ago at my parents' home.

BAHLOOL   But I thought you were late, I thought, she said—

ULA   We were late. We were.

BAHLOOL   But I thought . . . I thought . . .

ULA   Our papa sent us to the market at the last minute. He said, "We need more fruit. We need more fruit! I've underestimated. Ula, take Lamiya. Go!" The guests were beginning to arrive and we left to get fruit.

[LAMIYA *is dancing and dancing and dancing.*]

We took a long time at the market. I could hear my papa's voice, judging every piece of fruit I selected: "Unacceptable for a party." Lamiya was talking to everyone at every cart, telling them all about the wedding—

We were late. Soldiers stopped us at a new checkpoint.

BAHLOOL   They're everywhere.

ULA   It took such a long time. The soldiers apprehended several men ahead of us, took them away, in jeeps. And . . .

One soldier searched my sister, extensively, and she became . . . Enamored.

And . . . so, so late. I knew we had probably missed the ceremony. Finally, walking along the road home. Our papa could never have dreamed we'd be this late. Running. So late. In the distance they were shooting, firing the Kalashnikovs into the air—in celebration. Shooting shooting shooting.

Running running running. Lamiya and I had missed it. We had missed it. I tried to get my sister to move faster.

Fruit dropping everywhere—I was trying to pick it all up and—

[*Pause.*]

Suddenly, something knocked us to the ground. A sound. Deafening. The loudest sound I have ever heard. Planes. American warplanes. So low, right over our heads, it seemed.

Fruit falling all over, we fell into a ditch—

And then an explosion.

So loud. And flames and heat—

Screaming planes—

Another explosion and another and another and my sister and I huddled in a ditch—

Still another explosion and on and on and on and on and on—

Holding my sister so tight—

The explosions seemed to go on forever and then—

Silence.

I opened my eyes. The sky was filled with smoke. The sun looked pink through the haze. We stayed in the ditch, afraid to move.

So quiet. Now. Birds. The smell of burning. A cool breeze. And we moved, finally, and saw—

[*Pause.*]

Nothing. Where our house had once stood on the horizon, we saw nothing.

Nothing nothing nothing—

Walking down the road. . . we were lost.

And finally, through the smoke, the haze, against the pink sky, I saw something. Something I recognized.

This tree. I played under this tree growing up, out in the field near my parents' house. Exactly the same. This tree—this patch of earth, untouched by anything. But no house. No wedding, no wedding, no wedding . . .

[*Silence.* LAMIYA *continues dancing.* BAHLOOL *slowly turns, taking in the entire landscape until he is watching* LAMIYA *dance.*]

ULA I always believed we were safe. We weren't living in Baghdad. My papa thought we were safe.

BAHLOOL I . . . ummm . . .

ULA Now. My entire family. Lamiya and I were supposed to be there. Everyone was celebrating—

[LAMIYA *dances more passionately during the following.*]

My parents, my sister Khaireya and her husband Mohammad, my sister Fatima, her husband Ahmed and their son Raad, my sister Anood, her husband Talib, their son Inad and their daughter Kholood, my uncle Ali, my aunt Hamda, my uncle Mizhir, my aunt Marifa, my other uncle Ali and his wife Somayia, my aunt Fatima, my cousins Siham, Rabha, Zahra, Hamda, Ali, Hamza, Yasser, Raid, Daham, Wa'ad, Khava, my uncle Waldemar, my aunt Jasmin, my cousins Mostapha, Ahmad, and Isra, my sister Shilan, she was the bride, my sister Shilan and her new husband Hamid, they were just married and, of course, all of Hamid's family, everyone I think, my parents' friends, everyone I think, Shilan, just married, Shilan, who was probably the second prettiest of my sisters.

Lamiya is of course the prettiest.

[*Pause. Complete stillness. The only movement is the continued dancing of* LAMIYA.]

BAHLOOL You've been here for—

ULA Three days.

BAHLOOL No one's come? You said there's a town?

ULA People came. From the village. And some Americans. We were ghosts, sitting next to this tree. Chaos. People digging and yelling and searching. Focused on everything but us. And then they were gone.

BAHLOOL No one spoke to you?

ULA A woman. One woman. Asked, were we okay? I told her we needed some time, we'd leave soon. So hot and she left us some water. She was the last to go.

BAHLOOL You must be hungry—

ULA   We ate, a few pieces of fruit survived, from the market. We finished it off this morning.

BAHLOOL   Come with me.

ULA   I . . . my sister . . .

LAMIYA   Are you finally talking? Yay!

[LAMIYA *whispers to* BAHLOOL.]

> She's only talking to you because she still needs a husband. You're pretty young for her, but Ula is the smartest and funniest of my sisters.
>
> Come! Practice dancing with me!

[LAMIYA *returns to her dancing.*]

ULA   If I try to get her to leave, if we travel too far from this tree, too far down the road, she starts screaming and hyperventilating and I bring her back here and she's fine. I try again, to leave, move down the road—
> She panics.

BAHLOOL   What are you going to do?

ULA   I don't know.

BAHLOOL   Please come with me. Please.

ULA   We have nothing. Everything that mattered . . .

LAMIYA   Look at me! Imagine I'm dancing with my soldier! I am, I think I'm finally becoming graceful!

BAHLOOL   I can help you with her. Come with me—

ULA   Where? Where do you want us to go? Back to Baghdad with you?

BAHLOOL   Somewhere we can get food.

ULA   Then what? Where do we go after that?

BAHLOOL   I don't know. You have to eat.

LAMIYA   Have you two figured out the way yet? I think I'm ready. I'm not going to fall over my feet at this wedding. You watch. I love this music!

[*Beat.*]

Why aren't you two looking at the map? Have you figured out the way?

[*Beat.*]

Oh. Wait. Uh-oh . . . are you two falling in love?

[*Whispering.*]

Ula, he's pretty cute! Maybe this is your chance! I think Papa will approve of him. Please, can we go soon? Look at me! Look at me!

[LAMIYA *whirls around and around.*]

BAHLOOL   Let's go. Why not? She says she wants to go—

ULA   She's been saying that for three days. She tells me how she loves the American soldier, wonders aloud why I'm not yet married, and eventually she becomes aware of her hunger, and, I've tried a dozen or more times to . . . walk down the road, force her, carry her and it is the same. When we are beyond the fence line, the fence at the end of my papa's property, when we reach that fence, she becomes—

Hysterical. The look on her face . . .

[*Pause.*]

ULA   Who loves you?

BAHLOOL   What?

ULA   Earlier you told my sister, you told her someone loves you. Who?

[*Beat.*]

BAHLOOL   My wife.

[*Beat.*]

I haven't, I haven't seen her since the bombing began in Baghdad. I was at the restaurant one night, working late, and I know she's still alive.

ULA   Oh.

BAHLOOL   She . . . I know she's still alive. Because if she isn't, then . . .

ULA   Then what?

[*Pause.*]

BAHLOOL   Ula, you can't stay here.

ULA   When we go past that fence, I see it in her face, everything dies. She dies. If we go past that fence, I will never see my Lamiya again. I can't, I can't . . .

BAHLOOL   You'll both die if you stay here.

ULA   Even if . . . even if Lamiya could leave . . . I don't know if I . . . if I . . .
[*Beat.*]
This is my home.

[*Pause.*]

BAHLOOL   Which way is the village? I'm going. I wish you'd come with me. You can't die.
[*Beat.*]
I think I can get food and water. Bring it to you—

But . . . you see how it is. If nothing happens to me, I will help you. But if for some reason I do not return, it is because I was apprehended at a checkpoint or I was in the wrong shop when a bomb exploded. Not because I forgot you. You understand that it will be very difficult for me to get back to you. So please . . . I beg of you, if . . . if another day passes, if half a day passes, please go. Please.

I've lost a wife. And, we all do what we must, but—

Don't give up. I beg of you.
[*Beat.*]
Please say something.

ULA   I don't know how we will go on. We should've been at the wedding. How will we—

BAHLOOL   You will. You will.
Please say you will.

[*Beat.*]

ULA   If . . . if you do not return . . . I will . . . we will . . .

BAHLOOL   Yes?

ULA   Leave here.

BAHLOOL   Thank you. Thank you.
>   You're not alone.

[BAHLOOL *stands and throws his bags on over his shoulders.*]

LAMIYA   Are we going? The sun is setting—we're so late—

ULA   Soon.

LAMIYA   But do you know the way?

BAHLOOL   I have to go.

LAMIYA   But I thought you wanted food—

BAHLOOL   Another time.
>   [*Pause.*]
>   Your dancing is beautiful.

LAMIYA   Do you really think so? I've fallen at all of my sisters'
weddings.

BAHLOOL   Yes. You're very graceful. In fact, here.

[BAHLOOL *hands* LAMIYA *the boom box and CDs.*]

LAMIYA   But I told you I have no money—

BAHLOOL   It's a gift.

LAMIYA   Thank you.

[*Pause.*]

BAHLOOL   See you soon.

[BAHLOOL *exits.*]

LAMIYA   He was a lovely man.

ULA   Yes.

LAMIYA   Are you talking to me again?

ULA   Yes. It seems so.

LAMIYA   Are you angry at me?

ULA   Of course not.

LAMIYA   Good! Oh, I'm so glad. You're my favorite sister. You always listen to me. The others are too busy to care.

[*Beat.*]

Are we going to leave for the wedding soon?

ULA   Yes. Soon.

LAMIYA   Oh, I can't wait. My dancing has gotten better. Don't you think? I can feel it.

ULA   You're very graceful.

LAMIYA   Yay! Oh yay! Graceful. That's all I ever want to be.

ULA   You are.

LAMIYA   I wish so much that my American soldier could dance with me at the wedding. I love him. I do. Do you want to know why? Do you?

[ULA *nods.*]

After he finished checking me . . . for bombs and machine guns, he . . . he started to motion me on, through the checkpoint, so he could search the next person. And then he stopped. He just stood there and . . . he slowly reached up and took off his sunglasses and . . . oh, he had gorgeous dark brown eyes. And he just looked into my eyes. Really . . . it seemed like forever and I could tell, by the way he was staring into my eyes. The look, the look in his eyes.

I could see it.

My beautiful American soldier loves me.

[LAMIYA *and* ULA *sit beneath the tree as the sun slowly sets. We hear the sound of an American helicopter flying over.*]

• • •

The Mysteries of the Castle of the Monk of Falconara

James Armstrong

James Armstrong

James Armstrong is a member of the Dramatists Guild of America. His plays have been performed across the United States and Canada by such theaters as the Abingdon Theatre Company, the Epiphany Theater Company, and the Attic Ensemble. New York City audiences have seen the premieres of his short plays *The New Mrs. Jones*, *Searching for Saint Anthony*, and *When Ladies Go A-Thieving*, as well as his full-length play *Foggy Bottom*. *The Mysteries of the Castle of the Monk of Falconara* premiered in 2005 under the direction of Ken Kaissar as part of the Spotlight on Halloween Festival in Greenwich Village.

··· production note ···

The Mysteries of the Castle of the Monk of Falconara, a gothic comedy, premiered on October 14, 2005, at the Monster in New York City as part of the Spotlight On Halloween Festival. It was directed by Ken Kaissar and stage managed by Shawna Cathey. The cast was as follows:

MONK, Jonathan Brown
ANN RADCLIFFE, Eve Reinhardt
HORACE WALPOLE, John C. Fitzmaurice
MATTHEW LEWIS, Jonathan Monk
WOMAN IN WHITE, Jenna Kalinowski
MARY, Katherine Harte

characters

ANN RADCLIFFE, 29, one of the most skilled writers of Gothic novels, Mrs. Radcliffe is best known for *The Mysteries of Udolpho*, the novel parodied in Jane Austin's *Northanger Abbey*.

HORACE WALPOLE, 76, the founder of the Gothic movement in literature, Mr. Walpole wrote *The Castle of Otranto*, considered the first Gothic novel, and renovated his estate to look like a castle.

MATTHEW G. LEWIS, 18, also a poet and dramatist, Mr. Lewis shocked 18th-century readers with his scandalous novel *The Monk*. He died mysteriously in 1818 and was reportedly buried at sea.

The **WOMAN IN WHITE**
MARY

[NOTE: The MONK can double as MARY.]

time

All Hallows Eve, 1793.

place

A chamber in the Castle of Falconara.
In the center of the room sits a divan. On the wall behind it hangs an arras.

• • •

[*Italy. A mysterious gothic castle during a damp fall evening, 1793. As the lights come up, a* MONK *enters, followed by* ANN, *a petite Englishwoman in her late 20s.*]

ANN Is this where I've been summoned?

> [*The* MONK *motions to a divan in the middle of the room.*]
>
> Oh, cursed be the day I left my blessed England. Where is your master?
>
> [*The* MONK *motions again to the divan.*]
>
> I have a letter. It said I was to come here on the eve of—
>
> [ANN *produces the letter, but the* MONK *again motions to the divan.*]
>
> Very well. But tell your master I await his company. This is most irregular, you know.
>
> [ANN *sits down on the divan with her letter. The* MONK *exits.* ANN *reads.*]
>
> "To the Most Virtuous and Honorable Mrs. Ann Radcliffe: Your secret is known to me. Come to the Castle of Falconara at midnight on the eve of All Hallows, or else all shall be revealed!"

HORACE [*Offstage.*] Yes, yes, I'm coming.

ANN Oh, horrors! Who could that be?

HORACE [*Offstage.*] Not so fast! I'll get there soon enough.

ANN I, a married woman, caught with a stranger in a mysterious castle? Think of the scandal! I must secrete myself behind the arras.

[ANN *secretes herself behind the arras. The* MONK *enters, followed by* HORACE, *an elderly man with a cane.*]

HORACE They didn't used to make stairs quite so steep, you know. This is where he wants me, eh?

> [*The* MONK *motions to the divan.*]
>
> Don't know why I ever left England for this. Where is your master?
>
> [*The* MONK *motions to the divan.*]
>
> I've a letter someplace. It said I was supposed to come here on the eve of—

[*The* MONK *motions to the divan.*]

Very well. But tell your master I await his company. This is most
irregular, you know.

[HORACE *sits down on the divan with his letter. The* MONK *exits.*
HORACE *reads.*]

"To the Most Virtuous and Honorable Horace Walpole, M.P.:
Your secret is—"

ANN   Ah-choo!

HORACE   How now? A rat? Dead for a ducat, dead!

[HORACE *leaps up, and stabs the arras with his cane.*]

ANN   Ow!

HORACE   If only I'd brought a rapier. Ah, well. Is anyone back there?

ANN   No.

HORACE   I may be a day or two past my prime, but I'm not stupid.
Come out here, young lady. Let's have a look at you.

[ANN *emerges from behind an arras.*]

ANN   Most reverend and aged sir, do not reveal—

HORACE   Aged! Why, I'll have you know, young lady, I'm scarcely
seventy-six years old. One's not aged 'til one's at least four score.

ANN   I apologize. But you see, most reverend and—reverend—sir, my
presence here is a delicate matter. My husband knows nothing of
my flight to Italy, as I told him I went to visit a sickly aunt in
Brighton.

HORACE   Brighton, eh? You visit the Pavilion?

ANN   Sir, you misunderstand me. I have no aunt in Brighton. I came at
the behest of this letter.

HORACE   A letter? Now that is interesting.

ANN   "To the Most Virtuous and Honorable Mrs. Ann Radcliffe: Your
secret is known to me. Come to the Castle of Falconara—"

HORACE   "At midnight on the eve of All Hallows, or else all shall be
revealed!"

ANN   You know of my letter?

HORACE   I received an identical letter last month, only mine was addressed
To the Most Virtuous and Honorable Horace Walpole, M.P.

ANN   You're a member of parliament?

HORACE   Don't blame me. I didn't mean to be elected!

ANN   But being elected to parliament is a great honor. It's a sign of one's
success in the world.

HORACE   And therein lies my shame.

ANN   Where is the shame in serving one's country?

HORACE   Young lady, do you know who my father was? Think carefully
of my last name.

ANN   Not . . .

HORACE   Yes. Sir Robert Walpole. Prime Minister of England.

ANN   Why, he was the longest serving P.M. in history!

HORACE   And the most successful. Much to my despair.

ANN   Despair? You should be proud to have such a man as your father,
and to be able to follow him into the House of Commons.

HORACE   Mrs. Radcliffe, did you ever know of a man who wanted to be
like his father?

ANN   Not at all. I should say it's generally the reverse.

HORACE   Quite. Growing up the son of the most successful man in
England, I determined at a very early age that it was my mission
in life—to fail.

ANN   So what happened?

HORACE   Oh, blast it all, I've never been able to. I tried for years to get
kicked out of Eton. And what do they go and do? Graduate me!

ANN   Is that really so bad?

HORACE   Terrible! So I went to Cambridge, thinking surely I'd be able
to fail there. They tried to graduate me again! With honors,
nonetheless.

ANN I'm . . . sorry.

HORACE So before they could saddle me with a degree, my friend Tom and I took off for the Continent. I toured the back alleys of Europe, thinking, surely somewhere I'd be able to find disgrace. Nothing. Not so much as a scandalous word. I returned to find I'd been elected to parliament. In absentia!

ANN How traumatic for you.

HORACE I'll say. What's more, my father left me with a fortune. I knew if I were ever going to find the failure I sought, I would have to lose the whole amount. So I invested in the one industry guaranteed never to make a shilling.

ANN You went into publishing?

HORACE Precisely. I founded a press and printed a bunch of melancholy, brooding poems by my friend Tom.

ANN Did you lose it?

HORACE Unfortunately, Thomas Gray turned out to be a pretty good poet after all. I ended up with more money than ever. There I was, a member of parliament, filthy rich, with a successful press on my hands. I decided to write the worst book ever written, and publish it myself. *The Castle of Otranto* I called it. A ghastly tale of horrors and abominations. It became a bestseller, of course. Went through several editions. I used the profits to renovate my estate with the most monstrous bad taste ever devised. People came from miles around just to look at the place. I had to start issuing tickets.

ANN That does seem a bit odd.

HORACE You see, Mrs. Radcliffe, I've tried all my life to spite my father with failure, and have ended up richer, grander, and more famous than his wildest dreams. Despicable.

ANN Mr. Walpole, I don't mean to belittle your troubles, but all your life, you've striven to do nothing but fail, correct?

HORACE It's been my only ambition.

ANN But then, couldn't you say that you've FAILED at FAILURE?

HORACE By George, I think you're right. . . . Oh, damn it all! Success again!

ANN Ah . . . Well, at least your life has been extraordinary.

HORACE Which couldn't please my father more. I'll spite him one day. Of that, I assure you.

ANN But you have a dark secret. Perhaps that would displease him.

HORACE I'm in parliament, Mrs. Radcliffe. I have many dark secrets. But as Prime Minister, my father kept darker secrets than I could ever hold. What of you? Do not you have a dark secret as well?

ANN Oh, yes. A very dark and mysterious deed, deep, deep in my past. Something horrible I did long ago, Mr. Walpole. A most grievous and sorrowful act.

HORACE Might I be so bold as to inquire what it was?

ANN Oh, I haven't the foggiest. But I hope it was wicked!

HORACE Excuse me?

ANN Oh, nothing too wicked, understand you. Nothing irrevocably wicked, like adultery, or murder, but just wicked enough. Not so scandalous that people won't talk to me, but just so scandalous they'll talk behind my back.

HORACE You wish to be . . . mildly dishonored?

ANN Dishonored is too strong a word. But, oh, to have a secret! Why I'm sure that there's some mysterious shadow darkening my seemingly tranquil life. A tragic love affair, perhaps. A broken engagement. Secret trysts with a man beneath my station.

HORACE I'm a bit confused, Mrs. Radcliffe. If you had done these things, wouldn't you remember it?

ANN Mr. Walpole, have you never heard of amnesia?

HORACE Ah, yes! I'd forgotten.

ANN Only if it turns out that I do have amnesia, it's the most extraordinary amnesia that ever existed. For I remember my life quite clearly, you see. Every last detail. But when I remember it, it's all so boring. A simple marriage to William. Writing a few small stories for my own amusement. Settling down to quiet life in the country, where no one ever visits, and nothing ever happens! I am a unique and fascinating woman, Mr. Walpole. I must be! I couldn't bear to be ordinary.

HORACE   But if you're not afraid of your secret becoming known to the world, why come here at all?

ANN   To find out what it is, of course.

HORACE   Of course. How foolish of me.

MATTHEW   [*Offstage.*]
    Lead on, foul minion.

ANN   Oh, horrors!

HORACE   Yes?

ANN   Not "Horace." Horrors, horrors!

MATTHEW   [*Offstage.*]
    I'll seek your master, be it to the gates of hell!

ANN   Such foul language! I must not be seen in that gentleman's presence. Quickly! We must secrete ourselves behind the arras.

[ANN *grabs* HORACE *and they secrete themselves behind the arras. The* MONK *enters, followed by* MATTHEW.]

MATTHEW   So this is the devilish room.
    [*The* MONK *motions to the divan.*]
    I needn't have left England for a shabby stone chamber. Where is your master?
    [*The* MONK *motions to the divan.*]
    Shall I show you my letter? It commands that I come here on the eve of—
    [*The* MONK *motions to the divan.*]
    Very well. But tell your master I await his company. This is most irregular, you know.
    [MATTHEW *sits down on the divan with his letter. The* MONK *exits.* MATTHEW *reads.*]
    Ah-choo!

ANN   Bless you.

MATTHEW   Thanks. Wait a moment. . . .

> [*Goes to the arras.*]

> No one's back there, right?

ANN   Correct.

HORACE   Not a soul.

[MATTHEW *pulls back the arras.*]

ANN   Umm . . . except for us.

HORACE   We were, uh, studying the reverse side of the embroidery. The stitching's quite excellent, you know.

MATTHEW   Who are you?

ANN   I beg your pardon. I'm Mrs. Ann Radcliffe, and this is Horace Walpole, M.P., but it's not his fault.

MATTHEW   Is this your castle?

HORACE   No.

MATTHEW   Then what in hell are you doing here?

ANN   Good sir, please! Your language is quite uncalled for. We might just as well ask you what you are doing here.

MATTHEW   Me? Why, I have a letter!

HORACE   A letter?

MATTHEW   "To the Most UN-virtuous and DIS-honorable Matthew G. Lewis: Your secret is known to me. Come to the Castle of Falconara at midnight—"

ANN and **HORACE**   "On the eve of All Hallows, or else all shall be revealed."

MATTHEW   You stole my letter!

HORACE   Hardly. It seems we each have identical letters.

[HORACE *hands* MATTHEW *his own letter.*]

MATTHEW   Plagiarists!

ANN We were each brought here for a reason. But why? What links us three?

MATTHEW An M.P., eh? You an Oxford man?

HORACE Cambridge.

MATTHEW We'll forgive you.

HORACE So you are a scholar?

MATTHEW Matthew Lewis, sir. Poet, dramatist, and the most gifted student enrolled at Christ Church College, Oxford.

ANN And modest, as well.

HORACE So you're a writer? What have you published?

MATTHEW Well, nothing as of yet, but—

HORACE Mrs. Radcliffe, you mentioned writing some stories as well.

ANN Just a few slight tales to pass the time.

HORACE Nothing more substantial?

ANN I'm afraid I'm not capable of anything of that sort, Mr. Walpole.

MATTHEW But I am! Would you care, dear Horace, to hear my ballad of Alonzo the Brave and the Fair Imogine?

[*A bell rings.*]

ANN Oh, horrors!

HORACE Yes?

ANN No! Horrors, horrors! The bell. Quickly! We must secrete ourselves behind the arras.

[ANN *grabs* HORACE *and they secrete themselves behind the arras.*]

MATTHEW Secrete ourselves? What kind of a man do you think I am?

[ANN *runs out and grabs* MATTHEW. *They secrete themselves behind the arras. The* MONK *enters with a letter. He pushes the arras aside and hands the letter to* HORACE.]

HORACE Um, awfully drafty castle, you know. You really ought to do something about that.

[*The* MONK *exits.*]

ANN   Well, what is it?

HORACE   I have no idea.

MATTHEW   Don't keep us in suspense. Open it!

HORACE   I'm afraid to. Who knows what sinister plans our host may have in store for us.

ANN   And we'll never know unless you open it.

MATTHEW   Yea, though it call down fifty demons.

HORACE   Oh, dear, I'd better sit down.

ANN   Be brave, Horace, brave. You've come this far. There's no turning back now, no matter how devastating the contents of that letter.

HORACE   Very well. Pray for my soul.

[HORACE *opens the letter and reads it. His face is overcome with shock and horror.*]

ANN   What's wrong?

MATTHEW   Is it vile?

ANN   What does it say?

MATTHEW   Is it signed in blood by the Prince of Darkness?

HORACE   Worse! Worse! A thousand times worse!

ANN   What is it?

HORACE   It's from—my relatives!

MATTHEW   You mean it's not from our host after all?

HORACE   No. This calamity befalls me alone.

ANN   What's happened?

HORACE   They've named me Duke of Orford!

ANN   Oh, Horace, I'm so sorry.

MATTHEW   Sorry?

ANN   It's a long story, very funny, sorry you missed it, tell you later.

HORACE They may make me a duke, but I'll never sit in the House of Lords. Never, I tell you!

MATTHEW Where is our host, then, if this letter comes not from him?

ANN It's not yet midnight. We would have heard the chimes of the clock tower, else.

[MATTHEW *examines a pocket watch.*]

MATTHEW He has only a few more moments.

HORACE I'll need them to rest. I could not bear to face our grave host so soon after news of my misfortune.

MATTHEW Rest quickly, then. The hour is nearly upon us.

[*The clock chimes.*]

ANN Nay! It is at hand.

[*Chime.*]

HORACE Whatever shall I do?

[*Chime.*]

ANN Our host draws near.

[*Chime.*]

MATTHEW Let him come, be he Lucifer himself!

[*Chime.*]

HORACE Don't say that!

[*Chime.*]

ANN I'm frightened enough as it is.

[*Chime.*]

MATTHEW He'll come, whether we will or no.

[*Chime.*]

ANN I never should have come.

[*Chime.*]

HORACE   Nor I.

[*Chime.*]

MATTHEW   Midnight approaches.

[*Chime.*]

ANN   Hold me, Horace!

[*Chime.*]

HORACE   Angels and ministers of grace defend us!

[HORACE *and* ANN *grab each other and close their eyes.* MATTHEW *spreads his arms open in anticipation. Nothing happens.*]

ANN   The chimes stopped.

HORACE   It's midnight.

[MATTHEW *consults his pocket watch.*]

MATTHEW   He's late.

ANN   We've come all this way. Where's the man who summoned us?

HORACE   Perhaps we were not meant to see him.

[*Enter the* WOMAN IN WHITE.]

WOMAN   Dear friends, welcome to the Castle of Falconara. You are expected.

MATTHEW   Where is our host?

WOMAN   I am your host.

MATTHEW   A woman?

WOMAN   Of course.

MATTHEW   I must say, I am quite disappointed.

WOMAN   Do you prefer the company of men, Mr. Lewis?

HORACE   We simply expected someone a bit less . . . female.

WOMAN   Tonight will be full of surprises, Mr. Walpole. Or should I say, Your Grace?

HORACE   Blast that title! Call me Horace, young lady, or nothing at all.

WOMAN   Young! Now that is funny.

ANN   You look young enough to me, madam.

WOMAN   Yes. I suppose I'm aging well for someone who's six hundred and twelve.

MATTHEW   You're joking of course.

WOMAN   Not at all. I think I AM aging well.

ANN   You asked us here on account of our secrets.

HORACE   You said you knew all.

MATTHEW   And threatened to expose us.

WOMAN   And that I shall. But do you know what your secrets are? You've crossed seas, plains, mountains, braved the turmoil of Europe to come here, tonight, to the Castle of Falconara, but do you know why you came?

HORACE   Your letter, of course.

WOMAN   Not just a letter. A secret. A secret guilt tugged at your souls. Deep, deep down, each of you knew that your whole lives had been built upon sand, and all that was needed was one sharp blow to make everything you'd built come crashing to the ground. But do you know what it is? Do you know the lie that is embedded in your own breasts?

ANN   Good madam, please! To speak of being embedded is bad enough, but to mention . . . to mention . . .

MATTHEW   Breasts?

ANN   [*Covering her ears.*]
Vile tongues, corrupt not mine ears!

WOMAN   You must hear worse than that if you are to know your secret.

ANN   Oh, my secret! Is it juicy? Will I have to change my name?

WOMAN   You've wanted this for a long time, haven't you?

ANN   Don't get me wrong, madam. William is an excellent husband, and our life together has been everything I'd hoped. Except . . .

WOMAN   Yes?

ANN   Except . . . I can't help feeling that there's something more. All my life I've watched these other women who, on the surface, seemed so much like me. They grew up, had the proper education, fell in love in the ordinary way, got married, had children, grew old, died, were buried, all without having done the slightest remarkable thing in their entire lives. But I always knew, you see, that I was different. I didn't know why or how, but I knew that I was meant for something grander than some trite, dreary existence. I knew I was special. Then came your letter. A secret! A secret buried deep inside me, so deep even I couldn't see it. I have to know. Something makes me different from all those women I've watched throughout my life, all those women who lived, died, and were forgotten. Don't let me despair, madam. Tell me what it is.

WOMAN   I don't need to tell you, Mrs. Radcliffe. You know it already.

ANN   No. How?

WOMAN   Look within, Mrs. Radcliffe. Read the inscription on your own heart.

ANN   You must tell me.

WOMAN   I need not say a word. It is precisely the thing you fear.

ANN   I don't know what you're talking about.

WOMAN   Within, Mrs. Radcliffe, you know already.

ANN   Tell me!

WOMAN   You are those women, Mrs. Radcliffe. You are those women.

HORACE   What is that supposed to mean?

ANN   No!

WOMAN   You are ordinary, Mrs. Radcliffe. As ordinary as the grass that grows 'round your well-kept home. Your life, your dreams, those silly stories you've written, all will be forgotten. And you, too. Because you are just another one of those women.

ANN   Why should I believe you?

WOMAN   Because you know it already.

ANN   I have visions! Desires! Ambitions!

WOMAN   And so do all the others. And they go to their graves, just as you will, unfulfilled. Is it not true?

ANN   Please . . . don't say it. Just . . . don't . . . say it. . . .

WOMAN   Why not? Is that not why you came here? To learn the truth?

ANN   If I'm no different from all the rest, then why choose me? Why invite me here, and not the millions of others.

WOMAN   Because you need it more, Mrs. Radcliffe. The others will find out in due time. As they are having their soup, or ringing out the laundry, or throwing wood upon the fire, they shall realize that they are specks of dust to be swept away and never noticed again. And then they shall continue with their soup, and finish the laundry, and poke at the ash beneath the fire, and go on. But you shall not go on, Mrs. Radcliffe. You cannot live without the lie. You shall despair, and you shall die, and you shall never leave this castle.

HORACE   Now see here! You think I'll stand idly by while you force the young lady to stay against her will?

WOMAN   Who is forcing her? I see no chains, no dungeons, no armed guards. She is free to go, if she can.

HORACE   I think it's best if we all go. Come, Mrs. Radcliffe. Our journeys have been in vain.

WOMAN   And yet she stays.

HORACE   Ann! Get out of this place while you still can. There are darker things afoot than I ever imagined.

WOMAN   Far darker, Mr. Walpole. And yet she stays.

HORACE   Flee! There's nothing here for you. It was all a trick. Run for your life!

ANN   Oh, Horace, what life do I have to run to? The endless tedium of days and nights and days again without meaning?

HORACE   This is not the time—

ANN   I'll never be missed. Even William will forget me after a while. And I can't blame him.

HORACE   We have to leave. You could die here.

ANN   We all die, Horace! What difference does it make if I die here or at home in my bed when I'm eighty years old?

HORACE   [*To* WOMAN IN WHITE.]
Monster! You did this to her.

WOMAN   Did what? All I did was tell her a secret. A secret not unlike yours, Mr. Walpole.

HORACE   Then you hold my father's secret, not mine!

WOMAN   Your father's? A secret held by the most wonderful and successful man in all England?

HORACE   Successful, yes. Wonderful, hardly. I know how my father amassed the fortune he passed to me. That's the sand, no doubt, you spoke of, on which I've built my life.

WOMAN   He was Prime Minister.

HORACE   A post which, while rich in honor, did not provide to pay for the style of life in which he wanted to live. So my father sought out . . . other means. Bribes. Graft. Any corruption he could use to mint his precious honor into more precious gold. The Walpole fortune is a sham. And I've built my life on that sham. Why do you think I've tried every day of my life to disgrace that name I've always hated? My father was a villain. He would have stolen food out of the mouths of orphans to feed his ambition. And he probably did. He was a thief and a liar and a scoundrel and a rascal and a rogue and a whore!

WOMAN   And you loved him very much.

HORACE   I just told you he was a bastard!

WOMAN   And you loved that bastard more than you've loved anyone else in your entire life. What have you done in parliament, Mr. Horace Walpole, M.P.?

HORACE   Nothing. I stick to the back benches.

WOMAN   When did you speak?

HORACE   I never speak.

WOMAN   Except . . . to defend your father.

HORACE   Well . . . there was the one time. . . .

WOMAN   He was attacked. And you rose to his defense.

HORACE   The things they said about him . . . they were horrendous! They were slanderous and vile and. . . .

MATTHEW   And?

HORACE   And true. Every word. And worse.

WOMAN   Still, you defended him.

HORACE   Yes. That I admit. But no more!

WOMAN   And when he died, out of all the children of Sir Robert Walpole, you were the one at his bedside.

HORACE   All my life . . . I wanted to hate him.

WOMAN   And you couldn't. He was your father. You could no more hate him than you could hate your own self.

HORACE   Could that . . . could that be true . . . ?

WOMAN   Look into your heart.

HORACE   As he died . . . he cursed my name.

MATTHEW   Ouch. Even I'm not that cruel.

HORACE   Leave him alone! Oh God, God . . . won't someone end my misery?

WOMAN   All in good time. But first, Mr. Lewis, we turn to you.

MATTHEW   Expose all you like, I'm not ashamed of my secret.

WOMAN   No?

MATTHEW   You threaten to reveal my sinful nature to the world. Go ahead! Tell all England of my unnatural perversity and scandalous indecency!

WOMAN   I would, Mr. Lewis, were it not for the fact that much of England already knows.

MATTHEW   Oh, do they? Do they know of my heinous villainy and corruption of satanic proportions?

ANN   I did sort of get that idea, yes.

MATTHEW   But did you know my blackest of crimes? Did you know that within the sacred halls of Christ Church College Oxford, I've committed acts of such perversity and odium to make Sodom and Gomorrah blush with shame!?!

HORACE   Oh, please, Matthew. I knew you were a Molly the moment you walked in the room.

MATTHEW   You mean. . . . Don't you think I hide it?

HORACE   It's nothing to make a fuss over, Matthew. No one cares.

ANN   I care.

MATTHEW   You care when people use the dessert fork for the salad!

WOMAN   You surprise me, Mr. Lewis. You weren't supposed to become this angry until AFTER I revealed your secret.

MATTHEW   What secret is there left?

WOMAN   Do you not remember what you did during the summer of seventeen eighty-nine?

MATTHEW   Seventeen eighty-nine? I was in England the whole time. You can't pin the revolution on me!

WOMAN   It was before then, Mr. Lewis. The thirtieth of June.

MATTHEW   The thirtieth of . . .

WOMAN   You remember that summer, do you not? And the woman on High Street?

MATTHEW   But . . . no. How could you know about that?

WOMAN   I have many eyes and ears. Let it suffice to say my knowledge is not altogether natural.

MATTHEW If what you speak is true, I beg of you, please, by whatever demon you serve, do not reveal me to the world.

WOMAN On the thirtieth of June—

MATTHEW I'll never do it again!

WOMAN In the year of seventeen eighty-nine—

MATTHEW You can have anything you want!

WOMAN Matthew G. Lewis committed—a good deed!

MATTHEW Nooo! Calumnies and lies!

WOMAN You were loitering outside a tobacconist with your friends, when an old beggar woman passed by. After sending her away empty-handed, one of your comrades stretched out his foot and tripped her as she left. The boys began to spit upon her and kick dirt into her face.

MATTHEW And I kicked and spat with the worst of them.

WOMAN That you did. But after leaving the place with your friends, you made an excuse about having to be home. You returned to the woman, still lying there in the dirt, picked her up, wet your handkerchief, wiped clean her face, then you kissed her on the cheek, and apologized for what you had done.

ANN Is that true?

MATTHEW I am Matthew G. Lewis, the most villainous rogue the world has ever known!

WOMAN You may try to scandalize the world all you like, but deep down, in the core of your heart, you could never be intentionally cruel. Deep down, Matthew, you are good.

MATTHEW Good? I've rebelled against that word since the day I was born. I shall not be told what to do or how to act or what to . . . what to feel! I felt nothing for that old woman. Nothing! I felt . . . I am the master of my own compassions. I felt . . . I felt . . . Oh, just kill me now and get it over with!

WOMAN Do you see now? Matthew? Horace? Ann? Do you see now how your whole life is a lie? You are nothing. Your life has meant nothing. Your identity is nothing. You've built your castles on clouds of air, and now they've fallen to earth and crumbled to dust. All you believed in is gone. You are no one, and that is all you'll ever be. Follow me now to your graves, for you have seen the blackest night of hell. You have seen—the truth.

ANN Good madam, I think it is time for me to go back to England. But first, I should thank you.

WOMAN What do you mean?

ANN For better or for worse, I believe you have made me who I am.

WOMAN But you are no one. You are ordinary.

ANN Correction. I was ordinary. But you changed that. With this letter. Would an ordinary woman have lied to her husband, left her native land, traveled over vast distances to a place she never knew nor dreamed to see, all for the tender hope of a dream? That does not strike me as ordinary, madam. I have not been special until this very day. But today I have lived. And I shall not stop living.

WOMAN I invited you here because you are a worm.

ANN Yes. I was. But I stand before you now a woman. You have awoken me, madam, and I will not sleep again. I know that what I do now is no ordinary thing. You have made me special. And for that, I thank you.

WOMAN You are nothing. No more than these two miserable toads.

HORACE No more. But no less, either. And that is something.

ANN Yes, Horace. That it is.

WOMAN Don't tell me you believe her absurdities.

HORACE Perhaps absurdities, madam, are the only things worth believing.

WOMAN Have you forgotten the pain you felt a moment ago?

HORACE No. And I never shall. But I suppose I owe you my thanks as well.

WOMAN Thanks?

HORACE   Yes. It's true. I loved my father. And I've been ashamed of that love all my life. But love is a beautiful thing. Even if the object of that love is not all we should wish it. Love has brought me nothing but pain. But after staring it face to face as you have made me do tonight, I would not part with a jot of it.

WOMAN   And what of you, Mr. Lewis? What do you say to this?

MATTHEW   Good? Me? Is it possible that my heart could feel like any other's? Is it possible my swearing and blasphemy only sought to hide the fact that deep in my soul I was . . . No!!! It's a slander. I refuse to admit it.

WOMAN   I am afraid I have been mistaken. In all three of you. I had thought to have drained you dry. Left you lifeless corpses to crumble into dust. But no matter. I am your host. And you shall not go away empty.

[WOMAN *claps, and* MONK *enters.*]

Brother Ambrosio shall lead you to the refectory. There you shall dine, and when you have had your fill, you shall be free to leave in peace.

HORACE   We thank you, madam. For your hospitality, and for your honesty.

[*The* MONK *motions for them to follow.*]

MATTHEW   Good? You don't think I'm good, do you, Horace?

HORACE   Of course not. Don't be ridiculous.

[*The* MONK *exits, followed by* HORACE *and* MATTHEW. ANN *starts to follow them.*]

WOMAN   Mrs. Radcliffe? Might I first have a word with you alone?

ANN   Of course.

WOMAN   For nearly six hundred years I've been bringing people to the Castle of Falconara, crushing them, destroying them, sapping them of their very life. After a few centuries, the Italians wised up and stopped coming. I went on to the Swiss, the French, the

Spaniards, forcing them to gloom and despair. The Germans were just too easy, so I thought I'd try England. But in those six hundred years, never, not once, have I ever come across a woman of your courage and conviction.

ANN You flatter me, madam. But perhaps only we who most need our dreams are capable of seizing them.

WOMAN Oh, I can show you worlds beyond your dreams, Mrs. Radcliffe. I can give you powers of darkness you cannot possibly comprehend. I can make you live forever.

ANN That's very kind of you, madam, but there really can be too much of a good thing.

WOMAN Not good at all, Mrs. Radcliffe. Not good. Power. I can free you from your trite conventionality, and make you sovereign mistress of the night.

ANN But I don't wish to be anyone's mistress.

WOMAN When I brought you here, I thought to make you despair and drain every last drop of lifeblood from your body. I wished to sink my teeth into that white, plump, tender flesh of yours—

ANN Good madam, please! I'm not that kind of woman.

WOMAN I still long to suck the precious blood from your veins—

ANN Eww!

WOMAN But no longer just that. You shall also suck from mine!

ANN Madam, I am trying to be open-minded about this, and what you like to do with other women is clearly none of my business, but I have to let you know—

WOMAN I am offering you immortality.

ANN That may be what they call it these days, but personally—

[*The* WOMAN IN WHITE *seizes* ANN.]

WOMAN Show me that pale, sweet neck of yours.

ANN Unhand me at once.

WOMAN   I shall make you a Bride of Darkness!

ANN   Help! Help! I'm being attacked by a sapphist!

WOMAN   I can smell the blood already. Enter into the forbidden secrets of the nosferatu!

ANN   I'd really rather not.

WOMAN   Once we drink from each other's veins, the transformation shall be complete. You shall die, and be resurrected to the night!

ANN   Someone save me! I like my internal fluids where they are, thank you very much.

[*Enter* HORACE *with his cane.*]

HORACE   What's going on here?

[*The* WOMAN *releases* ANN, *who runs to* HORACE.]

WOMAN   Mr. Walpole. How kind of you to join us.

ANN   Horace! Thank goodness you're here.

HORACE   Leave us, Ann. I'll deal with this wretch.

ANN   But, Horace, you don't understand. She's a—

[*The* MONK *enters, unseen by* HORACE, *and grabs* ANN. *The* MONK *puts a hand over* ANN'*s mouth and drags her off.*]

WOMAN   That was quite a display earlier.

HORACE   I heard her screams. I know what you are now, and you shall not escape to kill again.

WOMAN   And I know what you are, and why you need me.

HORACE   What do I need with the likes of you?

WOMAN   Love, Horace. Love burns within your breast, searing your every memory. And what do you want? More love. I will give it to you, Horace. Nights of passion and desire.

HORACE   Madam, at my age, I merely long for nights of continence.

WOMAN   Drink from my veins, and all the vigor of youth shall return to you. Your body shall be supple and firm. You'll have the envy and love of every creature you meet. And if they do not love you, you shall bend their wills to love. You shall force them to submit while you suck from their hearts.

HORACE   If that were true . . . it would be tempting indeed.

WOMAN   I will give you that power. You have loved as no man ever has, yet none has loved you, Horace. Not your father. Not Thomas Gray. Not even that dear Mrs. Radcliffe you're so fond of protecting. You are no one to them. Drink of my blood, and you will make them love you.

HORACE   And shall that be love?

WOMAN   The longings you've felt all your life, they shall be requited.

HORACE   Yes. But upon compulsion? That is not love. Prison, rather.

WOMAN   All love is a prison. Until now you have always been the inmate of her walls. I offer you the key.

HORACE   So I can become the jailer?

WOMAN   Yes. The warden of another's heart. There's an ironic justice in that.

HORACE   I no longer long for justice. And even if I did, I know better than to seek it from the likes of you.

WOMAN   Do you even know what I am?

HORACE   I have encountered your soulless, bloodsucking kind before, madam. You forget. I am in parliament.

WOMAN   Then you know there is but one path to power.

HORACE   Yes. But what does it profit a man to gain the world and lose his own soul? Here I stand, madam, Horace Walpole, spurned and rejected by everyone he has ever loved. But I would be no other. I am at peace. And soon you shall be, too.

WOMAN   Do you think you can battle me, old man?

HORACE   Not only battle, but destroy.

WOMAN   With what? Your cane?

HORACE   If it is all I have, then I pray it serves me well.

[HORACE *forcefully swings his cane at the* WOMAN. *She stops it with one hand.*]

WOMAN   Really, Mr. Walpole, you're going to have to do better than that.

[*Holding on to the end of his cane, she uses it to force* HORACE *to the ground.*]

HORACE   Let me go.

WOMAN   Why should I?

HORACE   You promised we were to be let free.

WOMAN   And you trust the promise of one who has no soul?

HORACE   Please!

WOMAN   Beg of me.

HORACE   I beg of you!

WOMAN   Plead with me.

HORACE   I plead!

WOMAN   Kiss the dirt on my shoe.

[HORACE *kisses her shoe.*]

HORACE   Please . . .

WOMAN   Now DIE!

[*The* WOMAN *seizes* HORACE. *She opens her mouth and is about to sink her teeth into his neck when* MATTHEW *enters.*]

MATTHEW   That looks like fun. Can I join in?

WOMAN   Lie there, you pathetic old man. I'll deal with you later.

[*The* WOMAN IN WHITE *takes* MATTHEW'S *arm and they exit.* HORACE *lies sobbing on the floor.*]

HORACE   No . . . no . . . I've . . . no . . .

[ANN *enters.*]

ANN   Horace, thank goodness you're here.

HORACE   Ann . . . ?

ANN   I managed to free myself from the monk. Unfortunately, I used some very harsh language while doing so. I'm not accustomed to saying those sorts of things, but at least he won't tell anyone.

HORACE   Ann . . . I've . . . I've . . .

ANN   Yes? What is it?

HORACE   I've . . . failed.

ANN   That's wonderful news, Horace! But we have more important things to worry about right now.

HORACE   No! You don't understand. The woman . . . our hostess—

ANN   Yes, her . . . untraditional lifestyle choice. I know all about it.

HORACE   I don't think you do. Mrs. Radcliffe . . . have you ever heard legends of the nosferatu? Also known as . . . the vampyre.

ANN   Of course I have, silly. But everyone knows that vampyres don't exist.

HORACE   If only that were true.

ANN   Are you trying to tell me that our hostess—

HORACE   Is an immortal.

ANN   I try not to be judgmental, but—

HORACE   An immortal, Ann! A vampyre! A creature from blackest hell!

ANN   I don't approve of it either, Horace, but don't you think that's going a tad too far?

HORACE   She wants to drink from our veins, and worse yet, to turn us into demons just as foul as she.

ANN   But—

HORACE   A vampyre, Ann. You must believe me.

ANN   This is all nonsense, Horace. I'm sure there's a rational explanation for everything.

HORACE   Rational or not, you understand that she's dangerous?

ANN   Yes.

HORACE   And that we have to get out of here?

ANN Certainly.

HORACE Quickly, then. We have to find Matthew before she has her way with him.

ANN But why would she want Matthew if—Oh! You mean she's a VAMPYRE!

HORACE Yes!

ANN Let's find him, then.

[ANN *and* HORACE *start to go off. The* MONK *enters and blocks their way.*]

HORACE On second thought, Matthew can take care of himself.

ANN The stairs!

HORACE Yes!

[HORACE *and* ANN *run back toward the entrance. The* WOMAN *appears in the doorway and blocks it.*]

WOMAN Going somewhere?

HORACE I hate it when they do that.

WOMAN Mr. Lewis was not nearly so adverse to my proposal as you two were.

ANN What have you done with him?

WOMAN You'll find his body in the next room. But he drank before his death. Brother Ambrosio shall bury him, and tomorrow night he shall join me to fill the world with fear!

HORACE We know who we are now, and we shan't give in to your temptations.

WOMAN I don't expect you to. However, I am still quite hungry.

HORACE Run, Ann!

[ANN *and* HORACE *run away from the* WOMAN. *The* MONK *catches* ANN, *but* HORACE *runs past him.*]

WOMAN You shall find the door in the next chamber locked, Mr. Walpole.

ANN Please don't hurt me.

WOMAN   So you think you're special, Mrs. Radcliffe. We'll soon find out how special you are.

ANN   I take it back—everything I said! Just let me go.

WOMAN   No need to worry, Mrs. Radcliffe. Soon, you need not worry about anything ever again.

[*The* WOMAN *exits after* HORACE.]

ANN   Don't say that! I was wrong. I admit it. I'm not special! I never should have come! I'm no one. . . .

[*The* MONK *forces* ANN *onto the divan and pins her down.*]

WOMAN   [*Offstage.*]
   There's nowhere to run, old man.

HORACE   [*Offstage.*]
   Stand back.

WOMAN   [*Offstage.*]
   Or what? You'll attack me with this twig?

[*The sound of wood snapping in two.*]

ANN   All's lost! Forgive me, William, for ever leaving your side.

[*Half of the broken cane is flung onstage.*]

WOMAN   [*Offstage.*]
   Now, you have nothing.

HORACE   [*Offstage.*]
   Ann! Help!

ANN   I'm no one . . . No one . . .

HORACE   [*Offstage.*]
   Please!

ANN   Oh . . . oh . . . oh, bloody hell! Someone's got to do it!
   [ANN *knees the* MONK *in the groin and throws him to the ground.*]
   Oh, come now. You didn't need that anyway.

HORACE   Ann!

[ANN *grabs the broken cane.*]

ANN Coming, Horace!

[ANN *exits. The* MONK *stumbles offstage.*]

[*Offstage.*] Get away from him, you trollop!

WOMAN [*Offstage.*] AIEEEEEEE!

[ANN *and* HORACE *enter, out of breath.*]

HORACE Ann, thank God!

ANN Get me away from here, Horace. I don't want to ever look at that sight again.

HORACE When she broke my cane, it formed the jagged edge of a wooden stake. How did you know? How did you know the only way to kill a vampyre is a wooden stake through the heart?

ANN She wasn't a vampyre, Horace. A stake through the heart will kill about anyone.

HORACE In any case . . . thank you.

ANN And Matthew? Do you think he's really dead?

HORACE I'm afraid so.

ANN He'll never live to publish his ghastly writings, then.

HORACE No . . . but he may publish them dead.

ANN What do you mean?

HORACE She has already made him a vampyre. Something tells me that Mr. Matthew G. Lewis will rise from his grave to inflict his wretched prose onto the entire world.

ANN Is that possible?

HORACE Not only that, but now he is immortal. He could go on for centuries, faking his own death and changing his name, forcing his horrid tales of the macabre onto generations yet unborn.

ANN That's dreadful.

HORACE   Now, he is but a petty student, but after years of his dark ambitions, someday . . . he could be a King.

ANN   A King who writes bad horror novels?

HORACE   Yes. And I fear readers generations from now will be subjected to the hackneyed plots, half-baked premises, and shoddy characterizations of this . . . King.

ANN   We must do something, then!

HORACE   There's no time. We must away.

[MARY *enters.*]

MARY   Excuse me.

HORACE   Who's there!?!

MARY   I'm dreadfully sorry for having frightened you. Are you the master of this castle?

HORACE   Me? Certainly not.

MARY   I have a letter. It said I was to come to the Castle of Falconara one hour after midnight on the eve of All Hallows, or else all shall be revealed!

ANN   She invited others, then.

MARY   Please don't tell my husband I've come. He thinks I'm visiting a sickly uncle in Bristol.

HORACE   Young lady, I am sorry you have traveled so far in vain, but it is my duty to inform you that you must immediately—

ANN   Have a seat, madam. Your host will be with you shortly.

MARY   Thank you. I'm much obliged.

[MARY *sits on the divan.*]

HORACE   Are you mad!?!

ANN   Shhh!

HORACE   This castle isn't safe. We have to get her out of here.

ANN   Horace, when I came here, I was no one. Now, after the events of tonight, I feel I can do anything in the world.

HORACE   That's fine. But she can't!

ANN   I'll go back to England and . . . I'll write a novel! Not like those silly stories before, but a real novel, of a heroine imprisoned in an Italian castle, where she must learn to overcome the horrors surrounding her and take control of her own destiny. I'll call it *The Mysteries of Falconara*.

HORACE   That's all very well, but—

ANN   I should probably change the location.

HORACE   We can't simply—

ANN   How does Almalfi strike you?

HORACE   Fine, but—

ANN   Udolpho! That's it.

HORACE   Mrs. Radcliffe, please! There is a corpse in this castle that at any moment could be brought back to life. Do you want to subject this woman to that?

ANN   Look at her over there—so meek and humble. Perhaps after a night in this castle, she too will find that she is special—no longer a meek child, but a woman, capable of doing anything she wants. Who knows? Perhaps that meek young thing will go on to write novels of her own.

HORACE   If she lives.

ANN   She has yet to live, Horace. That's just it. And if she never learns to believe in herself, then she never shall.

HORACE   We have to at least warn her.

ANN   She would never believe us anyway. Let's leave this place, Horace, and let come what may.

HORACE   With all we know of this castle? No. I have to say something.

[HORACE *approaches* MARY.]

MARY   Do you know why I've been asked here, sir? I've come quite a ways.

HORACE   That I realize, but I really must . . . I mean, I have to tell you . . . That is to say . . .

ANN   She'll be fine.

[ANN *starts to go, but stops at the door for* HORACE.]

HORACE   Yes, well, um . . .

ANN   Trust me!

HORACE   Madam, I have to say . . . I apologize. What did you say your name was?

MARY   Oh! I didn't. My name's Mary. Mrs. Mary—

ANN   Come on, Horace! Let's go!

[ANN *exits.*]

HORACE   Madam . . . Good luck!

[HORACE *runs off. A crash of thunder. Blackout.*]

• • •

Small Things

Cary Pepper

Cary Pepper

Cary Pepper has had work presented throughout the United States and in Europe. *The Walrus Said* won the Religious Arts Guild Playwriting Competition; *Small Things* won the Robert R. Lehan Playwriting Award and the Tennessee Williams/New Orleans Literary Festival 2006 One-Act Play Contest; and *The Maltese Frenchman* was a finalist for the National Play Award. He is represented in print by *The Walrus Said* (Aran Press), *Audition Monologues for Student Actors II* (Meriwether Publishing), and *Scenes and Monologs from the Best New International Plays* (Meriwether Publishing). Cary is a member of the Dramatists Guild and a founding member of the San Francisco Bay Area playwrights group ThroughLine.

characters

HOYT, 50s. Tall. Deliberate. Tired.

DREW, 19. Clean-cut, well scrubbed. Innocent, sincere. Gives the impression of being almost fragile.

setting

HOYT's apartment.

• • •

[*Stage right, a couch, in front of which is a coffee table. Stage left, an easy chair. HOYT sits on the couch, cleaning a revolver. The doorbell rings. HOYT glances at the door, but doesn't move. The bell rings again. HOYT thinks . . . then tucks the pistol under a couch cushion, goes to the door, and opens it. In the doorway is DREW, who has started to walk away. When HOYT opens the door, he stops. DREW is clean-cut and well scrubbed. He wears a suit and tie, neither of which look natural on him. He carries a briefcase, which also seems out of place: it should be carried by an accountant or a businessman twice his age.*]

DREW   Oh. I didn't think anyone was home.

HOYT   No one is.

DREW   Uh, I represent the Assembly of Hubristic Evangelicals. We . . .

HOYT   The what?

DREW   The Assembly of Hubristic Evangelicals. Have you experienced the one true god?

HOYT   Not lately.

DREW   Well, if you'll give me just a few minutes, I'll tell you how you can experience the one true god.

HOYT   Right now?

DREW   There's no more perfect time to experience the one true god than the moment he comes to you.

HOYT   *Has* he come to me?

DREW He will, if you open yourself to his love and his power.

HOYT Right now?

DREW There's no more perfect time to experience the one true god than the moment he comes to you. May I counsel with you?

HOYT Now?

DREW There's no more perfect time to . . .

HOYT Experience the one true god. Got it. To tell you the truth . . .

DREW There is only one truth. That of the one true god.

[HOYT *gazes at* DREW.]

DREW That truth will save you.

     [HOYT*'s gaze becomes a stare.*]

     And when . . . you . . . experience . . .

     [*Something in* HOYT*'s stare causes to* DREW *to hesitate . . .*]

     this . . . experience . . .

     [*Then falter . . .*]

     it . . . strikes . . . you . . . dumb . . .

     [*Then stop.*]

     . . . with awe.

[HOYT *continues to stare. . . .* DREW *stands there . . . dumbstruck with awe. . . . Long pause.*]

HOYT Oh, this . . . is . . . perfect.

DREW Well . . . Sorry to have . . .

[*He turns to go.*]

HOYT Come in.

DREW What?

HOYT Come in.

DREW Really?

HOYT Yes. I want to be struck dumb with awe.

[HOYT *steps back.* DREW *enters uncertainly.*]

DREW   Thank you. For allowing me to . . .

HOYT   Sit down.

     [DREW *starts for the couch.*]

     Not there.

DREW   Sorry.

[HOYT *motions toward the chair.*]

HOYT   Here. Sit there.

     [DREW *sits in the chair.* HOYT *sits on the couch. His hand automatically goes to the cushion, on top of where he put the pistol.* DREW *seems to be thrown, uncertain of himself.*]

     [*Pause.*]

     So . . . Strike me.

DREW   Excuse me?

HOYT   Strike me dumb with awe.

DREW   Oh . . . There is only one true god.

HOYT   Is there?

DREW   Yes. And he . . .

HOYT   And you know who he is.

DREW   Yes. He's the . . .

HOYT   When you say you know who he is . . . You mean you, personally? Or the entire Assembly of Hubristic Evangelicals?

DREW   Oh, yes. All of us. For we have . . .

HOYT   How old are you?

DREW   Nineteen. Well, I'll *be* nineteen in two days.

HOYT   Aren't you a little young for this?

DREW   We all do it. Everyone in the assembly does a year of missionary work when they turn eighteen.

HOYT   You're nineteen.

DREW   Yes.

HOYT   So . . . you're . . . extra evangelical?

DREW   I'm finishing my year of missionary service. Today's my last day.

HOYT   And how does that make you feel?

DREW   Relieved! Uh . . . To experience the one true god . . .

HOYT   What's his name?

DREW   Who?

HOYT   The one true god.

DREW   His names are many. His spirit is omnipresent. . . . His power is omnipotent. . . . His love is . . .

HOYT   But what do you call him?

DREW   Who?

HOYT   The one true god.

DREW   . . . God.

HOYT   That's it? God?

DREW   Those who know the one true god need no other name. His spirit and power dwell within us. His essence flows through us like an endless stream of eternal sustenance. His glory . . .

HOYT   But he has no name.

DREW   Who?

HOYT   God.

DREW   Once you experience the one true god, he is within you, and you within him. Only the uninitiated need an earthly name for him. For they have not felt his power and glory.

HOYT   And you want to . . . initiate me?

DREW   Only the Initiated can experience the one true god.

HOYT   So, the rest of us can't?

DREW   Until you're Initiated, you have no true concept of god.

HOYT   What about *my* religion?

DREW   There is only one true faith.

HOYT   Yours.

DREW   Only the Initiated know the true path. Only the Initiated see the true light.

HOYT   So the rest of us are just stumbling around in darkness.

DREW   Only the Initiated experience the true sublimity of knowing the one true god.

HOYT   OK. How do we do this?

DREW   What?

HOYT   How do I get to see the true light?

DREW   You become Initiated.

HOYT   Right. How do I do that?

DREW   What?

HOYT   Get initiated.

DREW   You join the Assembly of Hubristic Evangelicals.

HOYT   How do I do *that*?

DREW   What?

HOYT   Join the club. Become a hubristic evangelical. I want to see the true light. I want to experience the one true god.

DREW   Oh . . . I have some pamphlets here. . . . These explain, pretty much . . .

[DREW *takes pamphlets out of his briefcase and puts them on the table.* HOYT *picks up the pamphlets and reads their titles.*]

HOYT   "The One True Path to the One True God" . . . "The One True God and You" . . . "Being Hubristic" . . . "Be God and Be Good" . . .

DREW   [*Handing over another pamphlet.*]
And this pamphlet will tell you about our bible . . . The One True Book. We combined the Old and New Testaments, took out the parts that are wrong, and revealed the one true message of the one true god. You'll get your own bible when you're Initiated.

HOYT   Yeah, let's do that.

DREW   What?

HOYT   Get initiated.

DREW   Well, if you come to a meeting, you can speak to a . . .

HOYT   No, I want to do it now.

DREW   What?

HOYT   Get initiated. I want you to initiate me.

DREW   Now?

HOYT   There's no more perfect time.

DREW   Here?

HOYT   There's no more perfect place.

DREW   No! I can't do that.

HOYT   Why not?

DREW   Uh . . . I only came to give you some literature.

HOYT   That's it?

DREW   Yeah. That's all we do in our missionary work.

HOYT   Well, I want more.

DREW   Well, come to a meeting.

HOYT   I don't want to wait for a meeting. I want to be initiated now. And I want you to do it.

DREW   I've never done that!

HOYT   No one's ever asked you to?

DREW   No one's ever let me in!

HOYT   You've been doing this for a year and no one's let you in?

DREW   No!

HOYT   That must be frustrating.

DREW   It totally sucks!

HOYT Well, you've hit the jackpot this time. You're going all the way, son. Initiate me.

DREW Uh . . . Why don't you read the pamphlets. And then you can . . .

HOYT I'll read the pamphlets later. Just go ahead and do . . . whatever needs to be done.

DREW I can't.

HOYT Why not?

DREW Um . . . uh . . . I'm not an elder.

HOYT But you've been initiated, right?

DREW Yeah. When I was, like, seven.

HOYT OK. Do to me, what they did to you.

DREW I can't!

HOYT Why not? What'd they *do* to you?

DREW They . . . had me stand before the Assembly . . . and . . . they . . . gestured over me . . . and they . . . questioned me . . . and I answered rightly . . . and they . . . gestured over me some more.

HOYT That's it?

DREW That was it.

HOYT Did you feel initiated?

DREW Yeah.

HOYT Did you feel different?

DREW Yeah! I was Initiated!

HOYT Did you know the one true path?

DREW I was Initiated!

HOYT Did you know the one true god?

DREW We all did! We were all Initiated!

HOYT Did you see the true light?

DREW   Well . . . no. They said that would come later. All the older people said they saw it.

HOYT   What did you feel?

DREW   When?

HOYT   When you were initiated.

DREW   Feel? I'd been initiated!

HOYT   Did you feel happy?

DREW   Yeah!

HOYT   Did you feel special?

DREW   YEAH!

HOYT   Did you feel at peace?

DREW   I was seven.

HOYT   Right. OK . . . So. Just do to me what they did to you.

DREW   I can't.

HOYT   Why not?

DREW   I shouldn't.

HOYT   Why not?

DREW   It wouldn't be right.

HOYT   Why not?

DREW   I'd rather not say.

HOYT   I won't tell anyone.

DREW   No. I'd rather not.

HOYT   C'mon. It's just you and me. And I'm about to become one of you. You've done your job well. You've got a convert. Your first one. They'll love you for this.

DREW   They'll hate me.

HOYT   No they won't.

DREW They already hate me.

HOYT Would that be the one true hate?

DREW Might as well be.

HOYT Do they believe in hate?

DREW Not officially.

HOYT Well, they sound like everyone else on that one. So . . . Convert me! Initiate me!

DREW It wouldn't be right.

HOYT [*He will not be denied.*]
Why?

DREW Because I'm leaving the Assembly.

HOYT Something you haven't mentioned?

DREW Could I . . . have a glass of water? Or something?

HOYT Sure. Would you prefer water? Or something?

DREW No . . . water will be fine, thanks.
[HOYT *goes into the kitchen.* DREW *sits looking at the floor, deflated.* HOYT *returns with a glass of water and gives it to* DREW.]
Thanks.

[*He gulps down all the water.*]

HOYT We're a little thirsty.

DREW I guess.

HOYT Want some more?

DREW No, thanks.

HOYT So . . . why are you leaving?

DREW I'd rather not say.

HOYT It's a little late for that.

DREW What do you mean?

HOYT You started this.

DREW   What?

HOYT   The forced intimacy.

DREW   I don't know what you're . . .

HOYT   You ring my bell . . . you interrupt what I'm doing . . . you come into my house . . . and you immediately question my religious beliefs. Then you challenge my beliefs . . . invalidate them . . . and try to impose your beliefs on me.

DREW   I . . . I never thought of it that way.

HOYT   What did you think you were doing?

DREW   Spreading the one true word.

HOYT   Why do you want to do *that*?

DREW   They tell us to.

HOYT   So you just go out and do it?

DREW   We all do.

HOYT   What makes you think I *want* to hear about your religion?

DREW   It's the one true faith.

HOYT   For *you*. Maybe I've got my own faith.

DREW   Ours is the one true religion.

HOYT   How do you know mine isn't the one true religion?

DREW   There can be only one true religion.

HOYT   Well, maybe it's mine!

DREW   It can't be.

HOYT   Why not?

DREW   Because it's mine.

HOYT   How do you know that?

DREW   The one true book tells us it is.

HOYT   Who wrote this book?

DREW   The one true prophet.

HOYT   This is one hot belief system, huh?

DREW   It's the one true religion.

HOYT   So why are you quitting?

DREW   I'd rather not say.

HOYT   And I say you owe it to me.

DREW   I do? Why?

HOYT   Because you've not only imposed all this on me, but you've caught me at a very . . . vulnerable time. I was doing fine before you walked in here. No, I wasn't doing fine at all. In fact you caught me a real low point. And you ring my bell, and I open my door, and what you do you offer me? Salvation! And what did that do? It made me hopeful. By doing that, you interfered with the natural order of my misery. In that misery, I'd found answers. But then there you were, and suddenly there were other answers. That took me out of my place and brought me to another. Yours. Now you're telling me this place is a sham. But where does that leave me? Disturbed, desperate, and in despair . . . which I was before. But now it's your fault. So I tell you I want to know . . . I *need* to know . . . what's wrong with your one true religion? And it's important that you tell me. More important than you know. And . . . I think you want to.
[*He waits. . . . DREW is silent. . . .*]
Why are you leaving the assembly?

DREW   I'm gay.

HOYT   So?

DREW   So . . . in their eyes . . . I'm an abomination.

HOYT   The assembly you've given a year of your life to . . . the religion you've given your heart and soul to . . . considers you an abomination.

DREW   Yes.

HOYT Because you're gay.

DREW Yes.

HOYT Bummer.

[*Pause.*]

DREW Can I use your bathroom?

HOYT Down the hall.

> [DREW *leaves.* HOYT *retrieves the pistol from under the cushion and thoughtfully rubs it with a cloth. The sound of* DREW *returning . . .* HOYT *puts the pistol back under the cushion.*]

> So . . . the one true faith for all humankind . . . hates some people. Because *they* don't love the people they're supposed to.

DREW I guess you could put it that way.

HOYT Why? A sin of Onan thing? A don't-disturb-the-natural-order thing? Or are you just a generic abomination?

DREW Uh . . . the last one, I think.

HOYT And how do they know this?

DREW It's in the one true book.

HOYT How can you be part of this thing?

DREW I can't. That's why I'm quitting.

HOYT Then how can you go out there and ask other people to be part of it?

DREW It's what we're brought up to do. You're taught to *want* to do it. You look forward to it. You don't even think about it.

HOYT So what happened?

DREW I started thinking about it. . . . I started *thinking*!
  All these years, I'm getting the message, this is the one true religion. But I'm also getting another message: I'm no good. At first I accept that, because I think maybe I *am* no good. Like, I've got . . . this affliction . . . or this . . . bad gene . . . or a disease. Maybe it's a test. And I'm always being told that if you have

enough faith, any test can be met. So if you're sinful ... or you have sinful thoughts ... or do bad things ... you have to have more faith ... pray harder ... go to more meetings ... work harder for the Assembly ... and it'll be OK. But the older I get, I begin to realize ... I'm not hurting anybody. I don't kill. I don't steal. I don't wish anyone evil. I don't lie. Except about one thing, and I only do *that* because of them. But, except for that, as far as I can tell, I don't sin at all. But ... according to them, I'm bad. And I begin to think, "What *is* wrong with me?" And I realize ... nothing. So why do they say I'm bad? I begin to ask more questions. ... And they tell me, have more faith. It's in the one true book. It's the will of the one true god. But those answers don't work for me any more. And I'm just beginning to *really* question everything, when it's time to begin my year of mission work.

HOYT   So off you went?

DREW   I was still working things out. And also, I'd made a commitment to do it. It felt wrong not to honor my commitment.

HOYT   So, on a scale of one to ten, ten being the worst, where was the missionary work?

DREW   Twenty-seven! They tell you you're doing something important. Spreading the one true word. Bringing people to the one true god. ... So why was it that every time someone opened the door, as soon as they realized why I was there, what I wanted, there was That Look on their face? They tell you it's because people don't know how much they need help. Everyone's walking around in darkness, unable to see the one true light, so when you come to the door, they think you're just another one of those other groups that does missionary work. And they react that way out of their own ignorance. So it's all the more important that you keep doing it, because people really need to hear about the one true faith.

So, OK ... that makes sense. But not for very long. Because you keep seeing That Look. And *no one* wants to hear what you have to say. And everyone is always *doing something* when you ring the bell. And I begin to think ... is this really helping anyone? Or is it just bothering people?

Six months into it, I decide it's just bothering people. I mean, if people really needed help . . . wouldn't they be out *getting* it? Wouldn't they be somewhere, talking to someone, instead of sitting around the house, as if they were hoping someone would ring the bell and save them? Or, if they are home, maybe they're on the phone, talking to someone who can help them. And I come along and interrupt them! So I'm *stopping* them from getting help! So the whole thing just isn't working for me at all. It just doesn't mean anything.

Unless . . . Unless you happen to ring someone's bell just when they're in the middle of a crisis. And you happen to be the exact person they need, because what you have to say, *helps* them. If *that* happens . . . If you come along just at the right moment, and you make a difference in someone's life . . . *then* it means something.

HOYT Well, you've hit the jackpot.

DREW And for a while *that* works. It keeps me going. Until I realize that I'm *terrified* it *might happen*. Because . . . I'm eighteen! I don't know anything! How can *I* help anyone?! "But you're not supposed to know," I tell myself. . . . It's the one true religion that has the answers. The one true god, and his one true book. So just tell them about that, and it'll be OK.

Except, according to Them . . . that religion . . . that book . . . I'm no good. So *I'm* their messenger, spreading the one true word, but, according to that word, I'm . . . what? . . . The one true evil? And everything starts to fall apart. I'm walking around in a daze. *I'm* the one who needs help, and even *I'm* not turning to the one true faith!

So now when I ring bells, I'm glad no one's home. And I'm hoping that anyone who is, *won't* let me in. And somehow, I get through my year.

Today's my last day of service. . . . It ends at five o'clock. With any luck, yours is the last bell I have to ring. And what do you mean I've hit the jackpot?

HOYT You know that crisis you were talking about?

DREW   Yeah?

HOYT   I'm having it.

DREW   What . . . kind . . . of . . . crisis?

HOYT   What's the difference? Call it a crisis of faith . . . sanity . . . finances . . . stability. . . . Doesn't matter. Not any more. You rang the bell. I opened the door. You said you had answers. I let you in.

DREW   But I don't have any answers.

HOYT   Afraid you're going to have to do better than that, son.

DREW   But I can't help you.

HOYT   Well, then, we're both in a pickle.

[*He reaches under the cushion and takes out the revolver.*]

DREW   Oh . . . shit . . . !

[HOYT *calmly resumes cleaning the gun.*]
Is that . . . loaded?

HOYT   Clean a loaded gun? I considered it. . . . But it's too chancy. You've got to be more precise than that for something like this.

DREW   Something like . . . what?

HOYT   Don't go stupid on me, son.

DREW   You're saying you're going to use that . . . on yourself? But why . . .

HOYT   Like I said . . .

DREW   . . . clean it first? I mean, why bother?

HOYT   You do something, do it right. Neat. Clean. And . . . I figured it'd be a . . . cooling-off period. See what happens between the time I start cleaning it and when I finish. See if anything came along to make me change my mind. And you know what happened? You rang the bell.

DREW   Yeah, but that's because no one else in the building was home. Or maybe they were, but they didn't answer. I mean, if anyone else answered the door, or maybe even let me in, I wouldn't be here now.

HOYT   But you are.

DREW   But that doesn't mean what you think it does. It doesn't mean anything.

HOYT   You said you had the answer.

DREW   But I don't!

HOYT   The one true answer.

DREW   There is no one true answer!!

HOYT   Then we're both in trouble.

DREW   *We?* You said you were going to . . .

HOYT   I've got no life. . . . You've got no religion.

DREW   So you're not gonna . . .

HOYT   Sure I am. There's a bullet here with my name on it.

DREW   I mean . . . me.

HOYT   Why would I do that?

DREW   People do all sorts of crazy things.

HOYT   Like ring doorbells of people they don't know?

DREW   You . . . seem so calm for someone who's about to . . . do that.

HOYT   How do you want me to be?

DREW   I don't know.

HOYT   Should I shout? Jump up and down? Wave my arms about? Say crazy things?

DREW   I don't know, but . . .

HOYT   [*Studying the gun.*]
I never was much of a screamer. Even when I got hurt as a kid. I never cried. Just wondered why the world hurt me, and marveled at how quickly things can change so much.

DREW   But this is so beyond *that.*

HOYT Maybe not as much as you think. And don't mistake calmness for lack of resolve. I am going to do this.

DREW Why? What happened, that you think this is the answer?

HOYT Oh . . . everything.

DREW Like . . . what?

HOYT You really wanna know?

DREW If you want to tell me. And if you don't . . .

HOYT Kind of hoping I do, terrified I will?

DREW No. Well, yeah, I guess.

HOYT Relax, son. I'm not gonna. You're off the hook.

DREW No . . . Y'know what? I asked. I really do want to know.

[*Pause.*]

HOYT Like I said . . . everything. Lost my job . . . lost all my money. . . . I'm not eligible for unemployment . . . can't pay my rent. . . . I'm gonna lose my apartment at the end of the month. . . . Got nowhere to go. Nowhere to live. No one to live with . . . and no will to keep going. I guess I'm just real, real, real, real tired. So . . . fuck it.

DREW That's it? That's why you're going to kill yourself?? Well, that's pretty stupid!

HOYT Watch the insults, son. I've got a gun here.

DREW No, I mean, really. You can get a job. Some job, somewhere. You can get another place to live. You can start over. I mean, out of all the reasons to kill yourself . . . that's . . . really lame!

HOYT Shows you how tired I am.

DREW Well, you know what? That sucks!

HOYT Yeah, it's a sin.

DREW It's . . . it's lazy! That's what it is!

HOYT Lazy? Look at how much effort I'm putting into this.

DREW   No, you stop putting in any effort at all! You're just quitting!

HOYT   I'm a bad person.

DREW   And . . . it *is* a sin.

HOYT   Well, maybe I need more religion. I asked for yours. You didn't give it to me.

DREW   Wait. . . . If I Initiate you . . . will that change your mind?

HOYT   You said you can't.

DREW   Well, what if I did?

HOYT   But you can't.

DREW   But what if I *did*!? Would that make a difference?

[*Pause.*]

HOYT   But you can't.

DREW   . . . Why *not*?

HOYT   You're not an elder.

DREW   Yeah, but I'm leaving, so there's an opening. You can take my place.

HOYT   Yeah . . . I've seen how much good it's done you.

DREW   Maybe it'll be better for you.

HOYT   The religion that says hate people just because of who they are?

DREW   The religion that says no matter how bad things get, there's always hope.

HOYT   Not good enough. And I don't think I like this religion.

DREW   Well, neither do I! But *all* the religions say that. That's what religion's for! To give us hope!

HOYT   And sometimes it just doesn't. Come to think of it, I've never been all that religious.

DREW   So why'd you let me in?

HOYT   You rang the bell, said you had the answer.

DREW No! I ring your bell, I tell you I have the one true word . . . someone like you slams the door in my face in three seconds.

HOYT Now how do you know that?

DREW You had That Look. As soon as I opened my mouth. I even started to walk away. You called me back and said to come in. Why'd you do that? I say it was so I could talk you out of it.

HOYT I say you're wrong.

DREW I say you're lying. You wanted to be talked out of it. You don't really want to do this.

[*Pause.*]

HOYT Know why I let you in? To talk me *into* it. To show me it really was the way to go.

DREW What?

HOYT Here I am . . . getting ready to stop it all. And . . .

DREW And cleaning your gun to see if anything would happen that *would* stop it!

HOYT . . . And the doorbell rings. And there you are. Someone offering religion. And I think, well, isn't this perfect. Isn't this a sign? Let's see what this one's got to say. And when he says absolutely nothing that makes any difference . . . *That's* the sign. There really is no reason *not* to do this. That's what I was thinking. That's why I let you in.

DREW And . . . I haven't given you a reason . . . have I?

HOYT You're kidding, right?

DREW Well . . . how about, maybe you just shouldn't do it.

HOYT Maybe?

DREW OK, you just shouldn't do it.

HOYT Is that your religion talking?

DREW No, it's me talking. It's got nothing to do with religion. I just think you shouldn't do it.

[*Pause.*]

HOYT   You're a good kid. But this isn't working.

> [*He gives the gun a last wipe, reaches under the table, and comes up with a box of bullets.*]

> And I think it's about that time.

[*He loads the gun, slowly—almost thoughtfully—putting each bullet into the cylinder. DREW watches his every move. After three bullets, HOYT spins the cylinder and stops.*]

DREW   So . . . you're saying . . . there's nothing I can say . . . to make you change your mind.

HOYT   I think we've established that.

[HOYT *resumes slowly loading the gun.* DREW *watches. . . . Finally, the gun is loaded.* HOYT *closes the cylinder and spins it.*]

DREW   Y'know what? You're right.

HOYT   I know.

DREW   Yeah . . . OK. If that's what you need to do, go ahead.

[HOYT *gazes at* DREW.]

HOYT   Reverse psychology? You stop trying to talk me out of it, I'll decide not to?

DREW   Huh? Oh . . . no. I mean it. I have been trying to talk you out of it. But it's your right. And who am I to talk you out of something you need so badly? You're even willing to kill for it. I mean, we don't even know each other, and I'm trying to stop you. But if this is what you need to do . . . It's who you are. . . . And saying don't do it, I'm trying to stop you from being who you are. Which is exactly what they're doing to me. So . . . if this *really* is what you need . . . I should just shut the fuck up.

HOYT   I guess you should.

DREW   Just one more thing?

HOYT   Which would be what?

DREW   . . . Wait until I'm gone. Please. I don't want to . . .

HOYT   When are you going?

DREW   . . . I guess I should go now?

HOYT   I guess you should.

[*Pause.* DREW *stands and heads for the door.* HOYT *sits back on the couch and studies the gun.* DREW *gets to the door, stops, turns . . .*]

DREW   I did it. Tried it . . . a couple of years ago, it got so terrible. . . . I knew who I was. . . . And They were telling me that was bad. And I believed them. . . . I couldn't live with it any more. I decided to use pills, and I lay down with a bottle, and put it on my chest and stared at it. And nothing happened. No one rang the bell. So I took the pills. And I'm lying there, waiting for them to kick in. . . . And . . . a song gets into my head. And I can't get it out. I can't stop thinking this song. And it's got words, and sometimes just the music's in my head, and sometimes it's the words, too. And it's . . . the theme song from *The Beverly Hillbillies*.

And no matter what I do, what else I think of . . . it won't go away! And I start thinking . . . How fucking stupid is this? My last fully conscious moments, and this is the best I can do? *What—is— wrong—with—me?*

At first, that did it. I mean, talk about signs. If *this* is the best you can do with your last moments . . . Absolutely, pull the trigger, kick the chair out from under you, pour the bottle down your throat. But then I start to laugh. . . . And . . . I don't know exactly what happened next. . . . I lost consciousness or something. But not from the pills. But next thing I know, I'm laughing. I mean, really, really, really laughing. Like, when you're laughing with everything you've got. . . . You're laughing so much it hurts. . . . It completely, totally, fills you. You *are* laughter.

And . . . I didn't want to die any more.

And . . . that's when the pills kicked in.

I started to go all hazy, and I knew that if I didn't get off the bed, soon, it'd be too late. But . . . I didn't want to die any more.

[*Pause.*]

HOYT   Nice story.

DREW   Yeah ... Well ...

[*He turns to go.*]

HOYT   Hey, kid.

[*He stops, turns.*]

DREW   Yeah?

HOYT   Congratulations.

DREW   Why?

HOYT   You're out of the assembly.

DREW   I am?

HOYT   You said today was your last day. If you meant it ...

DREW   I did. I really did!

HOYT   Well ... it's 5:30. You've been out for half an hour.

DREW   Yeah.

HOYT   You're a free man.

DREW   [*Softly.*]
      Yeah!

      [HOYT *spins the cylinder of the gun ... looks at it ... then opens the cylinder and shakes the bullets out.*]
      You're ... not ... gonna ...

HOYT   No.

DREW   Why not?

HOYT   Now you want me to justify *not* doing it?

DREW   No! Sorry. I was just curious. Forget it. I'm sorry. That was stupid. I don't know what I was thinking.

HOYT   It was something you said.

DREW   No way!

HOYT Don't argue with me. I still have the gun.

DREW But all that one true faith crap . . .

HOYT It wasn't crap.

DREW You're saying it *means* something?

HOYT Oh, geez, of course not! I'm saying it wasn't one-true-anything crap. You weren't in it when you said it.

DREW So what'd I say?

HOYT I think I'd like to keep that for myself.

DREW You're not gonna tell me?

HOYT Son . . . did you do all that for me, or for you?

DREW For you.

HOYT Then your job's done. Walk away.

DREW Yeah . . . OK.

[*He turns. . . .*]

HOYT No, wait a minute. You're entitled to know.

DREW [*Turns back.*]
OK.

HOYT You lying there, full of pills . . . with the theme song from *The Beverly Hillbillies* stuck in your head.

[*He laughs.*]

DREW [*Singing.*]
Come and listen to a story 'bout a man name Jed,
A poor mountaineer, barely kept his family fed,
Then one day he was shootin' at some food . . .

HOYT Son—don't sing that song.

DREW Sorry. But . . . what? You were afraid it would happen to you?

HOYT No, that wasn't it.

DREW   Then . . . ?

HOYT   It was, you told me the story. You weren't doing it for them. . . . You weren't doing it for you. I don't think you were even doing it for me. You weren't *doing* anything. You were just telling a story. You were just *with* me.

DREW   Someone else could have . . .

HOYT   Someone else? A priest? A rabbi? A shrink? They would have been doing a job. And spouting doctrine. You were just there. You were just . . . you.

DREW   Yeah . . . the walking freak show.

HOYT   Hey . . . I had a gun here, and you didn't run away. Most people's first words would've been, "Don't shoot me." Yours were, "Are you gonna use that on yourself?"

DREW   Actually, I think they were, "Is that loaded?"

HOYT   Yeah, but you weren't thinking about saving your ass.

DREW   Uh, yeah . . . I was.

HOYT   OK, of course you were. But once you saw you were safe, you didn't haul ass first chance you had. You stayed. You grappled. You tried to help.

DREW   I'm not . . .

HOYT   Son, you're not an abomination. Get used to it.

[*Pause.*]

DREW   . . . S o you're saying now it's not so bad?

HOYT   Oh, it's just as *bad*. But now it's . . . open-ended. Not a closed box with no way out. That what I needed to know. I'm not even sure why it mattered, but it did.

DREW   All I did was tell you a story.

HOYT   Sometimes that's all it takes.

DREW   That's not what They'd say.

HOYT   Son, you're not one of 'em any more. Get used to it.

DREW   But, just a story?

HOYT   It's the small things. For some people it's big things, but what I needed right then was something small.

DREW   I don't think I know what you're talking about.

HOYT   For you, it was a song. For me, it was someone telling a story. Sometimes it *is* doctrine. Could be a look on someone's face . . . graffiti in a bathroom . . . a book . . . a painting. A pizza. Doesn't matter what it is, as long as it gets you to the next moment.

DREW   You sound like *you* have the answer.

HOYT   I do. The one true answer.

DREW   What?

HOYT   Now, how stupid was *that*?

DREW   But you just said that *was* the answer.

HOYT   For me. For this moment. And you know what?

DREW   What?

HOYT   The moment's gone. You gonna be all right?

DREW   Am *I* gonna be all right? You're the one with gun! You're the one who's so tired!

HOYT   You're the one who's about to walk away from the last eighteen years of your life.

DREW   I've got a feeling the next eighteen years are going to be a lot better than the last eighteen! But you still have no job, no money.

HOYT   I've still got choices. I picked this one to get out of making other decisions I didn't want to make. Now that I've given this up, I think I can live with some of those others. I'll be all right.

DREW   So . . . I . . . did it.

HOYT   What?

DREW   Saved someone.

HOYT   Yeah. You. Not them . . . Not the one true religion. You.

DREW   [*Smiles.*]
Yeah . . . me.

• • •

Love on
the B-Line

Adam Kraar

Adam Kraar

Adam Kraar's plays include *New World Rhapsody* (Manhattan Theatre Club commission); *The Spirit House* (premiered at Performance Network of Ann Arbor); *The Abandoned El* (Illinois Theatre Center); *The Lost Cities of Asher* (Finalist, 2005 O'Neill Playwrights Conference); and *Freedom High* (Handel Playwright Fellowship winner). Adam's plays have been produced and developed in New York by Ensemble Studio Theatre, Primary Stages, NY Stage and Film, NY Shakespeare Festival, Cherry Lane Theatre, The Lark, Urban Stages, Ryan Repertory Company at the Harry Warren Theatre, Queens Theatre in the Park, and Theatreworks USA; and regionally at Geva Theatre, New Jersey Rep, NY State Theatre Institute, Bloomington Playwrights Project, and others.

Awards/fellowships: Sewanee Writers' Conference, Southeastern Theatre Conference, Inge Center for the Arts, and the Millay Colony. Plays published by: Dramatic Publishing, Smith & Kraus, and Applause Books. Adam grew up in India, Thailand, Singapore, and the US, earned an MFA from Columbia University, and lives in Brooklyn with his wife, Karen.

characters

MARIE, 28
ROBBIE, 28

place

An elevated subway station in Brooklyn

time

The present. Late summer.

• • •

[*A deserted, elevated train station. Enter* MARIE, *28, and* ROBBIE, *28.*]

ROBBIE   Here we are again. My home away from home.

MARIE   Look, over the water tower: Mars!

[*Pause.*]

Robbie.

ROBBIE   What?

MARIE   [*Kindly.*]

When the train comes, you stay.

ROBBIE   It's 2 a.m. You think I'm going to let you go home alone?

MARIE   You're such a gentleman. And you're very sweet. Your neck drives me crazy.

[MARIE *starts to kiss* ROBBIE's *neck.*]

ROBBIE   . . . Let me be.

MARIE   [*Gently.*]

Don't be like that.

ROBBIE   It's just . . . I mean . . . This . . . situation—

MARIE   [*For the fourth time tonight.*]

I can't stay over your house.

ROBBIE Why not?

MARIE I told you.

ROBBIE Why can't your father feed the cat?

MARIE Because he only eats if I feed him.
[ROBBIE *shakes his head in disbelief.*]
Hey. Don't you love that breeze?

ROBBIE It smells up here.

MARIE You didn't think it smelled when you wrote me that poem.

ROBBIE That was in April. Over a hundred subway rides ago.

MARIE So you don't think I'm the brightest star in Brooklyn anymore?

ROBBIE I do! I just—

MARIE You once loved riding the train with me. I have it in writing.
[MARIE *crosses to an advertising poster on which* ROBBIE *had once written her a poem.*]
See?
[*She reads the poem.*]
"When I ride with you, I'm not riding through Brooklyn
I'm on an open-air streetcar, gliding past the palazzi of Sicily
With the brightest star of the Mediterranean Sea: Marie."

ROBBIE You are, but—

MARIE And when the lights went out between 36th Street and Pacific?
Was that so bad?

ROBBIE It was great.
[MARIE *kisses him passionately.* ROBBIE *responds for a couple of moments, but then:*]
I just don't understand how one night Fluffball can't skip dinner.
He's not a thin cat.

MARIE He depends on me.

ROBBIE I do too.

MARIE You do?

ROBBIE Yes!

[*Pause.*]

MARIE [*Changing the subject.*]

I remember taking this line out to Coney Island, when I was a kid, and when the train came out the tunnel, you could look right inside the windows of people's houses. I felt like we'd come up out of the ground into another planet. My brothers would open the windows of the train, and you could smell every kitchen and every parlor in South Brooklyn. Like, garlic and hot sugar . . . dough, Old Spice . . .

ROBBIE How old were you?

MARIE It was before my mother passed, so I musta been four. The ride seemed to go on for days.

ROBBIE I know what that's like. . . . That ride home, after dropping you off. Seems to go on forever. There's no one on the train, and I start to think there's no motorman, no conductor, no stops. The clacking gets louder and louder. I try to remember the smell of your hair, of your shoulder. But it seems like a dream. Like a foolish dream.

MARIE Aw, Robbie.

ROBBIE Stay.

MARIE Aww.

ROBBIE Stay.

MARIE I wanna stay . . .

ROBBIE Then?

MARIE I can't.

ROBBIE I don't believe it's 'cause of your cat.

MARIE Oh?

ROBBIE There's obviously some issue we're not dealing with. Your father doesn't like me. He gave your brothers this look, when I was talking about my job—

MARIE They don't understand what you do. To them, you're like E.T. They never met anybody from Virginia before. Who cares? I love hearing about the Historical Society.

[*Beat.*]

ROBBIE Maybe you don't respect me enough to stay over. You have your way with me, get a second helping of scalloped potatoes, and then you leave.

MARIE You're the only man I ever knew who makes such a big deal about stayin' over.

ROBBIE I'm so tired. There's a sleep I've been imagining for three months, when the night goes on and on and on, and there's nobody else in the world. The dreams I dream of having—but I never do.

MARIE [*Sympathetically.*]
Robbie . . .

ROBBIE My whole life I've been dreaming of that kind of sleep. If only you'd just stay tonight.

MARIE I'm sorry.

ROBBIE Why?! . . . Because your father thinks I'm not good enough for you, so you don't really want to be with me, in a fundamental way—

MARIE Come here.

[MARIE *takes him over to the bench, makes him sit down, sits next to him, and then pushes his head onto her shoulder.*]

ROBBIE It's not the same.

MARIE Shhh.

ROBBIE This bench is going to give me sciatica—

MARIE Shut up and close your eyes. Shut 'em—or I'll shut 'em for you.
[*Slight pause. He closes his eyes. She sings.*]
"Hush, bambino, close your eyes
Stardust's falling from the skies
The birds have all said good night—"

ROBBIE Marie—

MARIE [*Sings.*]
"Close your eyes, bambino, dormi."

ROBBIE Marie: I love you.

MARIE Aw, Robbie . . .

ROBBIE Am I always going to be waiting for the next train?

MARIE Close your eyes.—God, you're handsome.—Now just pretend we're in your bed. You can smell the garlic, the crisp new curtains, the Minwax . . . and us. And that Coney Island air. And you're lying on my shoulder, on the beach, on a cloud.

ROBBIE [*Half-asleep.*] There's no one else?

MARIE Just us.
[*After a moment,* ROBBIE *starts snoring.*]
Robbie? . . . You really asleep? . . . Wow. . . . What am I gonna do with you? Don't you know I love you too? I would crawl into bed with you and sleep with you forever, if only . . .

ROBBIE . . . Mom?

MARIE Sure, it's Mom. Now sleep.

[*Pause.* ROBBIE *wakes with a start.*]

ROBBIE Ah!!!

MARIE It's okay.

ROBBIE No. It's not.

MARIE What were you dreaming?

ROBBIE The train. Always the train.

MARIE Oh.

ROBBIE Come home with me. You're spending the night.

MARIE No, I'm not.

ROBBIE Either come home with me, or . . .

MARIE Or what?

ROBBIE Or give me a credible explanation. Not Fluffball.

MARIE I don't do ultimatums, Robbie.

ROBBIE Okay. Okay. Okay.

MARIE What's that s'posed to mean?

ROBBIE I can't do this anymore.

MARIE I can ride the subway alone. I'm a big girl.

[ROBBIE *shakes his head.*]

ROBBIE I just can't.

[ROBBIE *crosses away from her.*]

MARIE What? What?

ROBBIE I'll take you home tonight, but then . . . that's it.

MARIE You're dumping me. On 25th Avenue. I really—! . . . Just go home. I don't need you.

[ROBBIE *goes to a bench and sits down to wait for the train. Beat.* MARIE *takes out a cigarette and lights it.*]

ROBBIE You told me you gave it up.

MARIE You told me you loved me.

ROBBIE I do. But it seems like . . . the train only goes in one direction.
   [*She smokes.*]
   When you smoke . . .

MARIE What?

ROBBIE It's not attractive.
   [MARIE *angrily puts several cigarettes in her mouth, and one up each of her nostrils, then goes to* ROBBIE *and starts to light them.*]
   Stop that.

[ROBBIE *grabs the cigarettes out of her mouth and nose, and throws them away.*]

MARIE Hey!

[*She slaps his face.*]

God!

[*Slaps him again.*]

You're impossible! Do you realize how freakin' impossible you are? And you look at me with those eyes, what am I s'posed to do?

ROBBIE   Well . . .

MARIE   If I stayed over your house . . .

ROBBIE   Yes, things would change. We'd learn things about each other. God knows what could happen. But it would be better. It has to be.

MARIE   I been seeing you five months and four days. And you wanna . . .

ROBBIE   Could we at least have a time-table?

MARIE   No!

ROBBIE   Give me a hint. A sign? A light at the end of the tunnel.

MARIE   I thought I was your light.

ROBBIE   Am I yours? Do I do anything more for you than drive you crazy?

MARIE   God. You're gonna make me say it, aren't you? But if I say it, I can't ever get it back. I'm not gonna say it, not yet.

ROBBIE   Why not??!

MARIE   I don't ever . . . wanna live in a cage.

ROBBIE   Of course not! I know you're a wild bird, I love that. I just want to be with you.

MARIE   One year ago I was . . . You wouldn'ta recognized me.

ROBBIE   What do you mean?

MARIE   . . . I locked myself in a cage. Lost the key, and forgot I was in a cage. Smoked two packs a day, ate ravioli out of the can. Drank wine right from the box, and had conversations with Chef Boyardee. I wasn't livin' at my father's; I was on Lorimer Street, a very dark place. With rusty bars on the windows. I had been waitin' for someone . . . who was obviously never coming back, except it wasn't obvious to me.

[*Beat.*]

It was only when I started seeing you. . . . I felt free again. I love ridin' the train with you. The ride out here, the elevated tracks, the breeze. The way you look at me.

[*Beat.*]

I have this way . . . of losing myself, of taking care of guys so good—and I love taking care of you—but . . . I can't—I won't—go back to Lorimer Street. Or any place where I lose myself that way again.

. . . I can't stay over your house. And I can't say when I'm gonna. I'm just . . .

ROBBIE   It's okay.

MARIE   It's okay?

ROBBIE   Yeah.

[*They go to each other. MARIE sprinkles his face with kisses.*]

MARIE   I never touched a cigarette for the past three months. I swear.

[*MARIE throws away her pack of cigarettes.*]

ROBBIE   Tell me about the time you got caught smoking in school.

[*MARIE sits next to ROBBIE on the bench, and pushes his head onto her shoulder.*]

MARIE   It was second period. Williamsburg Middle School. People had been smokin' in that girls' room for thirty-five years—the windows were actually yellow from all the nicotine. And there was this new vice principal, Mr. Ventolieri, who'd lost his sense of smell during Vietnam. So we're in there, puffin' away, when there's this loud knock on the door . . .

[*We hear a train slowly screeching towards the station. ROBBIE turns to look at the oncoming train and, after a moment, stands up. MARIE looks at ROBBIE and then also gets up and stands next to him, taking his hand, as they wait for the train to pull into the station. Blackout.*]

• • •

Crab Cakes

Joan Lipkin

Joan Lipkin

Joan Lipkin is the artistic director of That Uppity Theatre Company, specializing in facilitating civic dialogue and creating work with marginalized populations. A playwright, director, activist, educator, and social critic, her work has been featured on network television, National Public Radio, the BBC, and in the Associated Press, as well as academic journals and mainstream publications. Her plays have been published and produced throughout the United States, Canada, the United Kingdom, and Australia. Honors include a Visionary Award, a Arts for Life Lifetime Achievement Award, the James F. Hornback Ethical Humanist of the Year Award, a Healthcare Hero Award, and the Missouri Arts Award, among others. Her work is published in *Upstaging Big Daddy: Directing Theater as if Race and Gender Matter, Amazon All Stars, Nice Jewish Girls: Growing Up in America, Mythic Women/Real Women: New Plays and Performance Pieces, One on One: The Best Women's Monologues for the 21st Century*, and *Radical Acts*, among other publications. For more info, visit www.uppityco.com.

characters

FRANKLIN, husband, 60-ish, upper-level management

MARGARET, wife, 60-ish, professional volunteer

WAITER, indeterminate age

setting

Upscale restaurant

• • •

WAITER   The crab cakes are very good.

FRANKLIN   We'll need a moment, thanks.

    [WAITER *exits.*]

    [*To* MARGARET.]

    So what do you think about the crab cakes?

MARGARET   The crab cakes? You brought me here to talk about crab cakes?

FRANKLIN   Well, you do like crab cakes.

MARGARET   I don't know.

FRANKLIN   You've always liked crab cakes.

MARGARET   Fine. I'll have the crab cakes.

[WAITER *reenters.*]

WAITER   You'll be having the crab cakes?

FRANKLIN   Yes.

WAITER   And for after . . .

MARGARET   We'll see.

[WAITER *exits.*]

FRANKLIN   You're upset.

MARGARET   No. Yes. Who wouldn't be upset? I don't understand. I just don't understand.

FRANKLIN I told you, Margaret. I thought you understood.

MARGARET Well, just because you told me doesn't mean I understand. I don't understand.

FRANKLIN I told you, it's this need. Things change.

MARGARET Why? Why do they have to change?

FRANKLIN They just do, everything changes, seasons, the market.

MARGARET The market.

FRANKLIN You change your hair.

MARGARET That's different

FRANKLIN No, not really. You used to be brunette. Then you went blond. Now you're back to brunette.

MARGARET I was trying to cover up the gray if you must know. That's all. Just trying to cover up the gray.

FRANKLIN Well, there you have it.

[WAITER *enters, carrying crab cakes.*]

WAITER The crab cakes, sir.

MARGARET Well, by all means, let's have the bloody crab cakes!

FRANKLIN Margaret.

WAITER Is something wrong?

FRANKLIN No.   **MARGARET** Yes

WAITER Can I bring you something else?

FRANKLIN The Chardonnay.

WAITER Very good, sir.

[WAITER *exits.*]

FRANKLIN Sweetheart, you're making a scene. You don't want to make a scene.

MARGARET That's why you brought me here, isn't it? I mean, instead of talking about this at home. Or might I add, not at all. You knew if we talked about it here, I couldn't make a scene.

FRANKLIN   I thought you liked the crab cakes.

MARGARET   Fuck the crab cakes.

FRANKLIN   Mags, try to be reasonable. How can you know if I don't tell you? I need to tell you.

MARGARET   Thirty-three years, Franklin. We've been married thirty-three years.

FRANKLIN   And I've been wanting to tell you for a long time.

MARGARET   Well, you took long enough. Have you been lying to me for thirty-three years?

FRANKLIN   No. No, I haven't. Things change. Like I told you. Like . . . your hair color. First you were brunette. Then you became a blonde, then—

MARGARET   [*Interrupts.*]
I know, Frank. I know. That's hair color. This is, is . . . sex. . . . This is different.

FRANKLIN   No, it's not. You were happy at one point being brunette and then you realized that something within you desperately needed to be a blonde.

MARGARET   Desperately?

FRANKLIN   Well, you became a blonde, didn't you? Didn't you?

MARGARET   Yes.

FRANKLIN   And I might add, you didn't even ask me about changing. You know, your hair color.

MARGARET   It's my hair.

FRANKLIN   Well. Maybe I liked you as a brunette. Maybe I was attached to that.

MARGARET   This is different. It's about us. The two of us. How long have you been feeling this way? Never mind. I don't want to know.
[*Beat.*]
No. How long?

FRANKLIN   A long time.

MARGARET   How long?

FRANKLIN   I don't' know. What does it matter?

MARGARET   It matters. It matters to me. Were you bored? Is that it? Was how it was between us boring?

FRANKLIN   It's nothing like that. It's more about work.

MARGARET   Work!? Are we going to talk about work? All you ever do is work. All we ever talk about is work.

FRANKLIN   Yes, That's it. That's what I'm talking about. So much work. So many decisions. All day long.

MARGARET   Yes.

FRANKLIN   So I'm played out, Margaret. I'm spent. Just spent.

MARGARET   Well, I thought you were going to cut back.

FRANKLIN   I will. But I can't. I can't right now with the merger. It's just not a good time.

MARGARET   When is it ever a good time, Franklin?

FRANKLIN   I don't know. But it's not right now.
   [*Beat.*]
   And it does something to me, Margaret. It really does. Today, I had to fire someone.

MARGARET   Who?

FRANKLIN   Tom.

MARGARET   Not Tom Allen?

FRANKLIN   Yeah. Well, he just wasn't cutting it.

MARGARET   But his wife! Didn't his wife just have surgery? We sent them the flowers and the pears. Harry and David. This is unbelievable.

FRANKLIN   It's not like I have a choice. Margaret. I don't have a choice.

[WAITER *enters.*]

WAITER   The Chardonnay.

MARGARET   I don't want Chardonnay.

FRANKLIN   We ordered the Chardonnay.

MARGARET   You ordered the Chardonnay. I want something different. I want the Riesling.

WAITER   The Riesling?

MARGARET   See, I have a choice, Franklin. I have a choice, so I am choosing the Riesling.

WAITER   So should I bring the Riesling instead?

MARGARET   I don't know what he wants. I want the Riesling.

FRANKLIN   Both. Bring a glass of both.

WAITER   Right.

[WAITER *exits.*]

MARGARET   Poor Tom. Millie. Was that his wife's name, Millie?

FRANKLIN   He'll be fine. He's got a golden parachute.

MARGARET   Well, okay, then. I just thought what, with the surgery...

FRANKLIN   Yes. And I had to tell him. I had to tell him and it did not feel good. It did not feel good, Margaret. But he knew. He knew it was coming. He saw it coming.

MARGARET   So he's okay, then?

FRANKLIN   Well, his ego took a beating. But, yeah, he's okay. It's the others.

MARGARET   What others?

FRANKLIN   The others. The whole division. In Fenton.

MARGARET   The whole division? But it's Christmas! These people have families.

FRANKLIN   Tell me about it.

MARGARET   Why didn't you say no?

FRANKLIN   I don't have a choice in these matters.

MARGARET   Of course, you do!

    [WAITER *enters with wine.*]

    I ordered the Riesling.

WAITER   Right. And for you, sir, the Chardonnay.

[WAITER *exits.*]

FRANKLIN   You think I have all these choices. You think I have all this clout, Margaret. But I don't. I don't.

MARGARET   They sent you to Brussels.

FRANKLIN   Nobody wanted to go.

MARGARET   They didn't?

FRANKLIN   No, they did not. See, there are a lot of things that you don't know, Margaret.

MARGARET   Well, why don't you tell me?

FRANKLIN   I'm trying. I'm telling you now.

MARGARET   Okay. Okay. So, tell me.

FRANKLIN   You think I don't feel bad? Laying all those people off? Fred wanted to send a memo. A memo! Can you believe that? At Christmas?

MARGARET   Jesus.

FRANKLIN   I said they deserve more than that.

MARGARET   Yes.

FRANKLIN   So he said, well, however I wanted to handle it.

MARGARET   I see.

FRANKLIN   So I didn't know what to do. They deserved a meeting or at least a phone call.

MARGARET   At least. Yes.

FRANKLIN   Yes. So here's the thing. I have all this responsibility. But then I don't. But then I do. You think I can choose but I can't. Not really. And it's frustrating. It really is.

MARGARET   I'm sorry, honey. I know it must be . . .

FRANKLIN   I need you, Margaret.

MARGARET   Anything, sweetheart.

FRANKLIN   I need you to tie me up.

MARGARET   Not again.

FRANKLIN   Well, I do. You say you want me to tell you how I feel, but then you don't want to hear.

MARGARET   How am I supposed to listen? This, this is pornographic.

FRANKLIN   No, it's not. It's between us. If it's between us, how can it be pornographic?

MARGARET   What was wrong with the way it was?

FRANKLIN   Because I need something different now. Now, I have more responsibility. All this responsibility. All these lay-offs.

MARGARET   So because you have more responsibility, you want to be tied up?

[*Beat.*]

FRANKLIN   And beaten.

MARGARET   Oh, Frank.

FRANKLIN   Nothing too much. Just a little light beating. You don't want to break the skin.

MARGARET   Frank.

FRANKLIN   I feel so bad. I don't know. This might help me to, you know, feel better. To relax. Maybe you could use your shoe.

MARGARET   I don't know. Aren't there professionals, you know, who do this sort of thing?

FRANKLIN   Well, I thought about that. But what if word got around? With my position and all? Besides, you're my wife.

MARGARET   Yes?

FRANKLIN   And I love you. I love you very much.

[*He cries.*]

MARGARET   Aw, I love you, too, sweetheart.

FRANKLIN   I really do. And I trust you. And I need you to do this for me. For us. I know it seems strange.

MARGARET   To say the least.

FRANKLIN   But where else can I go? I trust you. You're the one I trust.

MARGARET   Yes.

FRANKLIN   I mean, who am I going to tell about this, this thing? Fred? Tom Allen, for God's sake?

MARGARET   Uh-huh.

FRANKLIN   I want you to completely humiliate me. Completely.

MARGARET   Uh-huh.

FRANKLIN   Just there. In the, you know, the bedroom.

MARGARET   Right.

FRANKLIN   And only there. Nowhere else.

MARGARET   No.

FRANKLIN   Jesus, Margaret. Just thinking about it makes me feel so hot. Like I could, you know . . .

MARGARET   Uh-huh.

FRANKLIN   And I mean all night long.

[WAITER *enters.*]

WAITER   So will you be wanting anything else?

MARGARET   Check, please.

• • •

It's a . . . Baby!

Cara Restaino

Cara Restaino

An actor, director, and playwright, Cara Restaino found success with the stage as early as age four, earning the starring role of the Virgin Mary in the St. Anthony's School Christmas play. While a student at Muhlenberg College, she found a place for herself as a director, taking on, most notably, *The Vagina Monologues*, which earned over $20,000 for a local women's shelter. *It's a . . . Baby!* was written for an evening of one-acts, entitled *Getting Off in Brooklyn*, produced by Ryan Repertory Company at the Harry Warren Theatre in 2006. Currently, Cara Restaino is a high school English teacher in Basking Ridge, New Jersey.

··· production note ···

This is intended to be performed by one woman. She plays all characters. Distinctions are made through varying focal points, shifting voices, and adjusting postures. Other methods of character portrayal are open to interpretation.

· · ·

[*Lights up.* CARA *enters. A pause.*]

The Virgin Mary. The holiest woman in the Catholic religion. [*Pause.*] One day an angel messenger came to Mary and told her that she was going to have the son of God. *Surprise*, it's a *baby*! A pretty important baby... Then, two thousand years later, there is Stephanie. Stephanie Restaino, my sister. Three years ago, my sister thought she had a stomach virus. [*Pause.*] My sister had a baby. She didn't know she was pregnant until about twenty minutes before she had the baby. This, however, was *NOT* a virgin birth and there was no messenger.

[*Pause.*]

I know... you have questions. It's hard to understand. It's hard to wrap your brain around an idea that sounds like a side show attraction or a topic for *The Jerry Springer Show*. This story is true. It's true and it's completely correct. What I mean is, my sister *would* have a baby and not know she was pregnant. It's completely normal, completely obvious, completely *correct*.

When I called my friends to tell them what had happened, some were surprised.

"Pat, it's Cara... I have some news. I'm an aunt! [*Pause.*] No, she didn't get a kitten... she had a baby. Yes, a baby... well, *she* didn't either."

At the time my parents had a restaurant and we were all so excited—well, eventually anyway—so we put up IT'S A GIRL signs all over. And the costumers would come in, "Ooo! Who had a baby?"

"My sister."

"You have another sister?"

"No, I only have one."

"You mean, Stephanie? The girl who cooks back there? She didn't look pregnant!"

"Yep."

"Huh . . . I didn't know she was pregnant!"

"Yeah, funny thing . . . she didn't either!" And the conversations went on like that for weeks.

My friend Alana was driving when I told her. She had to pull over. And after she got her breath back, she said, "Stephanie had a baby and didn't know she was pregnant. Hmmm, that's about right."

You see, you have to understand my sister. She is different, unlike any person I have ever known.

When she was little, my sister had trouble spelling. She was a little . . . slow . . . a slow learner. . . . concepts didn't come as fast to her as they did to other kids . . . or to me, for that matter. I was a *fast* learner. But not Stef. My mother took matters into her own hands. [*Pause.*] She made flash cards. There were cards everywhere—all over the house, all over the car—especially in the car. Any idle time was time enough for a spelling lesson. "CAT! C-A-T CAT! CAT!" "MOP! M-O-P! MOP! MOP!" Hours on end, spelling simple three-letter words. I was trying to read some kind of *sophisticated* Judy Blume novel while my sister was caught up in hard and soft *G*s.

Anyway, one day, while in the car, interestingly enough, *not* having a spelling lesson, my sister made an announcement. "I can spell a word!" My mother perked up, could it be there has been some sort of recognition? Could she have mastered the notion of phonics? We would have settled for a two-letter combo—*us, me, on* . . . ANYTHING!

"Sex! S-E-X! Sex! SEX!" My mother swallowed hard. My eyeballs nearly fell out of my head.

[*Long pause.*]

SHE COULD SPELL! Oh, joy! The little darling could spell after all. A glimmer of hope emerged from behind the usual *bats, mats*, and *dogs*. Stef could spell! And she spelled SEX! Not easy for a five-year-old. We were impressed with her genius. [*Pause.*] Yes, impressed. Shocked? Not in the least. In addition to being a little on the slow side, my sister had a curious interest in the subject. Her favorite movie being *Porky's*, which she pronounced "Pokeys," because in addition to being slow, she suffered from a slight speech impediment. Maybe we were surprised, but shocked we weren't.

This incident . . . spelling *sex* in the car . . . began a sort of tradition with my sister that remains true today. No, no, we weren't shocked.

School, in general, was hard for her. She struggled with keeping up, but she didn't let that hold her back. What she lacked in intellect she made up in sheer originality, making her mark in other ways. She had spiky hair and lime green eye shadow; her eyelids actually became stained with hues of avocado. She went by the name "Donut"—she was "round and sweet." She had T-shirts with a *Q* on the front . . . it read, "What's round and sweet?" and on the back, "Answer: ME!" So, Donut was an original. She didn't do things the way that other kids did. She had to be different. She won Halloween contests all through high school as Aunt Jemima, the Quaker Oats guy, and Chef from *South Park*. Surprise, after surprise.

While other kids applied to Yale, Harvard, and, well, Rutgers, my sister decided to follow in my mother's footsteps and become a chef. She applied to the Culinary Institute of America and got in—which was quite a feat for a kid right out of high school and a long way from *d-o-g dog dog*.

Not long after my sister arrived at the CIA, she fell in love with Jason. [*Pause.*] Jason was a triple threat. By the time I got to know him, he had a criminal record for armed robbery, which led him to a year stint at Riker's, a child with another girl, and a life-threatening blood disorder. But when he met my sister, he was on his second time through culinary school. He had made it through the first time, but said he didn't learn enough, so they let him go through again. He didn't finish that time around. Although she had a good heart, my sister had *bad* judgment.

And, at the time they met, my sister Stephanie was still Donut . . . very round . . . and sweet. And Jason wasn't interested in the girl who looked like she *eaten* a bakery. They were just friends.

Eventually, my sister started coming home a lot on weekends. And one Sunday night, after my parents had taken her back to school, my mother went to throw away the newspaper and found an envelope underneath. Inside was a note. "Dear Mom and Dad, I hate school. I miss you. I'm coming home again next week. For good." Unfortunately, my father had just sent in my sister's next semester's tuition . . . in addition to having a flair for surprises, my sister has always had impeccable timing.

Once she got home, she began losing weight, fast. By that time, my parents opened the restaurant and she was working all the time. She was down over one hundred pounds. And, by the time Jason got out of the big house, my sister wasn't as big as a house anymore. She looked amazing, and I am sure that when he saw her for the first time, he was more than surprised.

Needless to say, love blossomed. They were up each other's asses night and day. He lived in Queens, so my sister was out there almost every weekend. "Be careful!" my mother would yell to her. "Watch what you're doing!" she would call. She wasn't talking about driving either. Even if my sister could *spell sex*, didn't mean she knew how to be responsible *with* sex.

Well, 9/11 happened, and with terrorist threats on the news every five seconds, my parents made a decision. Obviously my sister cared very much for Jason. We got the whole sob story from her—he could die from his disease, his mother treated him like shit, his friend framed him, the baby wasn't his . . . etc., etc. My parents are good-hearted people . . . good-hearted, well-intentioned Christian-minded people, but they're crazy! Within a few months, they had rented a Penske truck and moved this poor soul into our home. And when I graduated from college in June 2002 and headed back home, there was almost no room at the inn! Well, he didn't actually have a room. He had a sofa. And a job at my family's restaurant.

Everything seemed to be going all right for a while. He slept on the couch, my sister slept in her room with the door open. But you know how long those things last. Before long, he was sneaking in her room during the night and making it back to the couch before my father would get up. He was caught eventually, and instead of making permanent residence in sofa city—he moved into my sister's bed . . . first with the door open, then, of course, shut. So much for decency.

In July of that same year, we took a family trip, Jason included, to Cancun. Well, my sister and Jason were sick the entire week. They threw up from one side of Mexico to the other. And I got to play nurse because we shared a room. Apparently sharing a bed in New Jersey is different than sharing a bed in Mexico. After we got back, every so often my sister would be sick again—throwing up, stomachaches, etc.

And by December she was looking awful. She had these dark circles under her eyes and her hair was getting curly, which was strange because she had this thick poker-straight hair ever since she was a kid. We all begged her to stop losing weight. "Stef, you're getting too thin . . . you look sick . . . you look awful . . . " And she did!

Every once in a while I'd catch her throwing up in the bathroom and she would swear that her stomach was just upset. She'd say, "I don't know . . . ever since Mexico I haven't been right. Maybe I have a parasite or something." And then she'd go outside for cigarette. She's a tough girl. She looks tough, she acts tough, she talks tough. I believed her. But the fact of the matter was that she looked like shit.

Months went by like this, and by January 2003, she was in a bad state. She was working twelve-hour days and her skin had turned the color of a cold, fried veal cutlet. She was gray. I told her to stop smoking, to stop the late nights out drinking with her friends and actually go to bed early, but she ignored me. And on the Saturday before the most insane week of our lives, she worked all day. She made two cheesecakes during the afternoon, worked the line, and spun pies in between. Her friends came in around nine o'clock and she cooked dinner for them too. By the time she sat down she looked awful. But she helped them polish off two bottles of wine and several packs of cigarettes before she and Jason went home.

All day Sunday she didn't feel better either. And against our better judgement we all went to the Macaroni Grill for dinner and out to see *Lord of the Rings* later that night.

Well, on Monday morning, she was moaning and groaning about her stomach again. But my father was moaning and groaning too, so we figured it was food poisoning or something. [*Pause.*] As I said, we went to the Macaroni Grill.

So, around four in the afternoon, my mom told her, "Go home. You look like shit. It's just Monday night, I can handle it. If you don't feel better, go over to the Immediate Care Center or something . . . but call me."

Everything seemed OK until around eight when Jason called to say that they were headed to the Immediate Care Center because she was really in pain. "This Mexico thing really got her," he had said.

"Alright, alright. Just call us when you finish."

About an hour later they called to say that they were on their way to the hospital. The doctor at the IMCC said that she needed a blood test to test for a parasite and that the hospital would get the results very quickly.

"Well, what did the doctor say?" my mother had asked.

"He said I could get a blood test quick. I just want the pain to stop," my sister told her.

When she and Jason walked into the ER, my sister gave her name.

"I'm Stephanie Restaino. I was sent here. . . . " But before she could finish, the nurse ushered her in and Jason took a seat in the waiting room.

She was poked and prodded by several nurses and doctors. Then, finally, the doctor said, "OK, we're either going to take you to

Labor and Delivery or surgery."

"Labor and Delivery? For what?"

"Well, you're having a *baby*."

"No, I'm Stephanie Restaino. I have a stomach virus."

And instantly, she was surrounded by six doctors and two crash carts and a lot of silence. They knew she was pregnant. They knew *she* didn't know she was pregnant. And as they examined her, they could hear a heartbeat, but couldn't find the baby. My sister, as I said, was very thin. When they laid her on the table, her stomach was concave. And as the doctor listened for a heartbeat, the nurse mouthed to the doctor, "Where the fuck is this baby?" Her placenta had ruptured—when? They weren't sure, but toxins were released in her blood flow, lethal toxins that could kill both her and the baby if the situation wasn't handled fast.

In the meantime, a nurse was sent to retrieve Jason, who still had his black leather coat on as he sat watching *Fear Factor*.

"Are you Jason? Stephanie's boyfriend?"

"Yeah."

"Come with me, please."

"Oh wait," he said, "let me go pull the car around for her so it's warm." It was January after all.

"Oh no," the nurse said, "that won't be necessary." She led him to the emergency room, where my sister was waiting. The nurse closed the curtain and my sister had to tell him what was going on.

"Jay, I'm having a baby."

"You're pregnant?"

"No, I'm having a baby . . . *now*." And before she could say anything else, the curtain flew open and the nurses tore off her clothes and shoved them into an elevator.

They told her that she would have the baby in about twenty minutes.

"Wait! I have to call my mom! She has to be here!!!"

"Honey, if your mother lived next door, she wouldn't make it in time."

They taught her Lamaze on the way up to Delivery.

She had no drugs . . . a completely natural birth, but it wasn't easy. The baby was actually situated up in her rib cage, which accounted for the lack of a belly. The doctors had to actually work her down—she didn't want to budge!

Nevertheless, shortly before midnight on Monday, January 13, 2003, at 5 pounds, the baby was born. A girl.

[*Pause.*]

Oh! But that's not the end of the story.

While my sister was having a child, my parents went to Costco and my father was pissed when he got home and found their other car blocking the driveway.

"How many times have I told them to leave the driveway open for me! I have all this stuff. . . . " grumble, grumble . . . Little did the poor guy know that in a few hours *this* would be the *least* of his problems.

I went upstairs to my room and my friends called to see if I wanted to go out, but I had been going out lately and needed just a good night's sleep . . . riiiiight. So I went to bed thinking nothing was wrong.

Well, around midnight my mother was still up—they weren't home yet. "Where could they be?" My father told her that maybe they stopped at the diner for something to eat. But my mom was getting nervous. She said, "I'm either going to call the hospital or the police." Then the phone rang.

"Yeah, Stef." My dad had answered it. "Mommy? Yeah, she's here. Hold on."

[*Pause.*]

Now, this should have been a sign. A big, bad sign. Never, *ever* in a moment of crisis do you ask to talk to my mother. You want level-headedness in a time of emergency, Daddy. You talk to

Daddy. But *this*, this wasn't something that you could have told my father.

"Stef? Stef! Where are you? Are you still at the hospital?"

"Yeah, Mom, I'm at the hospital."

"Did they admit you?"

"Yeah, Mom . . . Mom, listen to me. Are you awake?"

"Yeah, Stef. I'm awake. What's going on?"

"Are you sure you're awake?"

"Yes, yes. What is it?"

"Mom . . . I had a baby."

"What?"

"I had a baby . . . it's OK . . . it's a girl."

Dead air. Silence.

"Mom?"

Meanwhile, my father had sat up and he was yelling in the background. "Don't tell me she's pregnant!!"

"Mom, you've got to come up here."

"OK, OK. We'll be there in a little bit."

"Mom, I'm scared."

"I know . . ."

[*Pause.*]

"No, I'm scared that Daddy is going to kill Jason."

[*Pause.*]

"I know." She hung up the phone and turned to my father.

"Somebody wanna tell me what the fuck is going on?"

My mother stood up and walked to the foot of the bed. She was trying to find the words to explain this . . . how to convey this information to this man in the most direct way possible. How she could communicate this so that there would be absolutely no confusion or question in his mind about what has happened.

So my mom looked at him and said, [*Pause.*] "Do you remember Victor and Helen?"

Victor and Helen were friends of my parents. And twenty-five years ago, they had gone dancing on a Saturday night. The next morning my father got a phone call . . . it was Victor.

"Jer, you gotta come to the hospital with me."

"Vic, what's the matter?"

"It's Helen."

"Omigod! Is she OK?"

"Yeah, she's OK. She had a baby."

"Shit, Vic, you didn't tell me she was pregnant!"

"I didn't know . . . and she didn't either."

In an instant my father was standing. "I can't! I won't! I'll kill her! I'll kill *him*!"

And my mother, now completely out of character, took charge of the situation. "*Listen!* Listen to me very carefully. She is *your* daughter. This is *her* baby. She's not the first. She won't be the last. It's 2003. Get over it." And she stormed out of the room.

And my father called after her, "Where are you going?"

"I'm going to wake Cara."

Now, let's go back to me. Remember me? I was *so* tired. I didn't go out that night so that I could catch up on some much needed sleep. Yeah, so me. I was all *schnuggly-wuggly* in my bed having good dreams . . . pleasant dreams where my door doesn't fly open to reveal my mother is standing in the doorway . . . yelling . . . loudly . . .

"Cara! CARA! Wake up!"

"What . . . what's the matter?"

"Get up! Your sister is in the hospital."

I got up and looked at the big, blurry figure in the door frame. I'm legally blind without my glasses . . . I couldn't tell if I was dreaming or if this was a ghost or what . . .

"The hospital? Is she OK?"

"Fine. [*Pause.*] She had a baby. It's a girl." And then she just turned around and walked out of the room.

A baby?!? What the hell was she talking about—a *baby*? I fumbled for my glasses and went into my parents' room. My father was sitting at the edge of the bed staring at the wall. My mother was standing in the doorway of her walk-in closet *chugging* a bottle of Grand Marnier.

"Wait, I don't understand. She had a *baby*?"

"A baby. Yes, a baby. She had a baby. Now hold this, I need to call your uncle. Your father is going to kill Jason."

I stood there is disbelief. I didn't know what to do next. I looked at my father.

"Dad? . . . Dad? . . . DAD! You gotta snap out of this. It's going to be OK. Everything is going to be OK."

[*Long pause.*]

He didn't look up. He didn't even blink. He just stared at that wall.

"Nick. It's me. No, no, everything is OK. Well, uh, actually, I need you to come up here. It seems that Stephanie had a baby. Yes, our Stephanie. Yes, a baby. Yes. You need to get up here. [*Pause.*] Jerry is going to kill Jason."

My father *was* going to kill Jason. Yes, I believe that wholeheartedly. As he stared at that wall he thought about all the horrible, torturous things he would do to him. I could see his fury being projected onto the wall . . . he nearly burned a whole right through it.

My mother grabbed the bottle back from me and threw me the phone.

"Call your aunt. You tell her what happened."

"Me!?! I'm not qualified to do this."

She didn't answer. She just looked at me. [*Pause.*] Just looked at me . . . and chugged.

"Aunt Re?"

"Car? What's the matter?"

"Nothing, nothing . . . well, something, yeah. Uh, listen, everyone's OK, but, uh, Stephanie's in the hospital. She had a baby."

And then the funniest thing happened. My aunt's voice got very high.

"Oh. A baby? Oh-kay. A baby."

"Yeah, a baby. Are you OK?"

"Me? Yeah. A baby. Wow. Of all the things you could of told me. A baby . . . didn't expect that."

"Yeah, uh, us either. You gotta come up here. We need all hands on deck."

"What do you mean?

"My father is going to kill Jason."

At this point, the bottle of booze was gone. My mother wiped her mouth and walked over to my father. "You. Get up and get dressed. We have to get to that hospital and see our granddaughter."

He didn't look up. He just stood and grabbed his clothes.

We all got dressed. My aunt and uncle got to our house and we piled in our cars and made our way to see Stephanie. No one in the car uttered a single word . . . not a sound. But silently, *feverishly* we prayed. "Hail Mary, mother of God, pray for . . . Jason."

We literally ran into the hospital and my mother got to the nurses station.

[*Out of breath.*] "I'm Josephine Restaino. Stephanie's mom."

The nurse smiled at her. "Oh, I could have guessed."

My mother looked at her.

"You've been drinking, Mrs. Restaino. I can smell it on your breath. And I got to tell you, I would too. Your daughter is on the 3rd floor."

As we got in the elevator, we could feel the tension. And then my father began shaking his head.

"What is it?"

"I'm just thinking. They're on the 3rd floor."

"Yeah."

"Well, that's not good. I was going to throw Jason out the window. The third floor won't kill him. He'll break his arms and then I'll really have to support him."

Ah, humor. Lighthearted humor. There was hope!

Once we got off the elevator, Jason was waiting. When he saw us, he completely broke down. We all did. Who could believe this was happening? It was surreal. My father was the first one to go up to him. Jason could barely lift his head. And then he extended his hand. But my father grabbed him. And he hugged him and we all finally felt like we could breathe.

He told us the whole story. How my sister almost died. How the baby almost died. How we were experiencing a miracle.

He led us to my sister, who was lying in bed with a blanket over her . . . over all of her . . . even her face. My mother stood next to the bed.

"It's OK." And then we all cried some more.

They told us that they had chosen to name the baby Angelina.

"Awww . . . ," I said, "Little angel."

Jason said, "Yeah, well, I had this cat named Angelina that I really loved when I was a kid."

"How poignant."

Angelina had no health problems despite the fact that my cigarette-smoking, wine-drinking, Stacker-pill-popping sister went through what the doctors say was nine full months of pregnancy without a single prenatal vitamin, let alone doctor's visit. And Angelina is the smartest kid I have ever seen, regardless of her parents' inadequacies. I guess two negatives do make a positive.

Now for the questions, I know you have them. You're wondering how the hell this could have happened. Well, it *can* happen. It happens more often than you think. As I said, this became a topic of constant conversation at our restaurant and the more and more we talked about it, the more and more we heard of similar stories.

"Oh, that happened to my aunt . . . that happened to my grandmother . . ."

"My mother brought home my brother and nine months later she gave birth to my sister . . . her head was so small that my mother would knit her baby bonnets on a potato."

It was an old wives' tale that if a woman was breast feeding she couldn't get pregnant. Not true!—which is why nine months after bring a baby home, women were seen running back to their cars with their husbands after their water broke again . . .

OK, so you're wondering about that too . . . her water breaking. The doctors say that my sister was probably in labor for three days and didn't even know it aside from the excruciating pain. How did she not notice her water breaking? Well, sometimes a woman's water can break while they're in the shower or going to the bathroom and they'd never know the difference.

And her period . . . well, ladies, if you've ever lost a lot weight or been through a severely stressful experience, you know that your body can get out of whack. My sister had lost over 100 pounds. She attributed her missed period to the drastic weight loss.

Didn't she feel the baby moving? Some babies aren't very active, and don't forget my sister was feeling *something*. She was basically sick to her stomach for nine months; [*Pause.*] she just thought it was a parasite . . . it sorta was . . .

Like a parasite, my niece sucked every last nutrient out of my sister, which would have attributed to her deathly appearance, and the curly hair is a side effect of the change in hormones brought on by pregnancy.

So, it's been 3 years. I should catch you up on what's gone on. My niece is fine. She's a lot like my sister . . . reeking havoc. But she's smart, like me . . . she can spell *dog*.

Jason left almost a year ago. Turns out he was having an affair with my sister's best friend. Shit happens. He gave her the best thing he ever could have . . . Angelina. My mother, who swore up and down that she would never be a Nana, is indeed Nana.

And in the most interesting turn of events, my sister has become something I never thought she could be. It's not that I don't love my sister or believe in her, but as you can imagine, I was worried about her. She was thrown into this situation—her life turned upside down in a few short minutes. She has handled motherhood with a sense of wisdom that overshadows anything that has happened in the past. She is a brilliant mother who loves her daughter with that innate compassion that they say girls are born with. She has it. I always knew that I could outscore my sister on any test. I could write better, I could add better, I could *certainly* spell better. But I don't know if I'll ever be half the mother that she is.

And my dad, my dad and Angelina are inseparable. In the hardest, most trying times I think that my father looks at Angelina and knows that somehow she was sent to save him.

And me, I've been given a rare gift. I have been able to travel back in time to see my mother and father as young parents—how they were with me when I was a baby. The years melt away when they are around Angelina and I can see them with a sort of immortality that defies fact that time marches on.

[*Pause.*]

I try to rationalize things. Why this happened. Why she came and why she came in the way she did. I think about headlines . . . about girls having sex and then giving birth at their proms . . . leaving their babies on doorsteps of churches and hospitals. How what should be a beautiful blessed thing can turn into a tragedy. And how it could have been a tragedy for us. And beyond some deep, philosophical message, I've only this. You needed a messenger.

I'm not sure what would have happened if my sister didn't make it to the hospital. If we didn't get that crazy phone call that changed everything. Nothing has been the same since . . . nothing has been the same, but it has all been for the better.

[*Pause.*]

> The Virgin Mary gave us Jesus Christ . . . my sister gave us Angelina . . . not quite the same thing, and yet she has saved us in a way. And if you would, *hear* this story. Listen to the message, from me, your less than angelic messenger. We can get ourselves into some difficult situations. But everything happens for a reason.

> You think you know things. You think you know about love . . . about sex . . . about how things work, the birds and the bees, but *some things* defy explanation.

> I know, it's nearly inconceivable . . . but this wasn't just a blessed event . . . [*Pause.*] *this* was a miracle.

• • •

The Highwayman

Julia Jarcho

Julia Jarcho

Julia Jarcho is a playwright, director, and performer. Productions include *Take Me Away* (*Il faut brûler pour briller* festival, Paris, 2007), *A Small Hole* (Performance Lab 115, FringeNYC, 2006), *All I Do Is Dream of You* (Sophiensaele and English Theatre Berlin, 2006), *Delmar* (Berlin, 2005), *The Highwayman* (NTUSA performance space, Brooklyn, 2004), and *Nursery* (Young Playwrights Festival, Cherry Lane Theater, New York, 2001). She was a writer in residence at the 2002 Eugene O'Neill Playwrights Conference and won a Berrilla Kerr Award the same year. She is currently a resident writer at the Playwrights Foundation in San Francisco. She is also a board member of Young Playwrights Inc., a participant in Just Theater's New Play Lab, and a member of the New York–based playwrights' collective 13P. For more information, please visit www.juliajarcho.com.

characters (in order of appearance)

BESS
MATILDA, a woman of the town
Two **GUESTS**, peripatetic traveling companions
THE HIGHWAYMAN
TIM
There is also a guitarist somewhere.

∙∙∙ production note ∙∙∙

The Highwayman was developed at the 2002 Eugene O'Neill Playwrights Conference. It was presented at The Stable (DUMBO, Brooklyn) in December 2004, directed by the author and with design and music by Harry Kimball.

This play was brought on by Alfred Noyes's poem "The Highwayman."

∙∙∙

[*Lights up on* BESS, *alone onstage with her eyes closed. A pause. She opens her eyes and addresses the audience.*]

BESS   Where is this?
    [*Pause.*]
    The land? The moor. Purple bog. Hi!
    [*Beat.*]
    Hello. Look out there. I can look out at the land. It'll get darker.
    [*Beat.*]
    It's nothing for you anyway. I could just make it up and you'd never know the difference. When they say "and it was all a dream," I think, who cares? Tell me a story! I don't care. God. Right there, over there a goat was buried. Many years ago. It didn't belong to the mother or the father in particular. It was a family goat. I know goats are popular in jokes, but this isn't a joke. It's a dream! Ha-ha, who cares, not really. It's a goat. How do I know? From the inscription. There is a goat engraved on the tombstone. It doesn't say Beloved Family Goat, but I know about

that for a fact. They loved that goat. It gave good milk. It ate the garbage. You could pet it at that time. Now you can only make yourself think so. What it said was, Here Lies, and then the name of the goat. Who cares? It wasn't Bess. Or maybe it was.

[MATILDA *stands and speaks from the audience.*]

MATILDA Bess—

BESS No! Guess what. It wasn't a goat. Now that I think, it was a donkey. All this time. That doesn't change much, except the milk and the garbage. But they adored that donkey. Most donkeys seem to be unwelcome on this God-given earth, but not that one. Not this donkey! Why? Because it was so sweet-tempered. You should see with its kids—all lined up? They were all mules, but it never complained. The family contemplated having a portrait done like that, not of themselves. Because you can't help it if she hands you a mule when the day's come, right? You really can't. It was a quiet life. I don't want to talk about the rest. I don't know why I started. Let's just say here lies and then the name.

MATILDA [*Walking onstage.*]
Bess—

BESS You didn't feel strongly about that. It's OK. I can't help what I dream. That thing about the goat, it was just—it was just a donkey, so to speak. More space and less milk. Ha. No, but I have the medal. I don't know what to tell you.
[*Beat.*]
Am I supposed to—

[*Two* GUESTS, *travelers, enter with a satchel and set it down. They may or may not be twins, and their lines come right on top of each other.* MATILDA *exits on their first line.*]

GUEST 1 Bess.

GUEST 2 Bess.

GUEST 1 Look at you.

GUEST 2 Last time I saw you—

GUEST 1   You were a little girl.

GUEST 2   Little thing.

GUEST 1   A child.

GUEST 2   No child now.

GUEST 1   Where's your Dad?

BESS   Oh . . . he's—

GUEST 2   Got a couple beds?

GUEST 1   Passing through along.

GUEST 2   We were afraid you might be gone.

GUEST 1   The whole inn, gone.

GUEST 2   Many have.

GUEST 1   These days done into root.

GUEST 2   Not much root.

GUEST 1   Old piles. Old empty hives and you mighta thought—

GUEST 2   You mighta thought it would be a big lux bath.

GUEST 1   Many did.

GUEST 2   Took their baths.

GUEST 1   Woke up dry.

GUEST 2   Woke up old.

GUEST 1   And no family.

GUEST 2   Where'd they go with it?

GUEST 1   And it's not a sentimental, but I saw a man cry more times—

GUEST 2   A woman—

GUEST 1   Saw a woman cry more times.

GUEST 2   Where's there to eat?

GUEST 1   Dig in the ground.

GUEST 2   Digging in the ground.

GUEST 1   Just digging up ripped.

GUEST 2   Till his own skin starts looking pretty juicy to him.

GUEST 1   I've seen it.

[*Pause.*]

So we were afraid—

GUEST 2   Much less a bed.

GUEST 1   Who can pay for it?

GUEST 2   Plenty of people'll take their luck by the side of the highway.

GUEST 1   Roll up your wescot, sleep on that, what we been doing.

GUEST 2   I'll tell you who can pay for it.

GUEST 1   That's another breed.

GUEST 2   So they consider.

GUEST 1   They wouldn't rot if you kept 'em in your mouth.

GUEST 2   They rot when they have to.

[GUEST 1 *laughs: short, harsh.*]

Those jump-up noses rot right off of them.

GUEST 1   Kings and queens.

GUEST 2   Clean white churches.

GUEST 1   Oh, clean.

GUEST 2   Until he comes through.

GUEST 1   The end to that.

[*Pause.*]

But tonight, though—

GUEST 2   We can do that.

GUEST 1   I said to him, you know that—

GUEST 2   Just one night passing this way.

GUEST 1   You remember those beds?

GUEST 2   Softest, a man could get ruined.

GUEST 1   And the beer?

GUEST 2   Almost a fable.

GUEST 1   That little kid of his?

GUEST 2   Said she's a cute little thing-

GUEST 1   I wonder how is she doing at.

GUEST 2   Doing fine.

GUEST 1   That's the truth.
[*Beat. They retrieve the satchel and start to leave.*]
Guess we'll put these upstairs.

GUEST 2   Join your dad in the back.

GUEST 1   He still makes that beer?

GUEST 2   Before we forget—
[*Beat.*]
Something we had to tell you.

GUEST 1   Oh. Yes.

GUEST 2   Man's riding.

GUEST 1   Saw him riding this way.

GUEST 2   You know who we mean?

GUEST 1   That coach to the North?

GUEST 2   Saw him riding.

GUEST 1   You know the ribbon?

GUEST 2   He's riding this way.

GUEST 1   You saw the moon? Whole moon?

GUEST 2   Through sometimes like a bullet.

GUEST 1   Shining like a ribbon on the land?

GUEST 2   Shatters everything.

GUEST 1   The Highway.

GUEST 2   Don't want wine stains on your pretty elbows.

GUEST 1   Watch out.

GUEST 2   Your pretty hair.

GUEST 1   Very pretty, very nice to see you again, Bess.

GUEST 2   Take care for yourself, Bess.

GUEST 1   Listen to that wind.

GUEST 2   Look at that.

GUEST 1   Trees . . .

GUEST 2   The wind . . .

GUEST 1   Listen out for ghosts.

GUEST 2   Not just ghosts.

GUEST 1   The moon is a ghost.

GUEST 2   I know it.

[GUESTS *exit.* BESS *addresses the audience.*]

BESS   Let me tell you about a time. I'm gonna, look, I'm . . . there are ghosts involved. Ghosts to keep you in your corner, so, warm, so, let it.
[*Beat.* MATILDA *enters and faces* BESS.]
It's not whether or not it was a dream. We have cover, here. It soaks all the memory. Gimme a bed. You know? Put me in a glass. Under a stool. Among the boots. Still. So down there now in fact I can't, I don't listen, see anything but my own roof. Rolled-up sleeping on myself. This is the inn.

[*Pause.*]

MATILDA   Can you say more?

BESS   It's like this:
[*Facing the audience.*]
Hello.
—Hello.
Do you love me?
—Yes.

[*Pause.*]

    Hello, do you have a room?

    —Who are you?

    You know me. Everyone knows me.

    —I never met you.

    You were just a little thing.

    —Swallow me—

    [*Beat.*]

    —in your hands.

    That's not what I do.

[*Pause.*]

    Do you have a room?

    —For you?

    Who else?

    —We don't want trouble.

    Trouble, ma'am?

    —We hear you shatter it.

    There may be some truth in that.

    —Well, so we don't want that. We don't want that here.

[*Pause.*]

    —We don't . . .

    You and who?

    —Me and . . . me and . . .

    All I see is you and me.

[*Beat.*]

    —Who are you?

    You don't know me.

    —You look familiar.

    Well, you can forget that, I only want a room.

    —Please . . .

    Please what?

    —Just please . . .

[*Enter* HIGHWAYMAN. *He looks at her. She addresses the audience.*]

> Please what? Am I expected to know? I had my whole life this room, whole life this hair, elbows. In the back, when I was sick, they'd give me a drink of beer. It's this and the land. The moor is wild. No one gets buried right out there.

[*To* MATILDA.]

> I'm used to talking like this. I know people are nearby, that happens a lot.

[*She casts a quick glance at the* HIGHWAYMAN.]

> I hear it. Little thing? Totally fine. I'd like a room . . .
>
> *Do you have a room?*
>
> —Yeah.
>
> *I'd like to stable my animal.*
>
> —Please.
>
> *I'd like a drink.*
>
> —In the back there.
>
> *Drink of piss. Drink of rain.*
>
> —No rain in these parts.
>
> *I know your parts. Drink of salt.*

[*She glances at him again.*]

> —You can't do that, sir. Salt is the opposite of drink.
>
> *So is liquor.*

[*Pause.*]

HIGHWAYMAN Don't stop.

BESS [*To* MATILDA.]

> So is . . .
>
> [*She turns and speaks to the* HIGHWAYMAN.]
>
> Listen, you know what? I slept under the stove sometimes. In the stove.

HIGHWAYMAN May I introduce myself?

[MATILDA *exits.*]

BESS In the . . .

HIGHWAYMAN That's all right.

BESS You weren't interrupting.

HIGHWAYMAN I'm glad.

BESS I heard you.

HIGHWAYMAN Gossip?

BESS No.

HIGHWAYMAN I've never heard about you.

BESS No.

HIGHWAYMAN It's strange, because they usually talk a lot about that kind of thing.

BESS What kind?

HIGHWAYMAN Yours.

BESS It doesn't bother me.

HIGHWAYMAN Indeed, why should it?

BESS It shouldn't.

HIGHWAYMAN What a kind of node logic.

BESS I know that.

HIGHWAYMAN What?

BESS I know what I'm saying.

HIGHWAYMAN Forgive me. I have a way of speaking that alienates people.
[*Beat.*]
It's a shame.
[*Beat.*]
Or perhaps . . .
[*Beat.*]
Are you alone?

BESS No.

HIGHWAYMAN Who else is there?

BESS My father?

HIGHWAYMAN Oh. I get it.

BESS The landlord.

HIGHWAYMAN The landlord's black-eyed daughter.

BESS Me?

HIGHWAYMAN They look black. So black as blind. But I know you're
not blind. But I wonder about them. May I?
[*He peers into her eyes for a moment.*]
Are you sure you're who you claim to be?

BESS Yes. No.

HIGHWAYMAN Because I've seen those before. Oh, somewhere. I don't
know where. I don't mean to denigrate them. I think now I've
totally blown it.

BESS What?

HIGHWAYMAN Look how late it is. What's your name?

BESS Bess.

HIGHWAYMAN Do you fight, Bess?

BESS Like how?

HIGHWAYMAN Muscles working, ends of fingernails pumping around
for the eyes, loud smacking sounds, droplets of gore? Bone to bone?

BESS Why?

HIGHWAYMAN Say because someone just put it to you in a loathing tone.

BESS I don't think so.

HIGHWAYMAN Well, do you give it away easy?

BESS Who?
[*We hear a strain from the guitar.*]
Am I supposed to . . .

[HIGHWAYMAN *sings the following with music.*]

HIGHWAYMAN When I was young, but I was never young
   I met a man who taught a certain song.
   "I never met a man who couldn't die,
   tragedy, tragedeye."

   The song went on, I trembled as I heard.
   "I never met a man whose final word
   Astounded or resounded through the room,
   Trageday, tragedoom."

   I begged the man, but I would never beg.
   I slapped him and I kicked him in the leg.
   I ordered him to stop his awful chant.
   "Relent, recant, old man!"

[*Music stops.*]

BESS I have to say, it's strange.

HIGHWAYMAN In what way?

BESS How do you know when to do it?

HIGHWAYMAN Bess is secret from the land. The land is where I
   operate. It doesn't seem quite fair.

BESS Are you here for a bed?

HIGHWAYMAN Are you?

BESS Not really.

HIGHWAYMAN But I am.

BESS I think upstairs.

[*Beat.*]

HIGHWAYMAN You see what it is, a lady is waiting for me.

BESS Upstairs?

HIGHWAYMAN Her eyes, all her qualities are very different from
   yours. I didn't plan it this way, I mean, I didn't count on the

landlord's daughter. Even barely existing. Beer-fed, I think that's what you said? I feel foolish. My chances, I don't claim they would have been total, but neither insignificant. Am I right? She's no short order herself, I wouldn't want to put her down, very pretty, well-intentioned, weak arms and good strong sex organs. Not hard to recoup. But that's not a nice way to hurt people, and I would feel low if I didn't follow up with her as planned. She has children, there are wild animals around, and they've burnt down her house once already. I want you to see the situation. That I'd try. I'm usually very aggressive. It's my meat and make, after all.

[*Pause.*]

BESS   Do you give to the poor?

HIGHWAYMAN   I guess so, if they ask me.

>   [*Beat.*]

>   They don't always ask me.

>   [*Beat.*]

>   Her name's Matilda, what about that?

>   [*Beat.*]

>   I'm getting excited. I think I'd better go upstairs or we can't know what'll happen. Can we?

BESS   No.

HIGHWAYMAN   No. Maybe I'll see you on the way out?

BESS   I don't know.

HIGHWAYMAN   Obviously I would like that.

>   [*He starts to exit. Stops.*]

>   See you.

[*Exit.*]

BESS   After this I have one dream. All right. I think it must be the darkest time of night. When is that? I think I know. No, I don't know, that was the dream. And I knew those things. And I could tell things from the position of planets. Which I recognized. Clouds. I could tell from the clouds what the earth would be? And when they would be on the road? So I would have to go off it. How to find a hedge to go off it into. And know if the hedge is hungry and not go into it then and look again. That this would sometimes be true for miles and I would have to remember that I would have to dig in the ground, because they're on the road now. I knew how to do that and I had to do that, or also, I wouldn't have to, because there was nothing but me out there, nothing, me moving. Going. Knowing. Looking. Knowing. Not knowing. Knowing again. Or also, a rain like a wind, a moon like a ship, all ocean. I thought, this is what I'm gonna be spraying like all these. Spraying out of here to be then.

[*Beat.*]

Here. Inn.

[*Lights down on* BESS *and up on* HIGHWAYMAN, MATILDA, *and* GUESTS *sitting around in an upstairs room.* HIGHWAYMAN *and* MATILDA *have obviously had wild sex.*]

[*Beat.* ALL *laugh.*]

GUEST 1 Yeah.

GUEST 2 Yup.

MATILDA Wonderful.

HIGHWAYMAN I said if you don't get up out of that ditch, people will think you're one of ours.

MATILDA You.

HIGHWAYMAN Actually she looked sort of attractive, with her front torn down, hair blowing around.

GUEST 1 Uh-oh.

MATILDA You didn't. Did you?

HIGHWAYMAN Did I?

GUEST 1 Did she?

[ALL *laugh.*]

HIGHWAYMAN By that time it was practically dark. Why would anyone do that, when I or someone like me, any moment . . . fitted out like that, like a ship! Excuse me a second.

[HIGHWAYMAN *exits. Lights down on* GUESTS *and* MATILDA. MATILDA *walks across the stage to where* BESS *is standing. Lights up on the two women.*]

MATILDA Was it a good dream?

BESS To be out there. When I'm always in here waiting. I dreamt I was out there.

MATILDA Because you'd just met him?

BESS I had that dream before.

MATILDA Recurring?

BESS But I had it when I saw him. While I was seeing him. After.

MATILDA Do you still have it?

BESS I'm having it.

MATILDA Do you like it?
        [*Pause.*]
        Is that what you wanted when you . . . I think I know the story.

BESS I didn't want anything.

MATILDA Not even to save him?

BESS How could I save him?

MATILDA You're strong.

BESS Nothing is strong. There's nothing. Just him.

MATILDA What about you?

BESS I'm here. I'm in here. I'm dreaming I'm out on the moor. I'm waiting.

MATILDA For what?

BESS When he comes back.

[*Lights down on* BESS *and* MATILDA. MATILDA *crosses back to the* GUESTS *and sits down with them. Lights up on* MATILDA *and* GUESTS.]

GUEST 1 You ready for another go?

MATILDA With you?

GUEST 2 You crazy?

MATILDA   He'd shoot.

GUEST 1   He's not a mean guy.

GUEST 2   Knows what's his.

GUEST 1   Ranger knows what's his?

GUEST 2   What should be.

MATILDA   [*To* GUEST 1.]
   What's your name, anyway?

GUEST 2   [*To* MATILDA.]
   You better get yourself together.

MATILDA   Tied up?

[MATILDA *and* GUEST 1 *laugh.*]

GUEST 2   Am I the only solid brain in the room?

GUEST 1   Solid belly.

MATILDA   Solid heart.

[MATILDA *and* GUEST 1 *laugh.*]

GUEST 1   I like you, Matilda.

GUEST 2   You're awash.

GUEST 1   I guess I am.

MATILDA   Don't anybody worry. Where's my man?

GUEST 1   Oh, lady, a lot of spirit been chipped that way.

MATILDA   Who're you talking in terms of? I know who I'm dealing
   with. He and I see in the same direction. We've got a friendship.

GUEST 1   Good you.

MATILDA   Right! I know how an egg fries. The top part's the best. The
   rest you take 'cause you can. I know that. He remembers my kids.

GUEST 2   They're not his kids.

MATILDA   Well, he does for 'em sometimes.
   [*To* GUEST 1.]

I don't know how I sit around your friend.

GUEST 1   He gets grouchy when he does.

MATILDA   Now that is a what I find difficult to abide. When can you laugh else? These days.

GUEST 1   These days. Said good.

GUEST 2   Look at you. Doing fine. Doing fine right now. In no position. You see out there? You gonna live out there? Talk "these days." You haven't seen it. Line stretching from the sky, you run into it, you even walk into it, cuts you in two, zip.

MATILDA   [*To* GUEST 1.]
What's he doing?

GUEST 1   [*To* GUEST 2.]
Hey—

GUEST 2   You "Hey." You kick. You gonna forget? I won't let you forget.

GUEST 1   You won't let me?

GUEST 2   Yeah, get mad. I got the breath, though. Remember that. I got three-fourths of it.

GUEST 1   That's why you look like you do.

GUEST 2   Sure. You save that.

GUEST 1   Save it why? So I can get another thousand time of you bawling in my ear when you think I'm sleeping? You trying to wake me up.

GUEST 2   Crow-bite bitch.
[*To* MATILDA.]
You should have seen what we were.

GUEST 1   [*To* GUEST 2]
You think everybody wants to know.

GUEST 2   [*To* GUEST 1]
I never told anybody.

GUEST 1   I see you. Crouching in it. Watching for when to slip it.

GUEST 2   You're stepping that out.

GUEST 1   She doesn't wanna know.

GUEST 2   You think I'm—

GUEST 1   When's the last time I put it to a woman without your skin hanging all over the room?

GUEST 2   You think this is the one for you? His one?

GUEST 1   Oh, now, Ruin, you know he'd give me this one. If I just asked. He's got a hundred.

GUEST 2   He needs what he's got.

MATILDA   Nobody gives me. You both gone away? I think I'd like to see you war.

GUEST 1   No, lovely, we don't do that.

GUEST 2   He doesn't have the breath.

GUEST 1   Bast with that!

GUEST 2   Night our daddy—

GUEST 1   [*To* MATILDA.]

He wasn't there we weren't born he's making it up.

GUEST 2   FORGOTTEN. Why even.

[*Beat.*]

Forgotten.

[*Pause.*]

MATILDA   Where's my friend?

[*Lights down on* GUESTS *and* MATILDA. *Lights up on* BESS *and the* HIGHWAY-MAN.]

HIGHWAYMAN   It was very good. I thought it was very well done.

BESS   That's nice.

HIGHWAYMAN   She seems to move variously at once. I'd estimate twenty-three vectors.

BESS   Wow.

HIGHWAYMAN I know. I'm really more, one to four. With dispatch. She likes it.

[*Beat.*]

You do that?

BESS Twenty-three?

HIGHWAYMAN No, I mean, any.

BESS I'm-it's a question.

HIGHWAYMAN I have to admit I was wondering.

[*Beat.*]

How old are you?

BESS I'm not sure.

HIGHWAYMAN Because it just occurred to me that you might be really seriously young, whatever that means. You have this sort of stupid look on your face. I know you're not stupid, I mean stupid like a lamb.

BESS Thanks.

HIGHWAYMAN I don't have assumptions about lambs. I mean, I find it attractive, honestly.

BESS Have you killed people?

HIGHWAYMAN Not since last week.

BESS I guess everyone loves that.

HIGHWAYMAN It's for survival. When you're a highwayman, you have to do it.

BESS You'd rather not?

HIGHWAYMAN It's impossible to say. It'd be a different life then.

BESS I guess.

HIGHWAYMAN Maybe not.

BESS Is she sleeping?

HIGHWAYMAN I don't think so. She's up there with those two brothers.

BESS   Oh. She's . . .

HIGHWAYMAN   No, I don't think so. She knows I'm coming back.

BESS   Oh.

HIGHWAYMAN   I said I would.

[*Pause.*]

You could come up too.

BESS   No.

HIGHWAYMAN   You could—she's very nice, she's clean.

[*Beat.*]

Well, no, all right. But now I have to.

[*He starts to exit. Stops and turns back.*]

Look—

[*Walks up to her. Stops.*]

Could I—?

[*Takes hold of her hair. Looks at it in his hand. Gives it a tug. Lets go of it.*]

Great.

[HIGHWAYMAN *exits.* GUESTS *and* MATILDA *exit too.*]

BESS   Things you'd probably trip over if you tried to go out there. Without muscle. Trip over, fall into. No one takes care of that. No one has the job to. So you have to be born a certain way and your ancestors have to've all been bleeding and go Fuck! Who cares? And not care and pull out the animal's teeth.

[*Beat.*]

You have to pull out the teeth and throw the animal away across the land. That way you teach a lesson. You teach the land to eat the animal and not you. Then you can be alone again. It's how you're born and how you don't die. The same when it's not an animal. It's you and then them and then you. When it's another man, when it's a girl, even a child. And they would be happier for that because otherwise it's the same sun and the questions. Right?

[HIGHWAYMAN *and* MATILDA *enter, talking to each other.*]

HIGHWAYMAN   You have the money?

MATILDA   It's in a safe place.

HIGHWAYMAN   And you know if anyone tries to take it on the road, what to do?

MATILDA   I say I had it from you.

HIGHWAYMAN   That should do it.

MATILDA   As a present.

HIGHWAYMAN   [*As imaginary mugger.*]
"A present? I just bet. What's he giving a whore like you a present for? 'Present' for a nice wet—"

MATILDA   "He's my friend. He plays with my children. And you better stop talking to me like that, or he'll be on you."

HIGHWAYMAN   "I think maybe I'd like to give you a present too."

[HIGHWAYMAN *pushes* MATILDA *to her knees in blow-job position.*]

MATILDA   "He'll kill you for this."

BESS   But you notice when you grew up in the inn, which I did, you notice, and you learn, there are things that are true, in here, out there who knows, but in here, and you learn—
[HIGHWAYMAN *moans.*]
about burials
[HIGHWAYMAN *moans.*]
and vectors
[HIGHWAYMAN *moans.*]
and horses.
[HIGHWAYMAN *comes. Beat. During the following line, lights slowly down on* HIGHWAYMAN *and* MATILDA.]
You learn behind the window and you're lucky about that.

[*Lights down on* BESS. *A pause in the dark, and then we hear the* GUESTS.]

GUEST 2   Get up.

GUEST 1   Not yet.

GUEST 2   We gotta move.

GUEST 1   Move beyond.

GUEST 2   Out on the highway.

GUEST 1   Bones underfoot.

GUEST 2   Get up.

GUEST 1   To ride—

GUEST 2   And ride.

GUEST 1   Day out.

GUEST 2   Roll up your wescot.

GUEST 1   Sleep on that.

GUEST 2   Get up.

GUEST 1   Sleep on that.

GUEST 2   Not yet.

GUEST 1   You get up.

GUEST 2   Your leg's on top of my leg.

GUEST 1   Sorry.
[*Beat. Sound of a thump.*]
OK.

GUEST 2   OK.

GUEST 1   We're up.

GUEST 2   Let's move.

GUEST 1   Into the wind.

GUEST 2   Or further.

GUEST 1   I love you.

GUEST 2   Sure, I love you.

[GUESTS *exit in the dark. Lights up on* BESS *and* MATILDA.]

MATILDA   Would you tell me, I'm confused, was it you who told us about all this initially?

[*No answer.*]

Did it happen or is it going to happen?

[*No answer.*]

Are you a ghost?

BESS What kind?

MATILDA Yes. What kind are you?

BESS I'm a brat.

MATILDA It's no picnic.

BESS This isn't what I was after.

MATILDA What were you after?

BESS I wanted it to be him first.

MATILDA The Highwayman?

BESS I'm sorry.

MATILDA He's dead.

BESS He's coming.

MATILDA He's always first.

BESS I know.

MATILDA What about you?

BESS He thinks I'm beautiful.

MATILDA You are.

BESS He knows then. He knows I am. He makes me . . .

[*Beat.*]

MATILDA Makes you what?

BESS He makes me.

MATILDA Is he the one who's talking?

BESS Do you see him here?

MATILDA No.

BESS Doesn't mean he's not.

[TIM *enters and stands near the entrance.*]

TIM Bess? I just wanna know if you're OK. It scares me when you're like that. I wish you'd call me. I think there're things we could— I—you could do that could be done to make things easier for you. I know you said it makes it worse when I'm worried, and it's not that I'm worried, so I try not to worry. I just would feel better if you'd call me. I don't like calling you this much, I'm afraid you're at home and not answering, I don't. I can't stand the picture of you just sitting there with me calling. I feel stupid. I feel stupid. I don't want you to talk to me if you don't want to. I'm not trying to make you talk to me. I just wanna know you're OK. I hate this. You could call and leave a message. I won't pick up unless you tell me to in the message. Are you there? Are you crying? I hate it but I keep thinking of you crying. You cry so much. I think there's something that could be done. Really. I don't think you have to feel this way all the time. I'm afraid of where you are. Where are you? I'll help you. I'll do anything you want. Please just . . . please just don't hurt yourself. I'm not saying I think you will. Please don't, because I know you won't, because you're not that selfish. OK? I—

[TIM *exits.* BESS *takes a few steps after him.*]

BESS Tim?

[*Beat.* BESS *addresses the audience.*]

This is my father's inn. My father is the lord. Lan-lord. I cover the window with ice. The ice is delivered on the wind. I don't have to move to put it over.

[*Beat. Very quickly.*]

So I decided to keep inside to be, I decided to be kept inside. So I inferred, so I would I realized I could be able to stay and look out, through the ice, at the land, that would be nice, so I did that, good, it was airless, not suffocating, just empty, just me, it would be warm, I had a dress on, I had the inn on, I had the glass, it wasn't cracked, that was nice, it was closed, that was all.

[*The* HIGHWAYMAN *enters. He sings the following to the audience, accompanied by music.*]

HIGHWAYMAN   The horse was a moon in the shadow
    The moon was a horse in the sea
    The moor never wore its waistcoat
    The road was a wasted tree
    I couldn't have stood in the shadow
    The shadow was deeper than time
    Where shadow dissolves in the riding
    Riding, riding
    The shadow runs cold in the riding
    And the riding runs cold in the rhyme.
    Bonny, bonny, bonny, bonny, bonny, bonny, bonny, bonny
    Bonny, bonny, bonny, bonny, bonny, bonny, bonny.

BESS   [*To* MATILDA.]
    Where is this?

MATILDA   You want me to tell you?

BESS   Show me. Where?

MATILDA   I don't know.

BESS   You have to show me. You have to help.

MATILDA   What can I do?

BESS   You don't know?

MATILDA   I—

BESS   Save us.

MATILDA   When?

BESS   Punish them.

MATILDA   Who?

BESS   Bundle 'em into the God damn outside.

[*Lights down.*]

[*There is a musical interlude in the dark. All the actors gather onstage to listen. When the music stops,* ALL *exit except* BESS, *who stays against the upstage wall. Lights up.*]

[GUESTS *enter.*]

GUEST 1 You hear?

GUEST 2 Did I.

GUEST 1 It's a new height.

GUEST 2 Say there's never been like this.

GUEST 1 Sure, I can remember. Never.

GUEST 2 Never.

GUEST 1 COME ON!

GUEST 2 Unh!

GUEST 1 Every day.

GUEST 2 Twice a day.

GUEST 1 Twice on Sunday.
[GUEST 2 *gives a short sharp laugh.*]
He's on 'em.

GUEST 2 Through 'em.

GUEST 1 All around 'em.

GUEST 2 Comes up outta the ground.

GUEST 1 Down outta the height.

GUEST 2 Cold speed on his skin.

GUEST 1 Cold proof.

GUEST 2 That's why he does it.

GUEST 1 Take it!

GUEST 2 Take that, Clean White.

GUEST 1 Gleamy teeth.

GUEST 2 Knock 'em out.

GUEST 1   Doctor.

GUEST 2   Lawyer.

GUEST 1   Banker.

GUEST 2   Preacher.

GUEST 1   Down!

GUEST 2   Gimme everything.

GUEST 1   Gimme everything 'cause I need it. 'Cause I need to take it.

GUEST 2   Twice a day.

GUEST 1   They're afraid to travel.

GUEST 2   No tea parties.

GUEST 1   Stay at home.

GUEST 2   They don't like it.

GUEST 1   So they're going after him.

GUEST 2   Of course they are.

GUEST 1   Trying to find him.

GUEST 2   Poor fools.

GUEST 1   Trying hard.

GUEST 2   They'll cut it out if they know what's healthy.

GUEST 1   They don't have enough men for it.

GUEST 2   And they got a lot of men.

GUEST 1   Not to survive that. Men they have.

GUEST 2   True.

GUEST 1   So . . . they're paying extra for anyone to sign up.

GUEST 2   No.

GUEST 1   Yes. They got posters.

GUEST 2   You can't read.

GUEST 1   I know what they say.

GUEST 2 Got his picture?

GUEST 1 Yeah. It doesn't look like him. It's a bad likeness.

GUEST 2 Figures.

GUEST 1 You think anyone'll do it?

GUEST 2 People do everything for money.

GUEST 1 There's a lot of people that could use some money.

GUEST 2 Serpents.

GUEST 1 We know what that's like.

[*Pause.*]

GUEST 2 What're you-

GUEST 1 I'm just saying.

GUEST 2 What're you saying?

GUEST 1 You know Annie?

GUEST 2 Of course I know her.

GUEST 1 Know how she was working up at the big white?

GUEST 2 For the ploggy?

GUEST 1 Yeah, well, it was the first decent post she had since she was a kid.

GUEST 2 Decent? You mean 'cause he liked her arse so much?

GUEST 1 Well, he'd to give her things.

GUEST 2 Rod the child.

GUEST 1 You know what I'm getting at.

GUEST 2 I don't.

GUEST 1 You know what happened to him on the highway.

GUEST 2 Sure.

GUEST 1 Well, and now she doesn't have that job anymore.

GUEST 2 One less of us slaving for one of them.

GUEST 1   You seen her lately?

GUEST 2   One less of them.

GUEST 1   She looks like a mess.

GUEST 2   Loyal mess. Honest mess.

GUEST 1   I'm just saying.

GUEST 2   No you're not.

GUEST 1   Not what?

GUEST 2   Just saying.

GUEST 1   I'm saying it's not so simple.

GUEST 2   That's what you're saying? That's not what I hear you saying.

GUEST 1   It gets like you wanna be able to do something once in a while. What it's like to have something.

GUEST 2   I don't credit this.

GUEST 1   You don't think about it?

GUEST 2   What's think about it? You tell me what you're telling me. You say it now.

GUEST 1   Just what I've been saying.

[GUEST 2 *grabs* GUEST 1.]

GUEST 2   SAY!

GUEST 1   Get off me.

GUEST 2   YOU'RE LEAVING AWAY TO THEM. RIGHT?

GUEST 1   Get the hell off!

GUEST 2   You SAY!

GUEST 1   YEAH, then, YEAH!

[GUEST 1 *breaks free and has a coughing fit.*]

GUEST 2   Look at you.

[GUEST 1 *coughs.*]

You're gonna be a great soldier.

[GUEST 1 *coughs.*]

Leftenant Wrack. Sure, general.

GUEST 1   I'm going the God damn out of here.

GUEST 2   Sure.

GUEST 1   Get me some God damn canal.

GUEST 2   Ladies love it when you wheeze at 'em.

GUEST 1   Ladies love it when your face.

GUEST 2   Get the hell off then.

[*Beat.*]

GUEST 1   You come.

GUEST 2   Hell.

GUEST 1   You'd be good at it.

GUEST 2   I don't hunt my friends.

GUEST 1   He's not your friends.

GUEST 2   Cough.

GUEST 1   We don't have friends.

GUEST 2   Cough cough.

GUEST 1   Just me and just you.

[*Pause.*]

GUEST 2   How come you didn't leave yet?

GUEST 1   I wish you would try to see what I see. There's a story involved.

GUEST 2   I don't see it.

GUEST 1   I see it.

GUEST 2   You're lying.

GUEST 1   I'm not lying. You don't see it. But I see it.

GUEST 2   Tell it me.

GUEST 1   I can't tell it. Just see it. You see it now?

GUEST 2   Nonsense.

GUEST 1   I know you believe me.

GUEST 2   Doesn't have to do with believe.

GUEST 1   You're gonna come with me.

GUEST 2   Crazy.

GUEST 1   No one else is gonna help me with breath.

GUEST 2   Serve you right.

GUEST 1   It's all right. I see it.

GUEST 2   You always see it.

GUEST 1   Not like this.
   [*Beat.*]
   Have some money.

GUEST 2   Don't talk about that.

GUEST 1   That's part of it.
   [*Beat.*]
   I swear.

[GUESTS *exit.* TIM *and* BESS *enter and sit in chairs. A long, awful pause.*]

TIM   There's nothing to eat.

BESS   You hungry?

TIM   No.

BESS   Nothing in the store is fresh, it's all covered up, you can't see it.

TIM   That's not true.

BESS   Weights and measures.

TIM   You're being a brat.

BESS   That's a kind of animal.

TIM   No it's not.

BESS   Three-toed. Four-toed.

TIM   Ten.

BESS   How do you know? Did you count?

TIM   I—

BESS   Is that what you've been doing?

TIM   Jesus!

BESS   You don't know shit about animals.

[*Beat.*]

TIM   Tell me about animals.

BESS   What's the point. If I say something . . . all I can say . . .

TIM   There are two kinds . . . ?

BESS   There's more than two kinds.

TIM   Domestic?

BESS   They don't talk in real life. And wild. They talk. But not talk. It's more they have what's like music.

TIM   Like coyotes?

BESS   No. Yes. It's not really for hearing. It's for hunting.

TIM   What about—

BESS   They're all hunting.

TIM   And the domestic ones?

BESS   I don't know.

TIM   They get hunted?

BESS   They don't hunt.

TIM   They're caught.

BESS   No . . . they just hold themselves.

TIM   Then who gets caught?

BESS No one you know.
> [*Beat.*]
> And that's it.

[*Pause.*]

TIM Your phone's not working.

BESS It's not?

TIM It says it's disconnected.

BESS Yeah.

TIM You should pay.
> [*Pause.*]
> OK?

BESS Yeah.

TIM That's it really?

BESS That's the basics.

TIM Of animals.

BESS Uh-huh.

TIM Not what I meant.

BESS That's it. Really.

TIM Do I ever come back?

BESS Why do you say it like that?

TIM Do I?

BESS Like it's something I read.

TIM What about him, is he?

BESS Are you asking me? What are you asking me?

TIM I'm asking, I'm asking you what you want me to do.

BESS I want it not to matter what I want.

[*Pause.*]

TIM I'm gonna just touch your hair?

　　　[*No answer.*]

　　　I'm gonna just do that, OK?

　　　[*No answer.*]

　　　No.

　　　[TIM *stands up.*]

　　　You know I can't walk very fast. Bess.

[TIM *exits.*]

BESS Here, in here it's the right heat. I cover the window with earth. People bring in the earth with their shoes. They don't talk to me. It's too dark for them to see me.

　　　[*Beat.*]

　　　Here, in here it's the right heat. I cover the window with fire. The fire lies flat against the pane. It lights up the room and I see my own hands. They don't look old. I know time is over. No one else knows. They can't get it. No one can get in.

　　　[*Beat.*]

　　　Here's the story. There was a girl. She kicked everyone. She said it was so they wouldn't miss her. But it was because they wouldn't miss her. It's a stupid—it's a stupid story. She could never kick anyone. Or do anything or want or think anything.

　　　[*Beat.*]

　　　I know what to tell you. It's only the truth. No questions. Of course this is where I am.

　　　[*Beat.*]

　　　You could come—

　　　[*Beat.*]

　　　—out . . .

　　　Why?

　　　—I'd like to remind you that the moor is habitable. Habitabitable. Habitabitabitable. Hospitababitle. With life-forms. Who savage. Someday something will come in and you'll have to go out there.

　　　[*Beat.*]

So I build up my strength. Emergency measures. I smell my skin.
I compare it with my other skin. Things like this'll be helpful.
Because I know I've been in here since I was born and no one
else. And if someone else was here, he didn't see me. And if he
saw me, he's coming back to get me.

[*Beat.*]

Because he would like me.

[*Beat.*]

Would he want me to go, I think he might want me to go with
him. I think that's what he would want. There's no way I can do
that. Look at me. I've been here my whole life. A quiet life. I used
to bring sugar lumps out to the stable. There's a cellar somewhere
here, no, a tunnel through, not the cellar, I think there are stairs
and there's a, stairs through a room where they keep . . . beets? Is
that possible? Through there, a passage to the stable. I go
through there with my hand full of sugar. My hand is dry. Or
both. That's how I carry it through the passage, wedged out of the
wet land. So I don't set foot out of the inn.

[*Beat.*]

I get there, I get to the stable. There are so many of them. I'm
saying this, it's like a pillar of my childhood. I'm not just any one
of those little girls. Because these were not a fantasy. They're,
they shit and they take a piss, they have spit foaming up, big sour
spit, they're covered with scars and their coats, you can't even say
coats, they're covered in their skins, is the most you can say.
They'll bite, I have the rents some still on me.

[*Beat.*]

I get to the stable, still inside, I have sugar in my hand, that I took
from the kitchen. There are so many of them. Everyone put an
animal there and went in to drink. When it's the busy season
there's fullness of them. And I'm coming down, there's a push-bell
the people do when they need something, but then I disappear, I
go get the sugar and I go down the stairs into the place and into
the place, to see them, to give them the sugar. I don't know how
to describe. I said. Filthy. Some are about to die. Some are on
their first trip. Whips. They all have four and some have five and

some are daughters. Grown-up. I'm here with the sugar. Just here. I put out my hand . . . a tongue comes down, no, teeth. You have to put your hand flat and not get bit. Big teeth. You can tell the work. Eyes like my dumb eyes. You know what they want, it makes them want it more, they want, they would say—they can't, but—no, they wouldn't—it makes them want, they want the saddle blanket and the saddle, the saddle bags and the rein, they want, and the spurs, reins and spurs and hands high, but even done like that they want to go, they want me to take them and go, and they would be better off to go, says their faces, go!

[*Beat.*]

And I say I can't. Just because it's not. What about wind and stripes? But it's not.

[*Beat.* HIGHWAYMAN *enters.*]

Anyway he might not come.

HIGHWAYMAN   Go on.

BESS   He might not . . . he has a dangerous life. His life is dangerous and violent. He really doesn't think about things like this.

[*Pause.*]

HIGHWAYMAN   Bess . . .

BESS   Yeah?

HIGHWAYMAN   I'm back.

BESS   Hi.

HIGHWAYMAN   How're things?

BESS   Things are OK. Yeah, they're OK.

HIGHWAYMAN   Can I ask whether you thought about me?

BESS   I don't know.

HIGHWAYMAN   Did you?

BESS   Yes.

HIGHWAYMAN   That makes me happy.

BESS   Good.

HIGHWAYMAN   I thought of you too.

BESS   You did?

HIGHWAYMAN   You understand why I couldn't come back sooner.

BESS   Yes.

HIGHWAYMAN   They're making it harder for me. There are more soldiers now. I have to be careful about where I go. I do a lot of hiding out.

BESS   I understand.

HIGHWAYMAN   But I've definitely thought about you. Know what I think?

BESS   No.

HIGHWAYMAN   I think often that you're the most beautiful girl I've ever seen. Do you believe me?

BESS   No.

HIGHWAYMAN   It's true, though. It's true that I often think that. That's what I meant, do you believe that I often think that. Not do you believe that you are. Do you?

BESS   I don't know.

HIGHWAYMAN   I wish I could convince you. It would be good for your self-esteem.

BESS   Thanks.

HIGHWAYMAN   You're sad, aren't you?

BESS   Oh . . .

HIGHWAYMAN   Your eyes look sad. Is that possible? Don't take it as a criticism.

BESS   OK.

HIGHWAYMAN   I think it's beautiful.

BESS   Thanks.

HIGHWAYMAN But I wish you weren't.

BESS Thanks.

HIGHWAYMAN Sad.

BESS I know.

HIGHWAYMAN Unless—well—it's awkward to say...

[*Beat.*]

BESS What?

HIGHWAYMAN I wouldn't mind it so much if it were because of me. Because of missing me. It isn't, is it?

BESS No.

HIGHWAYMAN Oh. I mean, I didn't really think it would be.

BESS It's not.

HIGHWAYMAN No. Not even a little?

[*Pause.*]

BESS I don't know.

HIGHWAYMAN The thing is, I was a little bit sad thinking of you. Because of wanting to visit you again.

BESS Oh. Well, I wanted . . . I felt like that a little.

HIGHWAYMAN Really? I hoped so. That's great!

BESS I didn't mind about—about Matilda. I didn't care about that.

HIGHWAYMAN She's not here now, is she? I mean, because I don't want to see her tonight. I want to make that clear.

BESS I don't think she's here.

HIGHWAYMAN Good.

BESS I didn't care about that.

HIGHWAYMAN That's very nice of you.

BESS And I can . . .

[*Beat.*]

HIGHWAYMAN Sorry?

BESS I don't, it doesn't bother me to do that.

HIGHWAYMAN What?

BESS Whatever Matilda . . . what you do, I just, I don't have an objection, for me, for you and me to do that.

HIGHWAYMAN Really?

BESS Yeah. It's OK.

HIGHWAYMAN Oh, Bess.

BESS Because, it's not a big deal to me.

HIGHWAYMAN You don't have to impress me, pretty one. I know you're very young.

BESS I'm not that young.

HIGHWAYMAN Let's not talk about this.

BESS OK.

HIGHWAYMAN Because it'll begin to ache.

BESS I'm saying—

HIGHWAYMAN I have to warn you.

BESS You don't have to warn me.

HIGHWAYMAN I warn you.

BESS No.
[HIGHWAYMAN *dashes over to* BESS *and bites her very hard on the shoulder. He holds his grip for a moment. Then he straightens up and looks at her.*]
It's all right.

HIGHWAYMAN [*Turning away from her.*]
You see, I was overcome.

BESS Don't worry.

HIGHWAYMAN What an angel you are.

BESS Thank you.

HIGHWAYMAN [*Turning back to her.*]
It's part and parcel of my way of life.

BESS I know.

HIGHWAYMAN It's because you're so beautiful.

BESS Thank you.

HIGHWAYMAN I wish you would say something.

BESS Are you going to stay with me?

HIGHWAYMAN Darling.

BESS It's the wrong thing to say.

HIGHWAYMAN No, no, it's not wrong. It's not wrong, it's very sweet.

BESS Because you're not. It would be stupid to think you would.

HIGHWAYMAN Not stupid.

BESS But you're not.

HIGHWAYMAN They're hunting me, Bess. I'm harried and I'm pressed. I can't stay anywhere. My defense is in moving. Because I know the moor better than they do. That's my chance of survival.

BESS I know.

HIGHWAYMAN I'll just have to ride around and think of you.

BESS You'll forget me.

HIGHWAYMAN No.

BESS It's all right.

HIGHWAYMAN Bess, let me explain that I won't forget you.

BESS I might forget you.

HIGHWAYMAN What?

BESS I won't, but—

HIGHWAYMAN Don't. Don't say that.

BESS I won't. I just meant.

HIGHWAYMAN   Don't say that.

BESS   No. I'll stay here forever and wait.

HIGHWAYMAN   Until I die?

BESS   I'll wait here.

HIGHWAYMAN   Bess.

BESS   It's all right.

HIGHWAYMAN   Oh, Bess.

BESS   Because you couldn't . . . take me.

HIGHWAYMAN   Take you out on the moor?

BESS   Yeah. I know you can't.

HIGHWAYMAN   Do you know how to ride?

BESS   I could learn.—But you can't do that.

HIGHWAYMAN   It would make things more difficult.
>   [*Beat.*]
>   I would like to, but it would make things very hard. They're already hard.

BESS   I know. That's what I'm saying.

HIGHWAYMAN   I don't think you'd like it.

BESS   I would hate it.

HIGHWAYMAN   There you are.
>   [*Pause.*]
>   Perhaps someday.

BESS   Right.

HIGHWAYMAN   You don't want to do this kind of thing forever. It's actually not possible.

BESS   You might stay somewhere.

HIGHWAYMAN   You could come.

BESS   We would stay somewhere together.

HIGHWAYMAN   It'd be very cozy.

BESS   Yeah. Cozy.

HIGHWAYMAN   Something nice to think about.

BESS   When you think about me.

HIGHWAYMAN   And you'll wait?

BESS   Yes.

HIGHWAYMAN   Then of course where would you go?

BESS   I don't know. I wouldn't go anywhere.

HIGHWAYMAN   Adorable. I can't get over it.

BESS   Thanks.

HIGHWAYMAN   Imagine if everyone could be this fortunate.

BESS   As me.

HIGHWAYMAN   As me!
  [*Pause.*]
  I ought to go.

BESS   I know.

HIGHWAYMAN   Sometimes I wish this weren't my life.

BESS   Don't.

HIGHWAYMAN   Well . . .
  [*Beat.*]
  What if I come back tomorrow?

BESS   Yes.

HIGHWAYMAN   I should have some take then. Should I bring you some?

BESS   It doesn't matter.

HIGHWAYMAN   I'd like to bring you something. Maybe something to wear.

BESS   OK.

HIGHWAYMAN   I'll come back tomorrow. Tomorrow night.

BESS   OK.

HIGHWAYMAN   You'll be here?

BESS   Yeah.

HIGHWAYMAN   Remember that I love you.

>   [*Beat.*]
>
>   I'll just—no I won't.
>
>   [*He turns and begins to exit. Stops.*]
>
>   Tomorrow, Bess.

[*Exit.*]

BESS   I'll see you tomorrow.

[TIM *enters. They look at each other.* BESS *glances at the guitarist, then sings to* TIM *without music.*]

BESS   [*Singing.*]

>   When I
>
>   Please be
>
>   Going to be
>
>   It'll happen here
>
>   I don't have to say
>
>   Riding riding riding daughter daughter moonlight moonlight my intended.
>
>   I would
>
>   Underway
>
>   In the oldest key
>
>   Gone over
>
>   I could only say
>
>   Riding riding riding daughter daughter moonlight moonlight my intended.

[BESS *exits for the first time.* TIM *stares after her. A pause.* MATILDA *enters.*]

MATILDA   Hi there.

TIM Hi.

MATILDA How'd you wind in here?

> [*No answer.*]
> You OK?

TIM No, I—where is this?

MATILDA No, you don't look it.

TIM Why can't it just be one place? I could handle that. What's she doing?

MATILDA Who?

TIM Her.

MATILDA The landlord's daughter?

TIM Yeah. Sure.

MATILDA I guess she's in love.

TIM She can't be. She's sick.

MATILDA She looks OK to me.

TIM No, she's sad.

MATILDA Always had that look to her. I wouldn't have said sad. I would've said, still.

TIM It's a sick sadness.

MATILDA Right. I guess she's in love.

TIM There are names for things. Real things.

MATILDA You ever know any poets?

TIM What are you doing?

MATILDA May I recite?

TIM God.

MATILDA "Follow the careless and happy feet of children back into the kingdom of those dreams which are the sole reality worth living and—"

TIM   OK.

MATILDA   "The sole reality worth living and dying for."

TIM   She doesn't believe that. "Why do people wanna tell you things?" She said. She said, "I hate when people tell you things." She doesn't believe any of it.

MATILDA   Tell you what I believe. I believe there are girls and there are monsters.

TIM   Oh, fuck. I know her. I know her before it was like this. She's not a monster.

MATILDA   No.

TIM   So what?

MATILDA   She's a girl.

TIM   OK.
  [*Beat.*]
  Am I a monster?

MATILDA   Girls are fragile. They need monsters to protect them.

TIM   I'm a monster.

MATILDA   Girls need monsters for infection. To want to wanna get out of you.

TIM   Out of the monster?

MATILDA   Out to.

TIM   Am I?

MATILDA   Monsters are murderers. Monsters murder girls. So girls are murderers.

TIM   I'm hate this. I'm tired of this. I want her to come back.

MATILDA   She can't come back. She's always been here.

TIM   That's just not true.

MATILDA   I been here the same time.

TIM   Where is she?

MATILDA   You know. I know.

TIM   Well, I don't want it.

[*Beat.*]

MATILDA   I'm sorry for you.

TIM   That's not it. She's the one. Somebody has to help her. Where is she?

MATILDA   In love.

TIM   He's gonna keep her here.

MATILDA   Nonsense.

TIM   I can't let him keep her.

MATILDA   What're you gonna do against a man like that?

TIM   Like what? What is it you all think he is? Anyone can get a gun and take stuff. I could do it.

MATILDA   Like lying down with the whole land's life.

TIM   I can do it.

MATILDA   Yeah?

TIM   Yeah.

[TIM *grabs* MATILDA *and pulls her toward him. A long, terribly awkward moment.* TIM *lets go and turns away.*]

I'm sorry, I—I don't know what I'm-but don't laugh, please, she has so much of me.

MATILDA   Be glad she has any.

TIM   Is she really in love with him?

MATILDA   Who knows?

TIM   Don't you?

MATILDA   Not my story.

TIM   Whose?

MATILDA   That's a way to go crazy.

TIM Why isn't it yours?

MATILDA You mean yours.

TIM I want it.

MATILDA It's all been his for a long time.

TIM I'm taking it.

MATILDA How're you gonna do that?

TIM I live here now.

MATILDA So do we all.

TIM He can't stay.
> [*Beat.*]
> Thanks.

MATILDA Don't.

[TIM *exits. Beat.* MATILDA *exits. Lights down, then up on the* GUESTS, *who are dressed as soldiers now, and* TIM.]

TIM Are you brothers?

GUEST 1 No.

GUEST 2 Yeah.

GUEST 1 Long story.

GUEST 2 Back to you.

TIM This is the right place to come?

GUEST 1 That's us.

TIM I don't really understand where we are.

GUEST 1 Look out there.
> [*Indicates audience.*]
> Does that help?

TIM No.

GUEST 2 You were saying.

TIM Tall? Yeah, I think they're engaged is what she said.

GUEST 2   She saw you.

TIM   No, I'm pretty sure not.

GUEST 2   All right.

TIM   It's hard to tell.

GUEST 1   Too intense?

TIM   For me?

GUEST 2   And?

TIM   He was tall . . . I just think he's the guy on the poster. I'm sure it's that guy.

GUEST 1   The Highwayman?

TIM   It was him.

GUEST 2   You never saw him before?

TIM   I don't live here.

GUEST 1   Ever day that goes by someone gets attacked.

GUEST 2   It's a serious thing.

TIM   I understand.

GUEST 1   Little Bess, huh?

TIM   Do you know her?

GUEST 2   Used to.

TIM   I used to live with her.

GUEST 1   At the inn?

TIM   What?

GUEST 2   Her father's not gonna allow that.

GUEST 1   Parents can't do everything.

GUEST 2   How old is she, anyway?

TIM   She's—

GUEST 2   You don't get the reward until we catch him. You know that?

TIM   The reward.

GUEST 1   Are you OK to be telling us things? Think about it for a second before you answer. I believe people know whether they're OK to be speaking if they'd think about it.

TIM   I'm OK.

GUEST 1   Think about it!

[*Beat.*]

TIM   I'm fine. I don't want to think about it.

GUEST 1   Did you think about that, or were you thinking about it?

GUEST 2   Jesus! We're gonna go. We don't have anything else.

GUEST 1   Fine.

GUEST 2   Look at him.

GUEST 1   His eyes are hollow.

GUEST 2   But we're gonna go.

GUEST 1   We have to.

GUEST 2   Life of a hermajesty's.

GUEST 1   Hismajesty's

GUEST 2   Is it?

GUEST 1   I think so.

GUEST 2   [*To* TIM.]
See you later.

TIM   Oh . . .

GUEST 1   We have to make plans.

TIM   Oh. Yeah. Thanks.

[TIM *exits.*]

GUEST 1   Vagrant?

GUEST 2   Yeah.

GUEST 1   Holy?

GUEST 2 [*Turning away.*]
  Doubt it.

GUEST 1 But we're going anyway?

GUEST 2 Yup.

GUEST 1 We could keep some of the reward, maybe.

[GUEST 2 *short sharp laugh. Beat.* GUEST 2 *looks back at* GUEST 1. *Pause.*
GUESTS *exit.* BESS *and* MATILDA *enter.*]

BESS Why're you so interested?

MATILDA I want to understand what happened.

BESS It turns you on?

MATILDA Are you asking?

BESS Don't be ashamed.

MATILDA I want to understand what you were feeling.

[*During the following speech,* BESS *gradually advances on* MATILDA, *who backs up
a little.*]

BESS What I was feeling. You know metal in your mouth? Sour? It's not
  you're naked, because he doesn't care about that. He opens your
  shirt. He doesn't care about that, it's so he can see where to put it.
  You're, What are you doing, because not that you don't know, you
  want him to say. He says, Pretty. He takes your eyes. He covers
  them with his eyes. All you know about is the wind around you.
  Land around you, wet with time. You bare foot feels the bone
  coming up under it, up from under the moss, this old bone,
  smooth as a lip, fills the arc of your foot. He says, Don't move. It's
  a shoulder bone. He says, Don't you make a sound. Your cheek is
  wet for me. Listen. You listen. You can hear for miles. Moldering,
  creeping, growing up against itself, the moor. He says, You're for
  this. You don't move. The bone under your foot doesn't move. He
  says, It's inside you already. Inside and outside are the same. He
  doesn't touch you with his hand. He has no skin. You hear the
  blood of him. He knows you hear it. Moving, he says. That's what
  you hear in me. I'm what moves on this land. He says, When I

take your last piece of movement you'll understand. Kept. You
know that word? And you feel kept on your face, he says Your face
is wet for me. I've made a place for your body. Do you
understand? And he kisses you with no mouth but with something
cold and sour. Mine.

[*Pause.*]

Do you understand?

[*Pause.*]

MATILDA   I don't believe you.

BESS   It's my only real story.

MATILDA   You're making it up.

BESS   I couldn't have made it. Look at me.

MATILDA   I'm looking.

BESS   You like?

[GUESTS *enter.* GUEST 2 *is carrying a long gun and a coil of rope.* BESS
hurries over to them.]

Oh—hi.

[GUESTS *look at each other.*]

Do you—do you want a room? Rooms? Beds?

GUEST 2   Hello, Bess.

BESS   Are you soldiers now?

GUEST 1   Yeah.

BESS   Is it a good experience?

GUEST 2   What are you doing here?

BESS   Waiting for—a friend? People? Just, friends to come? In case, for
a bed? Beds, late? Right?

GUEST 2   We didn't come to sleep.

GUEST 1   We came to ask you, because you know who we're talking about.

GUEST 2   To take him.

BESS Who?

GUEST 2 Don't cheat.

GUEST 1 Don't do that.

BESS Who? Is someone coming here?

GUEST 2 [*To* GUEST 1.]
　　Do it.

GUEST 1 We don't have to really do that.

BESS What?

GUEST 1 We're supposed to do this thing . . .

GUEST 2 We do it. It's procedure.

GUEST 1 There's a procedure that we do with you.

BESS What?

GUEST 1 We don't have to talk to you about it. We do it.

GUEST 2 Do it.

BESS What? Are you—

GUEST 1 It's not killing you. Or like that.

GUEST 2 [*To* BESS.]
　　Don't move.
　　[*To* GUEST 1.]
　　Do it.

GUEST 1 You. I can't breathe so good in here.

[GUEST 2 *goes to* BESS *and holds up the gun and rope as if to measure her. Retreats.*]

GUEST 2 [*To* GUEST 1.]
　　You have to hold her.

[GUEST 1 *goes around behind* BESS *and holds her still. Together the* GUESTS *tie her up, fastening the gun so it points to her head.* BESS *doesn't struggle. At some point during the process,* MATILDA *speaks.*]

MATILDA No. Don't do it.

GUEST 2 [*Not stopping.*]
    Why not?

[*When the* GUESTS *are finished, they step away.*]

GUEST 1 It's so you won't get away and warn him we're here. We
    weren't gonna hurt you.

BESS Are you gonna kill him?

GUEST 2 Yup.

BESS Don't.

GUEST 1 You'll meet someone else.

GUEST 2 Don't move.

GUEST 1 We'll wait now.

GUEST 2 Don't move or it'll go off.
    [*Beat.*]
    There's no safety on it. So.

[*Beat.* GUEST 2 *exits. Beat.* GUEST 1 *follows him off.* MATILDA *looks away from*
BESS. *Pause.*]

BESS What will you do after this?

MATILDA I'm not sure. What will you do?

BESS It doesn't work like that.

MATILDA Why not?

BESS I'm just here. This is it.

MATILDA Where?

BESS No. Just here.

MATILDA The inn?

BESS In here.

MATILDA Is that what you want?
    [*No answer.*]
    Do you want me to untie you?

BESS Do you want me to untie you?

[HIGHWAYMAN *enters. He addresses the audience.*]

HIGHWAYMAN One wants to say something, I mean. Here's the floor. Thanks. You want to keep people's hopes up, when you can, that's not, I'll admit that's not the first thing on one's mind all the time. I've tried to dress in a way that'd be appropriate to passing by at a gallop or stopping and saying Dismount. People don't always know what that means. This is a strange area. I've travelled, I travel a long ways, and it's hard to say where I'm originally from. They're entranced from the first word and I don't like to disagree. There's so much of the same for them. It's the same by the ocean as it is on the moor. In my opinion, a trance is what they're after. It seems to me to be the wrong prize. The last man I killed, I'd gotten him in the belly and he dropped his gun. So he asked me to. Or music. I find both of these helpful in trying to understand. But at the same time, I've never been entranced. It might have to do with the motion of the horse. Air blowing by. Through. And the night: at nighttime, light always changes. I mean, and the maneuvering keeps you unkept.

[*Beat.*]

It usually goes like this: they're riding and I'm riding. I pull mine out in front. I say, Stop. Give me everything you're carrying. And I don't give exceptions. They'll try to lie, but I can tell when they've been comfortable. When people have too much it sits ill on them. They're better off without it. Sometimes that can refer to the most essential things. Sometimes it's their hair. Sometimes some of their clothes. I have an idea, which I see as a picture, and in it the world is almost empty, and everyone I see is just the bare bones of a self, staggering through bright weather between days.

[HIGHWAYMAN *exits.* TIM *and the* GUESTS *enter. All stand in a line behind* BESS, *watching her.*]

BESS Do you hear that?

[*Beat.*]

Do you now?

[*Beat.*]

Are they deaf?

[*Beat. Trying to say "I."*]

Ah—

[*Beat.*]

Bess realizes. She'll stay in here in this inn here on the moor. This inn sinking every day into the peat, dry hole in the sick wet earth, and no one will come in for a bed, and her story will fall off like a baby's tail and crumble while the road curls up around her and she sits nose to feet in the dark and lives forever, and she hears the horse, she knows what it was, and she'll never be a highwayman, she knows so she does it . . .

[BESS *puts her hand on the trigger of the gun.*]

GUESTS, MATILDA, and **TIM**   Ten. Nine. Eight. Seven.

[*Counting continues steadily. After "One," all the lines will come right on each other's heels.*]

BESS   She does it to warn him.

GUESTS, MATILDA, and **TIM**   Six. Five. Four.

BESS   She does it to save him.

GUESTS, MATILDA, and **TIM**   Three. Two. One.

BESS   BANG!

TIM   NO!

GUESTS   [*Turning to face each other.*]
        Shit!

TIM   No. BESS, NO!

[MATILDA *comes downstage and talks to the audience.*]

MATILDA   The image . . . what an image.

GUEST 2   He'll come back.

GUEST 1   Why did she do that?

GUEST 2   You wouldn't get it.

TIM   No.

MATILDA I'm not the first to observe that—in Western culture?—dead girls are something of a turn on.

GUEST 1 What do we do?

MATILDA There's a lot to be said about this.

GUEST 1 What do we do?

GUEST 2 We wait.

MATILDA This image.

TIM NO!

MATILDA Let me get my notes in order.

BESS [*This line should be repeated or cut short as necessary so that it ends when GUEST 2 says "Someone."*]
She realizes. She'll stay in here in this inn here on the moor. This inn sinking every day into the peat, dry hole in the sick wet earth, and no one will come in for a bed, and her story will fall off like a baby's tail and crumble while the road curls up around her and she sits nose to feet in the dark and lives forever, and she hears the horse, she knows what it was, and she'll never be a highwayman, she knows so she does it . . .

MATILDA Somebody has to say these things. We have to say them or we'll never get anywhere. In this country-

GUEST 1 Where are we?

MATILDA In this country these things need to be said and these images . . .

TIM No!

MATILDA . . . need to be examined . . .

GUEST 2 He'll come.

MATILDA . . . and ultimately broken.

GUEST 1 Who?

TIM Bess . . .

GUEST 2   I don't know.

MATILDA   What I do know...

GUEST 2   Someone.

BESS   [*Stops saying her previous line.*]
         BANG!

TIM   Come back.

MATILDA   What I do know...

GUEST 1   I never liked it here.

BESS   She saves him.

GUEST 1   The wind—

GUEST 2   The wind was a torrent—

GUEST 1   The moon was—

GUEST 2   Darkness—

BESS   BANG!

GUEST 1   Tossed upon clotted—

GUEST 2   Cloudy.

GUEST 1   Tossed upon cloudy—

MATILDA   What I do know—

GUEST 2   Cloudy seas.

GUEST 1   That's nice.

BESS   BANG! BANG!

GUEST 2   He's coming.

BESS   BANG!

[*All but* BESS *look out towards the horizon. We hear, faintly, the sound of a horse gallop-ing. The sound gets louder and louder until the volume is unbearable. Then it cuts out. All keep staring out, except* GUEST 1, *who turns his head to look at* BESS. *Beat. Blackout.*]

• • •

The Hunchback of Central Park West

Murray Schisgal

Murray Schisgal

Murray Schisgal has an extensive career spanning plays, screenplays, fiction anthologies and as a producer of five feature films. His Broadway plays include *Luv* (Tony nominated), *Jimmy Shine*, *All Over Town* (Drama Desk Award, Outstanding New Play), *The Chinese and Doctor Fish*, *Twice Around the Park*, and *An American Millionaire*. His films include *Tootsie* (Oscar nominated), *The Tiger Makes Out*, and *Luv* (based on the play).

Murray's Off-Broadway plays include *The Typists and the Tiger* (Vernon Rice Award, Outer Circle Award, Saturday Review Critics Poll Award), *Fragment*, *The Basement*, *The Flatulist*, *Walter*, *The Pushcart Peddlers*, *Sexaholics*, *Extensions*, *Road Show*, *Jealousy*, *Circus Life*, and *Angel Wings* (Off-Off-Broadway Award for Excellence).

Published works include *Days and Nights of a French Horn Player* (novel), *Luv and Other Plays* (collection), The Best American Short Plays (twelve short plays over a number of years, published by Applause Books) and Great American One-Act Plays.

scene

At the rear of the stage, through a panoramic window, a lush, verdant view of Central Park from an apartment on Central Park West.

Mid-stage, a bare, unfurnished living room except for a cordovan, leather armchair. Beside it, a side table with several worn hard-cover books, yellow legal memo-pads, pens and pencils planted in a cup. Upstage, a glass-shelved portable bar.

time

Spring; mid-afternoon. It's a sunless day with soggy puffs of clouds dotting the sky.

sound

Mozart's Church Sonata 12 in C Major, K.263.

• • •

AT RISE: Lights up. The periphery of the living-room is lost in darkness.

THE PLAYWRIGHT is a fastidiously groomed man of mature years. He stands at the bar, his back to the audience, dropping ice cubes into a rocks glass. He is wearing an imported paisley dressing gown, an ascot, black pleated trousers, linen socks and patent leather loafers. Burgeoning out from beneath his dressing gown is a prominent hunchback.

He pours Irish whiskey, no more than a scrupulously estimated inch, from a litre bottle into the glass.

THE PLAYWRIGHT suddenly appears to have heard something; his body stiffens; his head turns to look at offstage entrance door. He listens intently for a beat, putting down the glass on the bar. Then, as if he's satisfied with what he's heard (we've heard nothing), he calls, loudly.

THE PLAYWRIGHT   Yes, who is it?
[*Listens a beat.*]
One second. I'll be right with you.

[*Taking remote from his dressing-gown's pocket, he clicks off CD player. He moves to the offstage entrance door.*]

> [*Offstage.*]
>> Come in, come in. So glad to see you. Kurt Sternheim of the New York Times, isn't it?
>
> [*Listens a beat.*]
>> My pleasure, I assure you. I haven't been interviewed by an American newspaper for . . . Oh, it must be at least a dozen years; quite a surprise hearing from you, I must say. But I am not ungrateful.
>
> [*A beat.*]
>> I'd better take this with me. Come in, do come in.

[THE PLAYWRIGHT *enters, carrying in a wood-framed, cane-seated chair, which he places a few yards opposite the upholstered armchair. He continues talking to his imaginary guest, who stands at the rim of the living room.*]

>> Do forgive the appearance of my apartment. My domestic deserted me and to date I haven't been able to find a reliable replacement. Do sit down. I just poured myself an Irish whiskey, would you care to join me?
>
> [*Listens a beat.*]
>> Of course, you're working, how thoughtless of me. You wouldn't mind if I . . . ?
>
> [*Listens a beat.*]
>> How kind of you. Do sit down. It's somewhat surprising to note that as we age, we gradually modify our daily routine without taking any particular notice of it.

[*He retrieves his glass of whiskey from the bar, talking to his imaginary guest, who is now seated in the cane-seated chair.*]

>> Not too long ago I wouldn't have dreamt of having a drink before five, a self-imposed prohibition that I adhered to for decades. But like all my resolutions, this one, too, has fallen by the wayside. I am, unfortunately, suffering from a period of excruciating, creative . . . What is the correct word?

[*A thoughtful beat.*]

    Impotency! Yes, let's grab the bull by the horns and call it for what it is, impotency! And I choose that word with due deliberation, noting that it is not a reflection of any physical deficiency of my own!

[*He chuckles, sits in the armchair, setting his drink on the side table; he fastidiously crosses his leg, folding his dressing gown over his lap.*]

    You've arrived by happenstance at a rather critical period of my professional life. Incidentally, you do look rather young for a *New York Times* journalist. Without meaning to be rude, how old are you?

[*Listens a beat.*]

    What? Twenty-seven? Heavens to Betsy, that is young. Your mother must be inordinately proud of you.

[*Listens a beat.*]

    Come again? Oh, yes. The fact is, Mr. Sternheim, that after a career of some thirty years as a professional playwright, I find myself at the end of my tether. Who . . . Who in the world would have believed that my once fertile, prolific and capacious imagination has finally exhausted itself, or, if you will, flown the coop, vanished into thin air like the bubbling effervescence from a bottle of cheap champagne.

[*A wistful beat after each sentence.*]

    Gone. Evaporated. Fizzled to extinction. Not leaving behind the wispiest trace of memory for one to dwell on.

[*Normal discourse.*]

    There's no escaping it, for the last six months . . . precisely one hundred and seventy-two days, I haven't been able to come up with a single viable idea for a new play that's worth putting on paper. Oh, that's not to say I haven't written anything. I've written, ad infinitum, summaries, outlines, titles, possible adaptations, possible characters, possible scenes, possible pages of dialogue, all of which, I confess with embarrassment, terminated in a cri de coeur of frustration and failure. What I find, however, completely incomprehensible is that I'm not merely speaking here of an inability to come up with an idea for a full-length play. Oh, no. I'm speaking here of an idea for any kind of play, a one-act play, a ten-minute play, a monologue, an aphorism, a parable, anything, anything worth putting on paper that has a modicum of interest for whatever audience remains out there. And . . . And, beyond and above that, what's so ironic, what's so out of left field, is for you to phone and ask for an interview at the most impoverished creative period of my professional life. That . . . That to me is shockingly ironic!

[*He picks up his glass, drinks.*]

Well, so be it. Life proceeds at its steady pace in spite of gaps, gullies and assorted calamities. To your health, Mr. Sternheim. I promise you'll have ample opportunity to ask whatever questions you wish. I have no plans for the rest of the day, nor, for that matter, for the rest of the week.

[*He finishes his drink.*]

[*Glass in hand, without interrupting his conversation, he rises to put the glass on the bar. He picks up a second glass, fills it with fresh ice cubes and once again scrupulously measures an inch of Irish whiskey as he pours it into the glass. He moves to sit in the armchair, puts glass on side table and crosses his leg, folding his dressing gown over his lap.*]

I believe my . . . creative impotency is commonly referred to as writer's block, two words that haven't passed through my lips until this very moment. Writer's block. Definition? The infectious, systemic disease that, at one time or another, invades and destroys a writer's ability to write. This can be attributed to a gradual depletion of imagination or a chronic illness or a psychological malfunction. So the question arises, what does a playwright do when he suffers from writer's block?

[*He remains seated.*]

Well, he sits . . . he stands . . . hands clasped behind his back he paces . . . he looks out the window . . . he turns away from the window . . . he scratches an itch . . . he fixes himself a drink, ice cubes and a scrupulously estimated inch of Irish whiskey, but he doesn't drink it, not yet, he waits several minutes so that the melting ice cubes will blend with the whiskey and increase the contents in his glass . . . he picks up a book . . . he glances at a page in the book . . . he puts down the book . . . hands clasped behind his back he paces . . . he blinks . . . he thinks: What's in my head? What was that idea I had last month, last year, the year before last year that I thought would make a powerful, prizewinning play? Was it last month? Last year? The year before last year? The playwright is befuddled. He admonishes himself: An idea for a play that's worth writing isn't forgotten that easily, lame brain! And how many times do I have to tell you to write down your ideas! You don't just let them rot in your head until they're indecipherable. Worthwhile ideas are serendipitous. They come from the labyrinth of memory, from a fragrance scented, a cookie ingested, a photograph, a quotation, an observation, an experience. Any one of those when planted in the fertile soil of imagination, grows and blossoms into compelling characters and riveting scenes that may, God willing, be of interest to whatever audience remains out there.

[*A beat.*]

The playwright continues to admonish himself. He remembers how it felt to be lost in another reality, a pretend reality of one's own choice, of one's own making. He remembers how it felt to spend hours and hours playing with words, locutions, nuances, alliterations, writing hour after hour, forgetting lunch, sleep, appointments, time, blight and death itself! The playwright is lost, felicitously, in the private gardens and chambers of his imagination. He remembers, lame brain, he remembers how glorious it all was.

[*He stares off into space for a nostalgic beat, then picks up glass and finishes off his drink.*]

[*Glass in hand, without interrupting his conversation, he rises to put the glass on the bar. He picks up a third glass, fills it with fresh ice cubes and the obligatory inch of whiskey. He moves to sit in armchair, puts glass on side table and crosses his leg, folding dressing gown over his lap.*]

What you should know is that when I'm writing, when I'm engaged wholeheartedly in the act of writing, I'm entirely indifferent to my health, my appearance, my commitments, my

phobias. You see, Mr. Sternheim, my wife, my second wife, that
is, left me some weeks ago, and I find myself somewhat
disoriented, at least for the present. By the way, she took nearly
all of my furniture and persuaded my domestic to go along with
her; for that I will never forgive her.

[*Listens a beat.*]

What? What is it?

[*Listens a beat.*]

Oh, I don't believe her leaving me prolonged my writer's block.
Our marriage, to be polite, was ill-advised. We both feel
enormously relieved that our divorce is proceeding expeditiously,
but enough, enough of my personal problems. As I said, I'd be
happy to answer any questions . . .

[*Listens a beat.*]

Ah, the article you're writing is for the Sunday entertainment
section of the *Times*. Go on.

[*Listens a beat.*]

The article is to be called "Eminent . . ."

[*Interrupts himself.*]

I can't understand a word you're saying. Start again. Slowly.

[*Repeats what he hears.*]

The article is to be called "Eminent Playwrights of the Past:
Where Are They?"

[*Listens a beat.*]

That's the title of the article? "Eminent Playwrights of the Past:
Where Are They?" You're not in earnest.

[*Listens a beat.*]

You are in earnest.

[*He rises, clearly upset by what he has just learned. He moves toward his imaginary
guest, stares directly at him, gestures and speaks in a sonorous voice.*]

What do I think? I think it's an abomination. You're categorizing
me as a writer of the past? How damn audacious of you! If I had
known that was to be the subject of your article, I would never
have consented to this interview!

[*Listens a beat.*]

Why? You have the gall to ask me why?

[*Disparaging his imaginary guest's surname.*]

First of all, *Mr. Sternheim*, if you had been half the gentleman you pretend to be, you would have informed me of the content of your article when you phoned asking for this interview. That would have been the decent, ethical thing for you to do. Second of all, *Mr. Sternheim*, I am not, nor have I ever been a playwright of the past! Although I haven't had a play produced in New York City for...

[*Sweats it a beat.*]

... some time now, I have been produced, continually and without interruption, throughout the United States and the major capitals of Europe! In fact, *Mr. Sternheim*, three original full-length plays of mine were produced in Europe and have not been produced in this city, my birthplace and residence for over half a century! And furthermore, *Mr. Sternheim*, for your further enlightenment, New York City is by no means the be-all and end-all of theatre in our country or any other county. Au contraire! Au contraire! And I am speaking here from personal experience accumulated over a period of innumerable years and not from the weekly entertainment pages of the *New York Times*!

[*He paces, speaking with increased agitation, giving vent to emotions that have long simmered within him.*]

For that matter, and with rare exception, it is my unbiased opinion that theatre in New York City has deteriorated to such an extent during the past few decades that it has become the absolute pits! The dregs of banality and vulgarity! It consists primarily of kitsch musicals and television melodramas to satisfy the intellectual cravings of nitwits and nincompoops!

[*Listens a beat.*]

You're mumbling again, Mr. Sternheim. Please do me the courtesy of taking a deep breath and speaking slow-ly and suc-cinct-ly.

[*Repeats what he hears.*]

You wrote down... the questions you wanted to ask me. Your first question is: What... What is the state of my health?

[*Expression darkening.*]

I'm sorry. You lost me on that one.

[*Listens a beat; forthright.*]

What has the state of my health have to do with "Eminent Playwrights of the Past: Where Are They?" Are you taking a medical assessment of my health as well as updating my biography? Or are you inquiring about the state of my hunchback? Is that what you're driving at, the state of my hunchback? Is that the purpose of your question?

[*Listens a beat.*]

There's no need to apologize. I have no qualms about discussing my hunchback or, as you so delicately put it, my "congenital disability." You don't think that after all these years I'm embarrassed by the use of the word hunchback, do you?

[*Listens a beat.*]

No, no, I am not saying there wasn't a time when I would crawl under a rock at the mere thought of being called a hunchback, but that was during childhood and adolescence. It might be of interest to you to know that my parents never used that word. They were in complete denial, clinging to the delusion that my . . . kyphotic spine, my . . .

[*Sardonically.*]

. . . "congenital disability" didn't exist, that I was as robust and carefree as the next child. Grant you, my mother did scold me, repeatedly: "Stop slouching!" "Stand straight!" "Raise your head!" "Pull back your shoulders!" "Look at me when I talk to you!" And from behind his newspaper my father murmured, so softly one could barely hear him, "Leave the boy alone. He'll grow out of it, God willing." But obviously I didn't grow out of it, "God willing." I remember once, when I was on my way home from elementary school, a cross-eyed, scowling kid I had never seen before came up to me and said . . .

[*Mimics his voice.*]

"Hey, what's that bump y'got growin' outta y'ur back? Y'u gotta pillow in y'ur shirt?"

[*Normal voice.*]

Crawl under a rock? You bet I would, if I could have found a rock to crawl under. I always assumed that the principals of the schools I attended informed the teachers and the teachers in turn informed the students that the word hunchback was never to be spoken in my presence. Still, this prohibition was occasionally ignored. In my sophomore year of high school, during assembly in the auditorium, I remember being tapped on the shoulder from someone seated behind me. I turned around to see this very attractive young girl, not a classmate of mine, but someone I had frequently seen in the hallways, someone whose physical attributes I borrowed to give a tad of inspiration to my nocturnal indulgences.

[*Mimics her voice.*]

"May I touch it for good luck?"

[*Normal voice.*]

She whispered in my ear, glancing at her girlfriends who sat beside her. I nodded, dumbly, not having the courage to refuse her. I turned to face forward, toward the auditorium's platform, where the principal was speaking on the virtues of tolerance for the less fortunate, while the girl seated behind me placed both her hands on the hump of my back and vigorously crunched it, as if she were kneading a bowl full of baker's dough. She didn't hurt me . . . physically . . . and yet . . . I was in pain . . . humiliated by the coarseness of what she was doing . . . in public . . . for everyone to see. I thought of pulling away from her invasive, spindly fingers or asking her to stop it, stop it, stop it instantly, but once again I lacked the courage to do so. And as she continued kneading the hump on my back, she started giggling and her girlfriends joined in and . . . the three of them were giggling. The students around us stirred in their seats, pointed at me and they . . . they too started giggling.

[*Horrified by the memory.*]

Insult added to injury. Salt exacerbating the wound. Ridicule heaped on humiliation. And soon . . . soon the auditorium rumbled, shuddered and howled in a delirium of laughter. I . . . I panicked. Perspiration sprouted on my face. My heart pounded wildly. I jumped to my feet, pushed my legs through to the end of the row, bumping into knees, thighs, books, apologizing . . . "Excuse me. Pardon me. If you'll please let me through . . ." Once I reached the aisle I ran toward the doors at the rear of the auditorium and I was out of there, out on the street . . .

[*Breathlessly.*]

. . . running for all I was worth, running up the stairs of the two-storied, shingled house where I lived . . . throwing open the door and racing into the bathroom where I locked the door, pressed my head against the wall and I cried my heart out until . . . until I had no tears left . . . until . . . until I had no heart left.

[*He lowers his head for a long beat; staring at floor.*]

[*Softly.*]

It came to me many years later. If I hadn't been born a hunchback . . . I would never have become a playwright. I would never have had *the need* to become a playwright, and for that . . . I am infinitely grateful.

[*Glass in hand, without interrupting his conversation, he rises to put the glass on the bar. He picks up a fourth glass, fills it with fresh ice cubes and the obligatory inch of whiskey. He moves to sit in armchair.*]

[*He doesn't put glass on side table. He doesn't cross his leg. He doesn't fold dressing gown over his lap. He shortly finishes his drink.*]

[*His imaginary guest says something.*]

Will you repeat that? I didn't hear you.

[*Listens a beat.*]

Yes, I was married twice, the first time for love, the second for revenge. The gist of what I'm about to tell you has already been published, so I see no reason to withhold anything from you. In any event, I met my first wife, Loretta Breen, partner in the law firm of McMillan and Breen, at an evening performance of *As You Like It*, a Shakespeare in the Park production at the Delacorte Theatre. And as luck would have it Loretta was seated beside me, unaccompanied, wearing khaki slacks, red-strapped sandals and a white, cotton shirt with the sleeves rolled up to the elbows. As soon as I saw her I was in love with her. It took a while longer for her to reciprocate. We were married in Atlantic City and we lived happily together as man and wife. I'd like to repeat that line. We were married in Atlantic City and we lived happily together as man and wife. After our fifth year of marriage we planned to adopt a child since we appeared incapable of conceiving one. And, of course, no sooner had we reached that conclusion, in consultation with a Park Avenue obstetrician, we learned from Loretta's dermatologist that she was pregnant. And not only was she pregnant, she was pregnant twofold with a pair of twins, a girl and a boy. I'd like to repeat part of that: "She was pregnant twofold with a pair of twins, a girl and a boy."

[*Ebulliently.*]

God in heaven, talk about happiness, talk about whether or not life is worth living! Who are those wailing doomsayers, those sterile, silver-spoon-fed literati who stare up at the stars and see nothing but darkness? What pestilence buried them in dunghills of cynicism and morbidity!

[*A beat.*]

I felt none of that. Au contraire. Au contraire. I felt . . . happy. Ah, there's that glorious word again. I had it all, Mr. Sternheim, I had it all for some ten years. A wife I loved, a daughter I loved, a son I loved, a career I loved. Wife, children, career, life dancing on a blank page of adversities. I was God's favorite, no doubt about that.

[*A beat.*]

Where, you may ask, is Loretta today? Where are my children today? The answer? I have no idea. I haven't seen them in years. The last time . . . Let's see. They were living in Japan, Tokyo, to be precise.

[*Listens a beat.*]

What went wrong? How in the world did they end up in Tokyo? I went wrong, Mr. Sternheim. I went wrong.

[*He paces.*]

I was working on a screenplay from a play of mine in Los Angeles, compliments of Warner Brothers. Several script meetings had been arranged with the director and the producers. I, of course, missed my family, but I felt footloose and fancy-free. I rarely let an evening get by me without a drink or two; on notable occasions, three or four, which led, inevitably, to a liaison between a young, pretty, amply scented and abundantly stacked assistant editor and yours truly. My reasoning was irrefutable: what value success and name recognition for a hardworking, generous, decent hunchback, if he can't avail himself of the more sumptuous delicacies of life? And who may I ask was more deserving of these social amenities than a family-friendly hunchback? After several drinks, it all seemed obvious to me.

[*A meditative beat.*]

Somehow, no doubt from a concerned friend of ours, my sweet Loretta got wind of it, and being a no-nonsense, up-front kind of a girl, unbeknownst to me, she flew out to L.A. Here's where being married to a lawyer does have its disadvantages. A few short months later we were divorced. A few short months after that she met a Japanese businessman at a fund-raising event for the Metropolitan Museum. A few short months after that they were married and moved to Tokyo. With my children, of course. Visitation rights required that I fly halfway around the world to spend a weekend and a month's summer vacation to see my children, which I did, dutifully, if not on weekends, certainly on the month's summer vacation. Those occasions, however, were not very fulfilling, whether I traveled to Tokyo or they came to Central Park West. The reason was simple. They fell into the habit...

[*With difficulty.*]

... of speaking to each other in Japanese, as if they were sharing a secret, as if I wasn't with them. Or... was it that they didn't want me to understand what they were saying? Or... were they mocking me? Laughing at me because of my...

[*Sardonically.*]

... "congenital disability?" My own children? Is that possible? Preposterous! Where did that horrible thought come from?

[*Dismissing it.*]

Whatever. It was their secret, not mine. In time even our summ
vacations waned. It wasn't fun being together... with my own
children ... twins, a girl and a boy. I haven't seen them in years.

[*A beat.*]

As for my second wife, Bridget Henley, that was a horse of a
different disposition.

[*Struck by a thought.*]

Come to think of it, you know her. Quite well. Can you guess
who she is?

[*Listens a beat.*]

But you do know her. I mentioned her to you only a few minutes
ago. Give it a try. Who do you ... ?

[*Listens a beat.*]

That's right! The girl who sat behind me in the high school
auditorium! Yes, yes, the giggler and her three friends!

[*Slaps his thigh; laughs.*]

That's her! My haute masseuse! Wait. Wait till you hear how it
started. After I had my first success off-Broadway, I received a letter
from her at the theatre, congratulating me and writing that I should
congratulate her for being happily married and an executive at an
advertising agency. I didn't hear from her for a good number of
years after that, but one day, from out of nowhere, I received
another letter from her addressed to my agent, saying she had
heard of my divorce and since she was divorced and I was divorced,
why didn't we have a drink one evening? Which we did. A dozen
or so times, the last with a bottle of Dom Perignon and, from me,
a proposal of marriage. The first year was fun. Surprised? So was I.
I actually enjoyed being married again. Especially on those sweaty,
lascivious nights when I straddled my new wife and felt her crunch
her invasive, spindly fingers into the hump on my back, only now
gasping and whimpering and begging me to stay the course!

[*Laughing.*]

What wild and woolly rides they were. In the throes of
fornication I'd shout: "Beauty and the Beast! United at last!
Whoopeeeee! Whoopeeeee!"

ghing.]

I would laugh so loud and so long that on reaching orgasm, I'd tumble off the bed, landing flat on my roly-poly, crunchy hump!

Laughing; recuperates.]

Evidently Bridget didn't share my sense of humor. We were divorced before our second anniversary. And once again I was left to reflect on the tentativeness of marital relationships.

[*Wistful silence.*]

You'll have to excuse me, Mr. Sternheim. I seem to have run out of steam. An exhausting day of doing nothing. How wasteful it's all been.

[*A beat; softly.*]

Please let yourself out. And feel free to call me if anything comes up that you would like to clarify or discuss further. Do close the door on your way out. Thank you.

[*He waits in vain to hear the entrance door open and close.*]

[*Taking remote from his dressing-gown pocket, he clicks on CD player.*]

[*SOUND: Mozart's Church Sonata.*]

[*With effort, wearily, he stands . . . hands clasped behind his back he paces . . . he looks out the window . . . he turns away from the window . . . he scratches an itch . . . he pours himself a fifth drink, no ice cubes, no estimated inch . . . he knocks it off in one swallow, leaves empty glass on the bar . . . he moves to pick up a book from the side table . . . glances at a page in the book . . . he puts down the book . . . hands clasped behind his back he paces . . . he blinks . . . he thinks: What's in my head? What was that idea I had last month, last year, the year before last year that I thought would make a powerful, prizewinning play? Was it last month? Last year? The year before last year?*]

[*Somewhere during the above or afterwards . . .*]

[*Lights and music fade out.*]

• • •

acknowledgmen

I would like to thank my publisher, Michael Messina of Applause Books—The Hal Leonard Group, and my agent, June Clark, for their support of this edition and my position with Applause Books.

Furthermore, I'd like to thank Rick Pulos, administrative/production coordinator of the theatre program at Long Island University, my graduate assistant Liliana Almendarez, and the administration of LIU—Dean David Cohen, Associate Dean Kevin Lauth, and Assistant Dean Maria Vogelstein.

I also like to express my gratitude to all the theatres around the country and their literary managers, as well as all the playwrights whose work I read, enabling me to compile my first edition.

I follow in the footsteps of more than sixty editions of The Best American Short Plays/The Best Short Plays series, and I would like to thank all the previous editors of this series: the late Stanley Richards, Ramon Delgado, Howard Stein, Mark Glubke, Glenn Young, and anyone I may have left out who came before these fine editors who helped make this series a success.

I would like to quote from the 1989 edition of The Best Short Plays, edited by Ramon Delgado:

> From the beginning of this series the past and present editors have sought to include a balance among three categories of playwrights: (1) established playwrights who continue to practice the art and craft of the short play, (2) emerging playwrights whose record of productions indicate both initial achievements and continuous productivity, and (3) talented new playwrights whose work may not have had much exposure but evidences promise for the future. An effort has also been made to select plays not anthologized elsewhere and, when possible, plays that are making their debut in print.... The value of these considerations is to honor the artistry of the established playwrights, encourage the emerging, acknowledge the promising, and offer a varied selection of new plays in one volume.

As the editor of this series, I plan to keep the tradition moving into the future.